LATE-MODERN ARCHITECTURE
and Other Essays

D1373662

LATE-MODERN ARCHITECTURE

and Other Essays

CHARLES A. JENCKS

NEW YORK

HICKSVILLE PUBLIC LIBRARY
HICKSVILLE, N.Y.

Front cover
PHILIP JOHNSON and JOHN BURGEE, *Pennzoil Place*, Houston, 1974-6. A Late-Modern version of the simple Modern skyscraper which has distorted and accentuated elements to increase visual interest in a familiar form. The 'twin skyscraper' has become common in Late-Modern practice but the thin wedge of 10 foot space between the two trapezoids is still extraordinary.

Back cover
NORMAN FOSTER, *Willis Faber Head Office*, Ipswich, 1972-6. Typical isotropic space of Late-Modern architecture taken to a sublime extreme. The sandwich space and open office landscape are endemic to Late-Capitalism because of their great economies: maximum coverage for the minimum expense.

Frontispiece
HANS HOLLEIN, *Richard Feigen Gallery*, New York, 1969-71. The use of Slick-Tech imagery and polished chrome with a set of ironic dualities (painted columns, lights and balconies) that recall twin parts of the human body. See pages 96 and 97.

For Cosmo, Justin and Johnny

First published in the United States of America in 1980 by

RIZZOLI INTERNATIONAL PUBLICATIONS, INC.
712 Fifth Avenue/New York 10019

Copyright © Charles Jencks and Maggie Keswick

Library of Congress Catalog Card Number 79-92260
ISBN cloth 0-8478-0293-0 paper 0-8478-0284-1

Printed in Great Britain

CONTENTS

Q
724.91
J

1. LATE-MODERN THEORY

1.1 INTRODUCTION – END OF AN ERA?

When the death of Modern architecture was announced several years ago by a variety of architectural medics including myself it was greeted with scepticism in certain quarters. The announcement was presumed false, the coroner's report a forgery and the patient – suffering it was admitted from a momentary bout of high-rise blues – was supposedly restored to good health. Modern architecture we were told was again alive and well, purged of its minor ailments such as *gigantitis*, and was living it up in High-Tech Paris and New York. Architects who persisted in calling themselves 'Modern' were there to prove it. British and American magazines published hard evidence that the obituary was premature. Recently completed buildings *looked* Modern and their authors, such as I. M. Pei, said they were. Post-Modernists themselves, Charles Moore and Robert Venturi, declared they didn't want to be 'Post' anything. James Stirling and Philip Johnson insisted, at times, that they were still Modern, and alive as well. So the demise of a style, the end of an era, the extinction of an ideology, had not occurred; or if it had there was a quick resurrection.

Well, such wishful thinking is wrong. The patient has died: not it is true 'on July 15, 1972 at 3.32 p.m. (or thereabouts)' – that was a symbolic date meant to bring a little drama to the scene.[1] No, Modern architecture was dying well before this, before indeed the Ronan Point high-rise suffered 'cumulative collapse' in 1967; it was dying in 1961 when Jane Jacobs came out with her book *The Death and Life of Great American Cities* and no Modern architect had a convincing answer to her condemnations. Its ideology was dead.

Actually, the life and death of architectural movements seems an absurd notion; periods of history, whatever they are, are not organisms and the major protagonists of an era do not wake up one morning saying – 'Here endeth the Romanesque'. Although historians can date the time and place of Early Gothic to the building of the retrochoir of St. Denis, and even point to Abbot Suger's written intentions, these do not include a phrase 'here beginneth the Gothic'. Architectural movements are complex affairs, part stylistic and part ideological, part unconscious practice and part conscious convention, and any transition from one era to another is bound to be a flowing thing, an evolution, fast or slow. Moreover it is bound to be a statistical thing, a matter of dropping many ideas and picking up many, and transforming the lot with a peculiar percentage of each quality. As the reader will find in my chart of variables, p. 32, affixing a label, 'Modern', 'Late' and 'Post'-Modern, is never obvious and hardly simple; so the life and death of such movements to which these labels presumably refer cannot be fixed with precision. Labels are convenient historical constructions, rather like buildings, except they are built up over time by many historians. To gain persuasive power, to command assent, they must refer to a complex nexus of identifiable ideas and physical attributes.

What then is being claimed? Is Modern architecture dead, do Late and Post-Modernism exist – statistically or in any manner of speaking? As might be guessed by the title of these selected essays and the lack of gravity with which this portentous question is treated, my answers to all three questions must be a guarded and ironic 'yes'. There have been major shifts in architecture since, roughly, 1960 that have to be distinguished from the coherent body of practice that was known variously as the International Style and Modern architecture. One cannot use the word 'Modern' for what is happening today if that word is to have any meaning – if it is still to apply to what architects fought for in the twenties. There are not the same beliefs now nor the same styles and sense of space. One may use the term modern (lower case) to mean anything contemporary, and one may sympathize with the architects mentioned above who dislike the prefixes 'Late' and 'Post' (implying they've arrived late or even dead). In that case propose new labels, 'brand X' and 'brand Y'; search for better classifiers which can describe, in their titles, how architecture has evolved from Modernism while still keeping genes from its progenitor. Alternative labels are hard to find, and yet the ones I propose do not enjoy complete assent. Hence the continual irony, here and in my previous book on Post-Modern architecture, an irony which is meant to convey the ambiguity and open quality of our transitional period. It is an irony which allows room for manoeuvre for contradictory propositions which reflect the facts: that architects like Venturi and Stirling have given up Modernism one moment to return the next; that a skilful performer such as Philip Johnson slaloms down the hill between Late and Post-Modernism, sometimes hitting flags; that we can't fix any creative period, or architect, into a single mould, and yet that we can't give up the moulds, either.

Definitions

The term 'Late-Modern' arose in 1977 as a convenient label to distinguish one group of creative architects from another, from the group with which they were often confused, Post-Modernists. In the popular press, as indeed occasionally in the professional, many architects were being lumped together because of their common divergence from Modernism. To disentangle the fundamental split within these divergences, a set of minimum definitions became necessary. In brief, and as a first approximation to the complexity, the definitions are these: Post-Modern architecture is 'doubly-coded', one half Modern and one half something else (usually traditional building), in its attempt to communicate both with

NORMAN FOSTER, *Sainsbury Centre for the Visual Arts*, University of East Anglia, Norwich, 1974–8. Metaphorically the building is, from afar, a single piece of domestic equipment, or punch card, or cassette. The emphasis on pure technology and logic has resulted once again in a striking sensuous image. From the end and inside, critics term it an 'airplane hangar'.

Sainsbury Centre exterior shows the aluminium panel and glass infill wrapped around almost all surfaces rather the way domestic equipment and automobile bodies use an homogenous wrap-around aesthetic. Traditional architecture distinguished different surfaces with different materials.

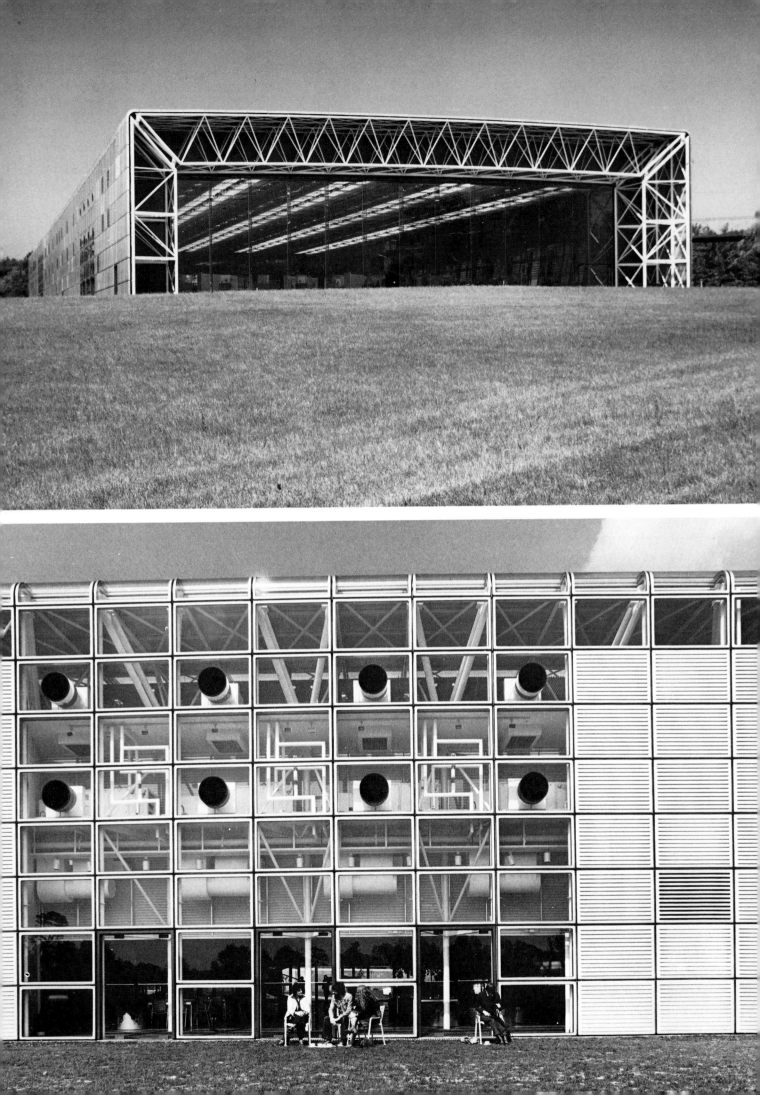

the public *and* a concerned minority, usually architects. By contrast, Late-Modern architecture, 'singly-coded', takes the ideas and forms of the Modern Movement to an extreme, exaggerating the structure and technological image of the building in its attempt to provide amusement, or aesthetic pleasure. This exaggeration the Modernists would have found unacceptable in the twenties; it sometimes merits the labels 'Slick-Tech', or 'Supersensualism'. Like the Late Gothic or Late Baroque architects these practitioners extend an already existing set of styles and values.

In the first essay defining aspects of this style are explored – extreme logic, extreme repetition of modular elements, an exaggerated emphasis on constructional details and structure, some amusing but unintended metaphors and a sensuous imagery. Norman Foster's recently completed Sainsbury Centre for the Visual Arts in East Anglia is a typical Late-Modern building. Like Arata Isozaki's Gunma Museum (p.116) it is an uncompromising image of technology and repetition, and like Isozaki, Foster repeats an aluminium grid-panel endlessly, as if it were the answer to almost everything – roof, wall and inside surface. This 'doing more' with 'less elements' is close to the Modernist incantation 'less is more' and like the former hocus-pocus it can sometimes work.

The excitement of the Sainsbury Centre is partly caused by such sorcery. The same 'superplastic aluminium' panel wraps around the (almost) flat roof, corner and wall thus giving a visual and semantic identity to elements which are conventionally distinguished by material and use. James Stirling plays the same trick in his Olivetti building (p.81) and also places the gutter 'where it shouldn't be' (on the ground). In both cases the distortion of traditional syntax becomes a kind of magic, making the building shrink in size and become a piece of domestic equipment: an Olivetti typewriter in the case of Stirling and a computer cassette, or punch-card, in the case of Foster. But, and this makes the Sainsbury Centre Late rather than Post-Modern, the metaphor doesn't seem either intended or particularly apt for the function – in this case viewing works of art. The criticisms of Sainsbury, and there have been some, concern this metaphorical unsuitability. From the end elevation it looks like an 'airplane hangar' and even on the inside the grand space dwarfs the activities and the (relatively) miniscule works of art, as an airplane hangar would.

Like the Pompidou Centre in Paris, another Late-Modern 'museum' among other things, a single, linear spatial idea dominates all other concerns. But, and this is the point of Late-Modern sorcery, the vices of the work are, in a different light, the virtues. We may overlook the homogeneity of the space *because of* its single-minded beauty. We suspend our disbelief, as we do before art, to judge it on its own terms; and these terms are, once again, extreme. The light quality of the ceiling is unlike anything we've seen before at this scale – shimmering, playful, irridescent, disturbing like 1,000 Bridget Riley optical vibrations laid end to end. It goes on buzzing and dancing overhead, with its 'motorized louvers', not for a hundred feet but for over four hundred.

The conceptual logic is even more extreme. Basically the art gallery is *all* one building, a zone of services (WCs, stores, darkrooms etc.) wrapped *all* around another building (the gallery and work areas). Like Cesar Pelli's work the 'skin membrane' (2.4 metres wide) is *all* extrusion in one direction, so that the end elevation is *all* section (or a projection of it). Like Superstudio's 'Contin-

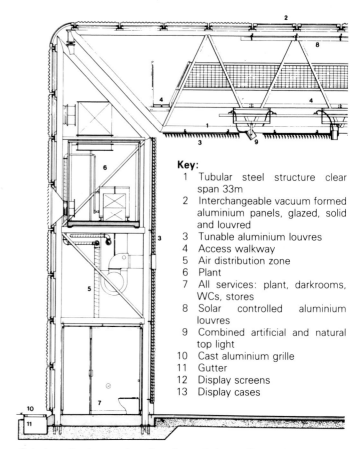

Key:
1 Tubular steel structure clear span 33m
2 Interchangeable vacuum formed aluminium panels, glazed, solid and louvred
3 Tunable aluminium louvres
4 Access walkway
5 Air distribution zone
6 Plant
7 All services: plant, darkrooms, WCs, stores
8 Solar controlled aluminium louvres
9 Combined artificial and natural top light
10 Cast aluminium grille
11 Gutter
12 Display screens
13 Display cases

Sainsbury Centre, section of wall panel shows like a Miesian detail where all the design effort is placed: in the neoprene gaskets, stainless steel screws etc. In Late-Modernism the construction is the decoration; in Post-Modernism the decoration is symbolic and applied.

uous Monument' (p.90) or Archizoom's 'No-Stop City' (p.94), the open space is isotropic – that is *all* the same in every direction (except for differences in length). Like the 'well-serviced shed' idea of the sixties, *all* the building fabric seems to come from functional requirements (structure and mechanical equipment). We might conclude that the Sainsbury Centre is an ultra-Modern building without exceptions, ambiguities or second-thoughts, summarizing all the extreme aspects of Late-Modernism.

However, some of these aspects are shared with Post-Modernism. Foster, like other architects, is reacting to the disenchantment with Modern architecture and trying to evolve a more accessible language of form. But he, and Late-Modernists, do not give up the commitment to technology and abstraction which characterized the previous period, nor will they use a conventional and representational language of form. So they are really closer to Modern architects than are the Post-Modernists who have rejected pure abstraction in a search for a richer symbolism.

* * *

The first section of these essays concerns these themes and the major debate which is now underway between Late and Post-Modernists. The second section analyses the heart of Late-Modernism, Japan, and treats several instances of it in the work of Italian designers and James Stirling. The fact that none of these designers would (or didn't then) take conscious note of the role metaphor plays in design is a recurring theme, and it also makes them Late-Modernists. But they do all have a commitment to sensuous form, or an 'erotics of design' in Oriol

Sainsbury Centre, interior shows the pure isotropic space of Late-Modernism. The ceiling's 'motorized louvres' give a soft, dancing light that is controllable.

Bohigas' words, and this idea can be traced through several essays here – 'The Supersensualists', Stirling's work etc. – to the third section where it becomes more explicit in the work of Philip Johnson and Bruce Goff. Much of this section is written in the Neo-Hysterical Style because, I believe, that combination of telegrammese and Tom Wolfe can express certain qualities that otherwise remain hidden. For some subjects it is appropriate, but certainly not for the last section, on historiography and theory, which is more closely argued. This part reiterates several themes – notably that of the Modernist *Zeitgeist* and morality – but in a new key.

The act of selecting and re-reading former essays is a chastening experience about which it is, probably, best to be silent. The mistakes of fact, the errors of tone, the sloppiness caused by the haste of architectural journalism become all too clear. These faults, at least the more obvious ones, I have tried to correct. But sometimes I have left an unbalanced or unhappy sentence, especially when it reflected the heat of the moment. Certain essays were written to engage an argument or reset a previous imbalance, and so I couldn't withdraw the offending lines without rewriting the whole piece. On the other hand, the enjoyable side of looking over past essays is seeing an idea recur and develop – for instance, here, the notions of multivalence and 'history as myth', which were first stated in 1969. I also became aware of concepts which may have clarified emergent design trends: 'Pop'

architecture, 'Camp', 'Supersensualism', 'Ersatz', 'Fetishism', 'Daydream Houses' and the 'kitsch' of Goff. All of these related and sometimes superficial trends had not been previously discussed for quite obvious reasons. While I found myself at first ambivalent towards them, I nevertheless started to develop an understanding and sympathy, perhaps through the process of writing.

The same can be said for my attitude towards the Late-Modernists. Partly against the movement because it has not entirely jettisoned the problems of Modern architecture, I am still attracted to aspects of its language and creativity. Because of this ambivalence and because these are selected essays, not a proper book on the subject, there are holes in my treatment of it. More could be said of the countless creative architects such as Denys Lasdun who were brought up within Modernism and then moved into its Late phase. Many developments, such as the late evolution of the curtain wall, remain unanalysed. But if the subject is far from exhausted here at least I hope to have clarified the outline of its existence.

I would like to thank the editors of *Architectural Design*, *The Architectural Review*, the *AAQ* (*Architectural Association Quarterly*), *Architecture Plus* and *Architectural Forum* (the same Peter Blake in the last two cases) for permission to reproduce essays which first appeared in their journals; also the students of the AA and UCLA who heard some of these ideas develop and talked them over with me; Tom Gorst and Frank Russell who helped with the production of the book; and lastly, once again, Maggie Keswick, who encouraged such limpid prose as happens to exist.

1.2 LATE-MODERNISM AND POST-MODERNISM

This essay, published in Architectural Design *1978, was a first attempt to distinguish Late-Modernists from the group they were confused with, both popularly and in the press. As can be seen from the list of definers (p. 13) it was not as complete or systematic a definition of each movement as I later arrived at (p. 32). There are only ten of some thirty classifiers; Hitchcock and Johnson, when defining the International Style, made it somewhat easier with only four major categories, but many would say they oversimplified the complexity of the Style not to mention the Modern Movement.*

The Modern Movement, capitalized like all world religions, had its Heroic Period in the twenties and its Classy Period, its dissemination and commercialization, in the fifties. By the late sixties, it had lost much of its ideological power and, with the death of Le Corbusier in 1965, it had lost much of its moral and spiritual direction. As a utopian movement, or at minimum an avant-garde attempt to influence society, it always had a normative role, a role which has recently diminished if not disappeared altogether. Recently heretical groups within Modernism have flourished that have revived one or another of the founding faiths – Futurism revived by Archigram, Neo-Constructivism by some Italians – there has even been Archizoom's Neo-Dadaism. But the essence of the Modern Movement became somewhat hollow at its core – in the academies and schools of architecture where it continued a prolonged existence under the heading of 'Late Mies', 'Late Kahn', or even the baroque appellation applied to Richard Meier's work – 'Post-Johnson-Corb'. All these trends grew out of the International Style, but were as different from it as Late Gothic architecture was from High Gothic. As we shall show, they have enough in common to be grouped together as a school of Late-Modernism, and distinguished from the other main, current approach of Post-Modernism. No doubt these labels are unwieldly, but they make the basic point which is often obscured today that the high period of the Modern Movement is definitely over and that current approaches have evolved out of it. Here we'll define the essential ways Modernism has transformed itself into something still recognizably Modern with aspects that are exaggerated, or 'Late'.[1]

Late-Modernism
To illustrate the overlapping of present architects into the two major tendencies, we can recall how they have responded to the general disenchantment with Modernism. The environmental 'crisis', the unpopularity of Modern housing estates, the boredom with Modern aesthetics are too well known to need recounting, but it is to these pressures that both Late-Modernists and Post-Modernists have reacted.

The Late-Modernists have, for the most part, taken the theories and style of their precursors to an extreme and in so doing produced an elaborated or mannered Modernism. By contrast Post-Modernists have modified the previous style, while building upon it, but in addition also rejected the theories almost completely. Brief illustrations of both new schools will bring out their similarities and differences.

HERMAN HERTZBERGER, *Centraal Beheer Offices*, Apeldoorn, 1968–1974. An office for 1,000 workers some of whom commute from Amsterdam. Hertzberger has broken up the Modernist slab office building into roughly fifty-six cubes or 'work islands' which are organized in a grid of interior 'streets' and coffee bars. The attempt to break down the image and function of hierarchical bureaucracy is partly successful. Nonetheless old Modernist problems remain: the repetitive machine aesthetic, unclear communication (the entry had to be marked '*ingang*') and unintended metaphors ('rabbit warren' etc.).

Centraal Beheer, interior street with its planting, omnipresent concrete block and overhead duct-work. If one accepts the aesthetic celebration of movement and technology then one has to applaud the intricate beauty of these parts – concrete block versus glass block versus silver light fixture and ducts. A Chinese puzzle of grey tones against which more colourful patterns are placed by the users. A deeper pluralism is however absent; traditionalists are excluded.

The work of Arata Isozaki and Herman Hertzberger is some of the most convincing Late-Modernism around. It responds to the anonymity of Modernism with extreme articulation and in the case of Hertzberger with extreme cellular multiplication, in an attempt to provide identity. Where Modernists emphasized mass, volume and linear circulation spines, Hertzberger emphasizes subcentres, various routes, and individual constructional elements. Where the International Style was purist and closed as a unified aesthetic, the Hertzberger aesthetic is impure and open to addition, modification and, to a degree, personalization. His Beheer office building is claimed to be a 'monument to democracy'; an open, anti-authoritarian building because it breaks down the centralized bureaucracy into a lot of little so-called 'work islands' and then invites these small centres to be used, decorated and modified at the request of the users. And yet on an architectural level one can see that Hertzberger hasn't in fact changed the basic style and ideologies of Modernism. There is still the fundamental idea that architecture can shape social behaviour, especially mass behaviour and that of large corporations, and the basic abstract style of concrete block, glass brick and constructional expression. A Post-Modernist, by contrast, might have used styles, spaces and social imagery more local to the area, or stemming from the Dutch tradition. When I interviewed several people there in 1977 I found that, although most of the young people liked the scheme and personalized it in various ways, the non-average employee was excluded by, or dubious of, its machine aesthetic. An older woman who commuted from Amsterdam would have preferred more soft wooden surfaces in a different ambience. I'm not suggesting that architecture *must* follow traditional taste cultures here, but rather that Late-Modernists do still have a commitment to a unified and exclusive aesthetic even when they talk of democracy and participation.

The same can be said of Norman Foster's and Richard Rogers' work, which, while trying to get closer to popular imagery than Modernism, still remains essentially wrapped in its thrall of technological fantasy. Indeed the so-called London School – Foster, Rogers, Farrell and Grimshaw, Derek Walker etc. – is all Late-Modernist precisely because it takes technological imagery to an extreme that the Modern Movement never reached. Partly this is due to the presence of this technology on a massive and efficient scale; something that the Pioneers never enjoyed. When glass, steel and ventilating technology allow one to do away with all the conventional elements of doors, walls, parapets and rooms, then it's likely that leading architects will make an expressive virtue of these absent parts, for expression is always partly dependent on a distortion of the accepted code. What gives Foster's and Rogers' work its peculiar, exhilarating quality however is the exaggeration of the distortion. Some is so stripped of familiar elements that, conceptually, the entire building is a wall, with no roof and bottom, with no joints and entry, rather like a magical box. Mies may have adumbrated this Mannerism, but his buildings always retained some scaling elements, many of them Classical.

Why is the Pompidou Centre Late-Modern and not Modern? Because, like a work of Art Nouveau, the expression of joints and structure is so obsessive and poetic that it dominates other concerns. The muscular 'gerberettes' and their accentuated curving sections have all the overtones of an Art Nouveau insect, such as

Adler's *Bat*, and the way pin joints are celebrated is reminiscent of Horta's Maison du Peuple. This 'structuralism' would have been condemned in the twenties as structural acrobatics, but quite clearly here the architects are trying to be popular, not Modern, and take advantage of the widespread love of the meccano-set image which is now deep in our society. They have succeeded because, as with all fantasy, they haven't compromised the basic image.

Thus if we read the service facade in depth we find five distinct layers of technology accentuated by different colours. The first layer of circulation is a black cage; then some green pipes to either side are followed by cross-bracing painted silver (the exoskeleton of this rectilinear insect) followed in turn by heavy blue ducts that taper downward – a veritable colonnade of paired columns reminiscent of Perrault's Louvre nearby. This, the strongest visual layer, is followed by a layer of orange metallic cabinets, and then finally a grey wall.

Although compositional rules appear to have played no part, there is an interesting Classical-Baroque air about this facade: a 'rusticated' basement level of extract units and heavy blue horizontals, then two storeys of building which graduate in openings like a palazzo, and at the top not a cornice line but instead an implied roof line – the continuation of the blue ducts. To complete the comparison with a Baroque palazzo there is the overall division of the facade into bays, a near symmetry and two stressed side verticals – all like Bernini's Palazzo Chigi-Odescalchi of 1664. The bay rhythm (A,A,BCB,A,A,A,A',BCB',A',D) bears comparison with the way this palazzo was altered (to 3,1,7,1,3 bays).

This historical parallel may seem absurd at first, especially since it is Post-Modernists and not Late-Modernists who refer to historical models. And yet there is an unmistakable palazzo feeling to the overall horizontal facade which is so strong that it won't disappear, especially since the Pompidou Centre is surrounded by a similar type, the Parisian hôtel. But, and this is typical of Late-Modernism, the coding is apparently unintended, the comparison, or metaphor, inadvertent. Piano and Rogers don't intend their building to be read symbolically much beyond its literal messages or celebration of technology. As opposed to a Post-Modern version of the same building, there is no real interest in making a comment on

G. BERNINI, *Palazzo Chigi-Odescalchi*, Rome, 1664, extended by N. SALVI, 1745, so that it had sixteen pilasters instead of eight. The typical Baroque palazzo had a rusticated base, giant order of pilasters, side entrances, complex rhythm of bays and a pronounced cornice. Note the window 'ears', a metaphor comparable to the Pompidou 'gerberettes', or 'arms'.

RICHARD ROGERS and RENZO PIANO, *Pompidou Centre*, Paris, 1971–1977. Architecture about construction, technology and movement – the three canonic subjects of Modernism are here given a Mannerist emphasis. The classical code of Perrault's Louvre, and other palazzos is implicit, but unintended? (Compare with Bernini's Palazzo Chigi-Odescalchi).

the language and context of Paris. True the building holds street lines and tries to be low, but there is no acceptance of a street-side entry, no conversation with the ground floor, indeed not even much use of this all-important level. The street floor, as in so much Modernism on stilts, is a grand desolation.

But if these are its faults as seen from a Post-Modern position, what are its Late-Modern virtues? Aside from the technological fantasy already mentioned, it has an extreme logic (repetitive sandwich slabs of warehouse space), extreme circulatory emphasis, extreme flexibility (which may not be used) and the extreme pragmatism of Modernism. One can find parallels with the Berlin Free University, the ultra-logic of Eisenman and the decorative structures of Paolo Portoghesi. Basically this is a decorated toy box of technical tricks which the French executive fancies as much as the common man and Monsieur Hulot. It is an oversized meccano set painted in French blues and reds and it is sitting in the heart of limestone Paris.

As a completely unlikely occurrence it is probably appropriate for its role as a culture centre, and as a supermarket of culture it is no doubt very successful, and as popular as the Eiffel Tower (the standard comparison). The problem is however that one can't support such supermarkets very far – one, for Paris, is enough.

Difficult cases

We can now summarize the qualities of Late-Modernism and contrast them with Post-Modernism: basically the approach is pragmatic rather than idealist, and *ultra*-modern in its exaggeration of several modern aspects – extreme logic, extreme circulatory and mechanical emphasis, a mannered and decorative use of technology, a complication of the International Style (e.g. Richard Meier and Michael Graves) and an abstract rather than conventional language of form. To these essentially Mannerist qualities ought to be added the most ultra-modern and mannered one of all: the tendency to shock by discontinuity, by newness, by being a self-sufficient, avant-garde statement cut off from traditional architecture. Norman Foster's buildings have those qualities as much as Peter Eisenman's. Other architects who should be added to this list are John Heyduk, Denys Lasdun, Cesar Pelli and Helmut Schulitz, Fumihiko Maki and most of the Metabolists, Gordon Bunshaft, Kevin Roche and many corporate practitioners, Piet Blom and Riema Pietila, John Andrews and a host of architects who are pushing the mainstream tradition hard in an attempt to deal with the failures of Modernism. Of the eight qualities or definers mentioned above these architects have five or six of them evidenced in their work, enough to group it together in spite of varying styles.

In like manner Post-Modernism must be defined as a loose overlap of qualities, although opposite to the previous ones: an interest in popular and local codes of communication (e.g. Portmeirion), in historical memory, urban context, ornament, representation, metaphor, participation, the public realm, pluralism and eclecticism (see the diagram on p.32).

Thus if we simplify from thirty possible attributes

MATHIAS UNGERS, *House types for Marburg*, 1976. Various models were developed sympathetic to the existing historic fabric. While the gridded geometry is very Modernist, the scale, variety and strong symbolic shapes are historicist. In other schemes Ungers returns to infinite repetition and the canons of Modernism.

(listed in the diagram) to ten definers, we may say that if six of the ten are present in a work that is sufficient to define it as Post-Modern. Unmentioned is perhaps the most obvious definer and one that is shared by both groups – the evolution out of Modernism and therefore the continued presence of the International Style, in some form. This aspect is most clear to a traditional architect, and why he continues to censor both Late and Post-Modernism without making distinctions. For us, however, it is crucial to make the distinctions between these two schools because of the significant, philosophical differences. Briefly they may be described as differences over an intention to communicate: Post-Modernists, in an attempt to reach the various users of their buildings, *doubly-code the architecture* and use a wide spectrum of communicational means whereas Late-Modernists remain within the restricted and hermeneutic language of Modernism.

Having drawn these distinctions in terms of number and degree however, it is not surprising that several architects fall between schools, or sometimes, as in the case of Philip Johnson and Mathias Ungers, go back and forth. This vacillation is not surprising given both the philosophical confusion of the moment and the opposite demands on the architect – that he should design both conventional glass and steel skyscrapers and contextual buildings. In fact if we were looking for stylistic definers alone, as historians usually do, we would only be partly successful in classifying schools. Thus we might speak of

a

b

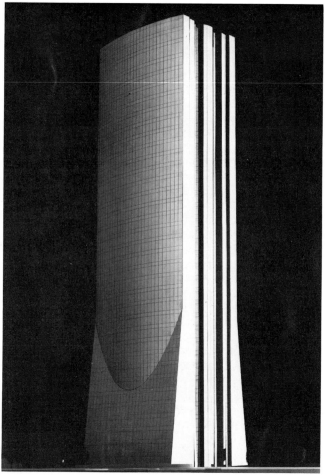

e

d

c

LATE-MODERNIST fragmentation of the slab. Kevin Roche's tower opposite the United Nations in New York (a) slides back three times and also decreases the scale by a small horizontal grid. Philip Johnson's towers in Minneapolis (b) and Houston play with the corner problem in a new way, either by increasing the articulation from one juncture to seven, or by making it triangular and splayed back. Anthony Lumsden, from DMJM, undulates the wall (c) or gives it a bevelled base (d), while John Portman uses the rhythmical set-back (e). There is enough in common between these schemes to characterize a shared approach to the skyscraper: an emphasis on the stretched skin, the ambiguities of reflection and scale distortion, and the exaggeration of single themes perceivable in an instant. The problem of the skyline created by these angular flat tops and the problem of minimal reference was engaged by Johnson's AT & T building.

the Late-Modern 'slick-tech' look, the faceted glass polyhedra which develops the stretched skin surface beyond Modernism. Here the work of Pelli and DMJM shares a lot with John Portman, Norman Foster, Philip Johnson, Arata Isozaki and so many commercial developers who use mirror-plate.

Generally speaking the surface of these buildings is isotropic and endless, a grid of repeated shapes which might be extended infinitely, but which has, in volume, many subtle variations. Johnson's Minneapolis tower staggers the corner so many times that it becomes a faceted wall; his Houston towers set triangular shapes in counterpoint to rectangular planes; Stubbins' and Roche's recent skyscrapers in New York also play these tricks in scale and massing in a way which might be called 'Picturesque-Modern'. Isozaki and others have developed the 'smash joint', that is a non-joint joint where two homogeneous surfaces going different directions are 'smashed' together without a change in articulation, without space, mouldings or the typical sculptural

modulations of Modernism. The ambiguities are as interesting as the break with tradition. The visual hallucinations caused by repeated reflections and layered transparency add an interest lacking in Modernist skyscrapers, but clearly they are Late-Modern rather than a complete break with the previous style.

It is instructive to look at several architects whose work appears to be going Post-Modern without, however, having the majority of P.M. definers. These I would term 'difficult cases' – that is difficult to classify in either school, not necessarily difficult architects. The recent work of Michael Graves and Paolo Portoghesi fits partly into both schools; it has historical roots, without the references being easily understood; it uses elements decoratively without wishing to use them conventionally. In short, it partly establishes a communication with the users as Post-Modernists do more thoroughly and it partly treats architecture as esoteric sculpture, as do the Late-Modernists.

The Casa Papanice in Rome starts, as many of Portoghesi's buildings do, from where Borromini left the Baroque: as an enjoyable game of walls sliding in and out to accent the doors and windows, the erotic zones of architecture. The Baroque slight curve *is* clearly recognizable, no one could miss it, and since Rome is largely a Baroque city one can find many contextual reasons for this revival including a response to the site, a curving in to frame a tree, or to catch light etc. Portoghesi has drawn an explanatory plan analysis which shows the three basic

PAOLO PORTOGHESI, *Casa Papanice*, Rome, 1970. Windows are treated in a variety of ways, but the horizontal bands are continued to keep the eye moving uninterruptedly as in Borromini's architecture.

PAOLO PORTOGHESI, *Casa Papanice*, Rome, 1970. View from the back shows the roof terrace 'organ pipes' surrounding concentric circles over the dining area. Bedroom balconies, 'striped candy-cane' and stepping stone 'coins' carry out the kitsch metaphors which are underscored by the glazed tiling in glistening stripes of green from the ground, blue from the sky and gold from the owner. The Rococo lightness to the overall building comes partly from the white background and delicate verticals.

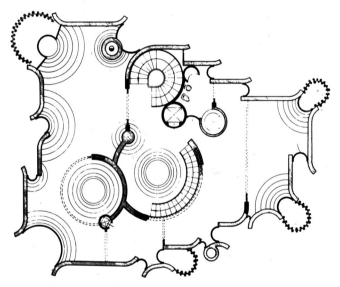

Casa Papanice, dining area is marked by concentric curves as are the fireplace and various lighting conditions, natural and artificial.

generators of curves (poles of access, light and function) and how they are organized on a grid set diagonally to the 'front' of the building.

The light-catching curves create a pool of lightness, emphasized by concentric curves above the windows. The explicitness of the metaphor here is Post-Modern, the desire to communicate on the literal level so that the viewer becomes sensitized to certain themes which he then seeks to find in more subtle instances. The metaphor of defining 'pools of place' is just as explicit above the twin 'hearts' of the house – the hearth and dining alcove which also receive their telescoping curves. It is a very convincing attempt to give back to the house those traditional centres which were overlooked by Modernists. But, as with Frank Lloyd Wright, who also accentuated these centres, they are dramatized with unconventional ornament and esoteric symbols: not mouldings but stepped 'saucers', not dados but horizontal stripes painted green (for children) and blue (for adults). Who would understand this symbolism, and the fact that Portoghesi used it partly to keep the client from covering the wall with his questionable paintings (a very Modernist stance to battle the taste of the client).[2] Furthermore the popular images latent within these forms call up metaphors which tend to undercut the seriousness of the work; the flying saucers look like an Art Deco restaurant lounge, the stripes like Christmas packaging.

Of course Portoghesi, like Charles Moore and others, intends these whimsical meanings and enjoys a flirtation with kitsch, especially in a building which asks for it. Here the client wanted his house to be featured in films – and it already has been a backdrop for three, including a science fiction film and melodrama with Monica Vitti. So a very sophisticated acknowledgement of opposed taste-cultures is being made: Borromini for the classes and Rockefeller Center for the masses. But it is arguable that the presence of these images – the 'organ-pipes' on the roof, the 'money-pavement' on the ground and the 'sugar-cane' balconies – distract us from deeper meanings. We are inclined to dismiss this work because of some superficial facility and aberrant readings. That is when we see the roof cylinders rising up and down in easy staccato rhythms, like organ-pipes in so many shlocky music halls, we doubt the presence of richer meanings. The glistening exterior tiles, in candy stripes of blue, green, brown and gold, also look trite.

Yet these surface images should not trick us into dismissing Portoghesi anymore than Rococo embellishments should make us disregard Balthazar Newmann. Architects and intellectuals are as likely to be taken in by superficiality as the general public, although in opposite ways, and both the Baroque and Rococo have been underrated by them until quite recently. For similar reasons I think Portoghesi's lightness and good humour have been underrated.[3] They are like the froth and cheerfulness of a German Rococo church, something that reveals *and* conceals a basic seriousness and creativity.

Casa Papanice, reflected ceiling plan showing graduated circles and the restricted gamut of inflected walls. 'Pools' of space with their ceiling 'ripples' are organized on a grid set diagonally to the basic axes, so that the eye is continuously moving to the corner views.

We have mentioned the ripples of circular motifs which define pools of space, and the way light is modulated on these curves. If we look closer at the curved window areas of the living-dining spaces we see how controlled is the quality of spatial differentiation. There is the general diagonal pull towards exterior views (marked V in plan) which keeps the eye moving laterally away from the dining and fire places to focus on exterior events. As in Baroque buildings the eye is further pulled across surfaces by the horizontal bands which, like a Borromini cornice, continue across interruptions. These swirling lines are then played in a different key in the ceiling, light fixtures and mirrors (which reflect views of the ground thus establishing yet another relation to nature). But the connection of inside and outside space isn't complete as in so much Modern space. The window articulation (what Portoghesi has called 'the dialectic window' to distin-

FRANCESCO BORROMINI, *S. Ivo della Sapienza*, Rome, 1642–50, entablature unifies the convex and concave shapes in a dynamic swirl of continuously alternating rhythms (A, C, A; A, B, A etc.) Portoghesi has written an extensive study of this architect's language.

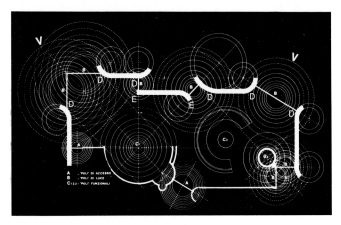

Casa Papanice, schematic spatial analysis of public area with zones of A-access, B-light, C-functions: dining, sitting, fireplace. In addition, different lighting and edge conditions can be seen when a wall curves out, D, or exposes an edge and turns in E. V signifies important corner views.

guish various types of treatment) varies the view in significant ways. The inflected walls curve back to back (D in plan) for major views, or alternate curved and flat surface for more hidden and mysterious views (E). Thus exterior space is implied rather than seen at these points and an element of expectation and surprise is introduced. The graduation in light intensity further intensifies both in the curved wall and graduated steps of the saucers. Such refinements both inside and out make this a subtle use of kitsch motifs for very non-kitsch ends.

If Portoghesi's work does not quite use conventional ornament to communicate directly neither does Michael Graves'. Rather they both use complex transformations of historical imagery which have to be analyzed, sometimes laboriously, to be perceived. Since about 1976 Graves has introduced recognizable mouldings, split pediments, keystones, lattice-work, Cretan columns – in short historicist recollections – into his work. Previously it had been restricted more or less to the vocabulary of the twenties and Juan Gris.[4]

His Cultural Bridge project – to unite the two towns Fargo and Moorhead with a cultural centre – consists of symbolic images of unity and division which relate to historic forms. First of all the bridge itself is, as Graves pointed out to me in conversation, a heavy Palladian type gesture rather than the thin shells of Modernism and Maillart.[5] It has the overtones of many existing bridges

including those with buildings on them such as the Ponte Vecchio. The placement of a heavy form over water, on the middle of two arms, is quite naturally a very strong symbol of unification, of meeting, of binding two halves, in this case two competitive communities, together.

Graves has shown the etymology of meanings in his exquisite thumb-nail sketches which we can follow in detail. First the rotunda of Ledoux, a massive cylinder surmounting a horizontal, bridge-like base (a), then a pyramidal form from Castle Howard is placed over another Ledoux theme of water spilling through a half cylinder (b). Next the pediment is broken in its centre so that the void, rather than solid, symbolizes unity (c). This created a problem with respect to the sky since Graves wanted to keep the tripartite organization of bridges – basement, piano nobile and attic. So he went to a new formal and historical solution, proposing a profile stepped up and relating to the *Serliana* (d) (a motif which can be seen in the final project, now quite thick and covered with an abstract grid).

The next step consists of simplifying this arch, thickening it and stepping up walls (e) rather than the profile (in the final project they've become overscaled glazed elements – giant windows, 'eyes'). Then, the last sketch shows an early synthesis of the central block: the dropped keystone out of which water pours (f) (or like Ledoux's Chaux, a sculptural mass of symbolic water frozen into rock); the 'legs', 'eyes' and strong anthropomorphic imagery which will become even stronger with the addition of a 'nose'; finally the thick vaults of unification.

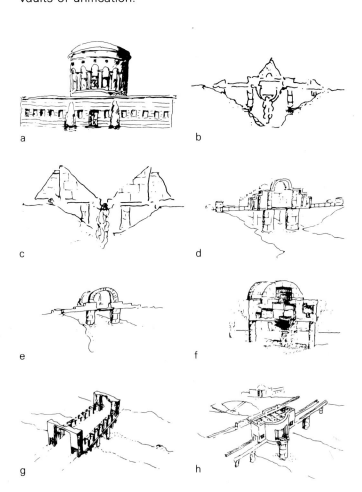

MICHAEL GRAVES, *Fargo/Moorhead Cultural Bridge*, 1977, referential sketches showing historical transformations from Ledoux etc. (see text).

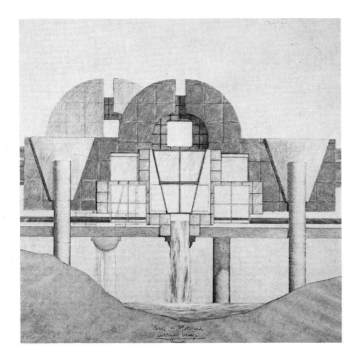

Fargo/Moorhead, rendered elevation, 1978. The basic theme of two communities unified by an arch, yet still separate – its break and twin in the background – comes through even if the specific references remain hidden.

In the adjoining sketches the evolution of the bridge may be seen, with its emphasis on the edges, and disunity, as well as the framed exedra of the centre. The distinctive step here is the addition of two end 'triumphal arches' with their jagged inside edges, what Graves calls his 'English-Muffin-fork-split' (g). Twin pergolas, later to become a heavy raised cornice of building, emphasize the duality once again. The inspiration for this was, apparently, the dual-centre projects of Asplund as well as a painting of an arch at Kew, by Richard Wilson, 1762. Finally, the inverted pyramid of glazing in the centre was partly inspired by the lantern of Borromini's San Carlo alle Quattro Fontane and its perspective effect of diminishment.

To all these explicit references should be added the bridge column capitals which relate to many Modern concrete constructions, the handling of the broken pediment related to Mannerist architecture and the blue, red and orange colouring present in Cubist painting. The references are thus quite specific and numerous. Two general points might be made concerning their efficacy and relation to the architecture we are discussing: as a precise set of meanings their significance would be totally lost to the citizen of Fargo and Moorhead. The codes are too esoteric, the meanings too private to Graves and architectural scholars, to communicate the depth of reference intended. For those willing to go through the above analysis the bridge is, no doubt, a multivalent work sending out a criss-cross of elaborated meanings quite marvellously complicated in their interrelations. But for the uninformed beholder there are not enough explicit cues for this rich interpretive process to take place: in this way the scheme is characteristic of the private language games of Late-Modernism. Secondly however, and in contradiction to this privacy of meaning, there is a general penumbra of historic meaning which would, I believe, be perceived.[6] It is a question of suggested metaphor, implicit rather than explicit coding, and here Graves' work has a breadth and particularity of reference which is quite apt.

In gross terms most people would probably perceive

the dominant images of unification and division. The 'arms' of the two arches reach out to meet each other, but don't yet touch, implicit metaphors of striving for civic unification. This theme of 'unified-duality' is repeated often enough – the broken arches are offset in plan – to be readily perceivable. Furthermore the repeated symmetries, like those of the human, are echoed forcefully throughout and we all know, because it is a fact of our bodies, that this symmetry of two things constitutes a single whole. As mentioned, the eyes, nose, mouth and legs are implicitly coded and they underline this basic body metaphor. For these reasons the Fargo/Moorhead Bridge is a very appropriate symbol of cultural unification, and Post-Modern in the clarity with which it expresses this symbol. Like all of Graves' work it is also very convincing as a sensual and sculptural composition.

Post-Modernism

Post-Modernists, to turn now to the other major school, double-code their buildings so that they communicate with their users as well as other architects and it is this attempt which ties them to previous traditions – the classical language, Queen Anne Revival and Art Nouveau, to name three.[7]

As an example of double-coding let me illustrate Philip Johnson's recent design for the AT & T building in New York, which has been called by Paul Goldberger 'Post-Modernism's major monument'.[8] As pointed out by Goldberger the top of this skyscraper looks very much like a Chippendale highboy or an eighteenth-century grandfather's clock. Furthermore it will function as an eighteenth-century fantasy scheme of Ledoux or Boullée if, as intended, smoke from the heating system pours out from the hole in the broken pediment. The bottom continues the historical allusions including, within, a 'forest of columns' and, without, a very Renaissance motif, the *Serliana*, or according to Johnson, the front of Brunelleschi's Pazzi Chapel.

The ambiguity of formal reading here is shared by the main shaft of the elevation which, at thirty miles an hour (the speed of a New York taxi driver) might look like a modern, granite sheathed skyscraper: or, more slowly and carefully, like a work of Louis Sullivan, that is, 'Pre-Modernist'. The divisions and syncopations come directly from the classical skyscraper tradition – the Auditorium Building in Chicago of Adler and Sullivan. But behind this, in fairly strong contrast, is a traditional modern skyscraper trying to get out, or rather stay in.

These codes are fairly explicit and some of them are shared by both the man in the taxi and the architect. Depending on how the granite and ornament are handled, I think further meanings will become equally clear.

If the reticence of the side elevation is anything to go by then the building will start to approach the Gucci Look, or better the Lanvin Mode. It will be perceived as in the Fifth Avenue or Bond Street Style, signifying fastidiousness and boredom, that combination of good taste and uncreativity which has made prestige commissions so remorselessly funereal. If the detailing follows the front elevation then there is more hope for the scheme: it will take the cosmetic associations and tie them with the more local sustaining meanings I have mentioned. This amalgam could be witty and even appropriate. The skyscraper as elongated grandfather's clock, as gigantic Lanvin perfume bottle, as Renaissance chapel, as Neo-Fascist colonnade, as imprisoned Lever Building, or Rolls Royce radiator. The New Yorker may be well pleased to

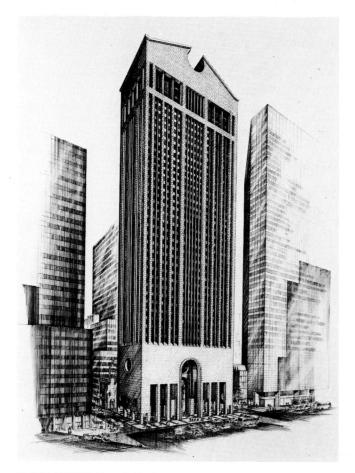

PHILIP JOHNSON, and JOHN BURGEE, *AT & T Building*, New York City, 1978–82?, re-establishes the conventional New York skyscraper code of an articulated masonry frame culminating in a pitched roof of classical provenance. Various historical codes underlie this form including the column (i.e. base, shaft, capital, entablature), the Pazzi Chapel (base), the Chippendale highboy (top) and the Rolls Royce radiator.

HANS HOLLEIN, '*Rolls Royce Grill on Wall Street*', 1966, predicts the recurrence of this temple image. The associations of business propriety with the Parthenon are not fortuitous as historians have shown.

HANS HOLLEIN, *Austrian Travel Bureau*, Vienna, 1978. Placed under a Secessionist gridded barrel vault are various conventional signs of foreign travel: a Lutyens dome for India, Moroccan palm trees, a ruined Greek column encasing a chrome support and other symbols not visible here.

Travel Bureau, cashier's till is marked by reticent Rolls Royce grills, another ironic use of a conventional sign. Hollein, an admirer of Johnson, has also recently moved towards a Post-Modern use of historical reference.

see these meanings come into his skyscraper, and delighted by the elegance with which the thirty foot pediment lifts up its ears, gently, at the ends. 'Chippendale indeed, we can put that grandfather's clock right opposite the front door.' The skyscraper has been given a diminutive model, a perfume bottle, or furniture case.

So the building makes use of quite contradictory codes in an entertaining way: it's not the most creative synthesis of double-coding and it will probably be heavily criticised for that (e.g. for being a conventional glass and steel building inside a conventional Louis Sullivan). But a degree of credit should go to Johnson, I feel, for the sensitivity with which he has combined local, New York

codes. Although it is not as confident as the Chrysler Building and other historicist skyscrapers of the twenties and thirties, it is still the first New York skyscraper for a long time to go beyond the flat-top look.

Probably younger designers working on smaller commissions have greater scope for developing historicist imagery than those trained in the International Style. Particularly those trained by the historicists at Yale (Venturi, Moore and Scully) have a freedom of expression denied to their teachers, who had to struggle against Modernism. James Righter and Peter Rose, who worked under Charles Moore, have developed his flat, wood-sheath aesthetic to the point where it can make quite

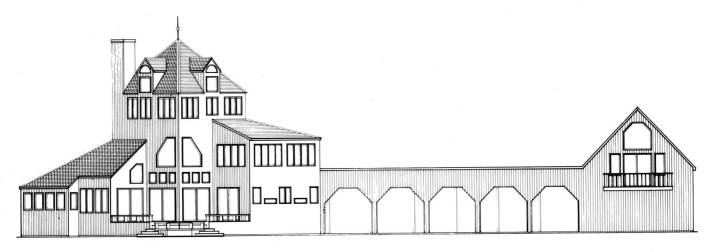

JAMES VOLNAY RIGHTER, *Osborn House*, Fisher's Island, 1972–3. Large volumetric shapes in wood recalling the Queen Anne Revival of a century before. A basic square geometry is rotated to forty-five degrees and then opened out to the view, arcade and studio.

straightforward allusions to a monumental architecture of the past, to Palladianism and the nineteenth century. Their justifications for these images appear convincing because they are tied very closely to the local context or the symbolic function of the building. For instance the ski-lodge, Pavillon Soixante-Dix, is given its steep roofs because of heavy snows, and the omnipresence of this vernacular form in the area. The cut-out arch motif relates to local buildings *and* acts as a symbolic gate welcoming the skiers. The sun-deck, a semi-circular Palladian exedra influenced by the Villa Trissina, also has a symbolic role of welcoming, as well as a practical function of sunbathing, and viewing the skiers' approach. The architects have underlined these symbolic considerations.

> The intention of the building is to affirm the importance of skiing as a social event, to give every participant a sense of the romance of being in the North, outside, with friends. To do this, the building itself must have a presence, a feeling of monumentality, even if that monumentality is derived from familiar images.[9]

If the exedra, symmetry, chimneys and entrance all remind us of monumental buildings, then other cues remind us of Modernism: the flattening of the arch at its top, the flat, skin surface and the absence of ornament,

except for a thin strip of neon light, under the arch. This is another kind of double-coding, half Modern, half something else, which is characteristic of Post-Modernism. We can see it in Peter Rose's Marosi House and James Righter's Osborn House buildings which relate as much to the Shingle Style and Neo-Queen Anne as they do to the Moore aesthetic. On one level these hybrids are disquieting as hybrids always are: they remind us of what is lost in translation as well as gained by historical allusion. In these cases we see the Shingle Style spaces without the detailing and scale of that exquisite domestic style. The Osborn House, for instance, has an attractive diagonal plan that focuses on dining-room and chimney, the twin symbolic centres of domestic life, but these important zones are then left embarrassingly free of adornment. It is not only the craft tradition which has died, but architects' desire and ability to sustain significant ornament.

One Post-Modern architect in Japan, Yasufumi Kijima, is really trying to resurrect significant ornament, even if he isn't altogether succeeding. Several of his houses use pan-tile and sliding screens in a traditional and modern way, but the results are rather strained. Like Robert Stern's applied ornament, the mouldings and repeated patterns are etiolated and brittle. Indeed one might characterize Post-Modern ornament in general this way and try to see this thinness as a positive quality. Since the nineteenth century, machine-made ornament has been over-precise as compared with the hand-crafted variety. Although this and other factors led to its rejection by

21

Osborn House, plan and view from open living room to dining-room and beyond to landscape. The chimney acts, as in Wright's work, as both centre and divider of space. Here it becomes part of a wall and alcove. Movement through the house is by a series of zig-zags organized on the diagonal. The ambiguities are typical of Post-Modern space.

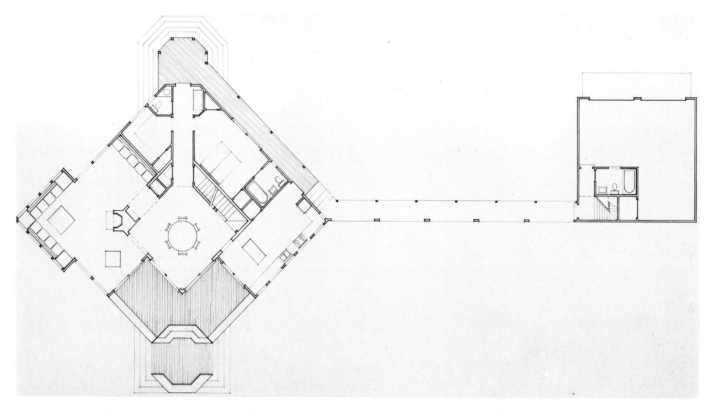

J. V. RIGHTER, P. ROSE and P. LANKIN, *Pavillon Soixante-Dix*, St. Sauveur, Canada, 1976–8. The skiers aim towards the embracing arms of the exedra, the social area and sun deck on which skiers always lounge about waiting for things to happen. The false front, reminiscent of local buildings, also reminds one of a cathedral porch with its two towers.

Pavillon Soixante-Dix, perspective shows pitched roof articulations common to resort hotels as well as mouldings, unfortunately not yet added.

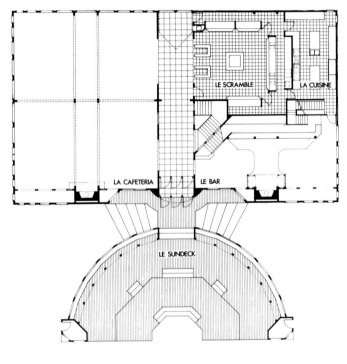

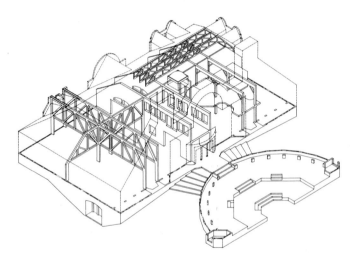

Pavillon Soixante-Dix, plan and cut-away projection show Palladian planning as well as the different articulations of space by a changing structure. The cafeteria, for 300 skiers, is twenty feet high, 'panelled and beamed in wood to recall the great Laurentian lodges of seventy years ago. The bar is more intimate, panelled again, and centred on an open fireplace.'

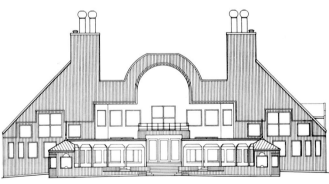

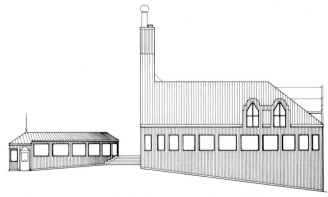

Pavillon Soixante-Dix, 'The facade was taken from the false front of a fine building at Ste-Agathe, but it was chopped to suggest the Second-Empire mansard of a great Montreal hotel. The chimneys came from the gable wall of a stone farm house of the early 1800s. A geometric panel was cut out to emphasize the entrance. Great windows were put in for the sun and view of the hills. And a classic plaza was placed in front.' (Quoted from the client brochure, 1977).

YASUFUMI KIJIMA, *Matsuo Shrine* in Kamimuta, 1975–6. A barrel-vaulted temple added onto a traditional Japanese shrine as an entrance narthex. This open-air front has an hallucinatory quality partly caused by the exquisite scale and machine-like finish and partly caused by the mixture of Eastern and Western references.

Matsuo Shrine, detail of columns touching water and meeting decorative capitals, decorated with fir motifs(?) and T-junctions. The precise curves of the arch make it look like an extruded metal section.

Modernists, I think the precision has its own virtue – a linear, elegant sleekness attacked by traditionalists. In a sense this is precisely the virtue of the Miesian aesthetic; and Kijima's Matsuo Shrine looks rather as if Mies had decided to detail coffered tunnel vaults and Japanese Doric rather than I-beams. The result is quite surreal. His conceptual drawing, made after the building was complete, as is his practice, reminds one of Escher's transformations of one thing into another. Here an upside-down Corinthian column and its fluting transform themselves into a colonnade, while the dome of the Pantheon transmutes into the coffering of the barrel vault. These two Western images are then attached to Eastern motifs, the lily pond and Japanese shrine. The contrast is just kept from becoming kitsch by the elegant smallness and detailing of the scheme. Here precise ornament is a help. Each pre-cast detail, each capital and entablature, fulfils its role like the part of a well-built machine. The copper shingles are stretched taught around the cylindrical roof like steel plates on the hull of a ship. The pristine entrance arch curves in an exact arc like a polished gear wheel. What could be more twentieth-century *and* traditional than this image of the extruded temple?

Kijima, as one would guess, discusses his use of hybrid ornament with a certain irony:

> Each part of a building should have its own innate life. Substantiating the boundaries among these various parts is architectural design . . . one of the major points in style is the ability of ornament within a style to communicate a definite mood. But this does not mean that a style is consequently fixed or that there is a fixed relation between ornament and style. Ingenuity and an original solution to the problems at hand must always play a part in architectural design. I employ beautiful decorative elements of both the East and West to ornament my buildings. People who cannot understand the essentials of what I am doing despise such work as mere imitation. I have no desire to refute their assertions. Each person has his own level of ability.[10]

Clearly Kijima's work is not imitative, whatever else it is. One is tempted to call it hallucinatory, a delirious combination of opposites, East and West, traditional ornament and machine aesthetic. The double-coding is there with a vengeance. What adds to the feelings of a reverie is the fact that symbolic forms, which had a precise historical role, are now being quite resemanticized *in their totality*. Whereas Michael Graves uses historical fragments, he keeps them implicit enough so that the previous meanings don't entirely dominate. My own view of Kijima's building is that in this particular context, as a shrine gateway, the hallucinatory meanings are plausible and almost appropriate. The comment of the machine metaphor on religious persuasion is also plausible today in the age of mass-cults, even if it is not a pleasant thought.

YASUFUMI KIJIMA, *drawing of Matsuo Shrine*. As in one of M. C. Escher's drawings elements transform themselves both in space and in content. Here a Corinthian column becomes the colonnade, while the coffers of the Pantheon become the barrel vault. The mirror of the water perhaps prompted these reflections.

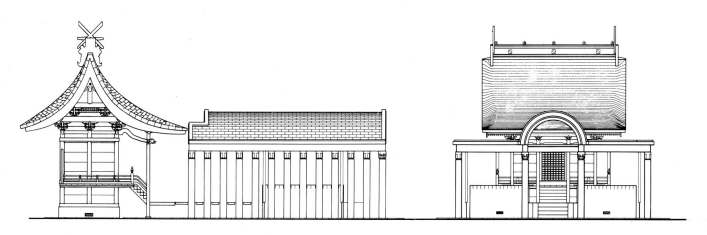

Certain problems of Kijima's shrine face all Post-Modernists and if these problems are not entirely solved at least here they are faced. First of course is the question of a plural culture and the corresponding double-coding – two traditions in Japan, or many subcultures in the West – a pluralism which Kijima tries to acknowledge rather than disregard like Late-Modernists. Second are the questions of ornament and beauty; concepts, indeed words, on which there has been a fifty year moratorium. Lastly there is the question of explicit versus implicit reference and the difficulties of going from one level of communication to the other in a free and intelligent way. No Post-Modernist has mastered these problems as, for instance, the Baroque architect did, yet one, Thomas Gordon Smith, who has studied Baroque, is beginning to find a way.

Smith studied painting and sculpture at Berkeley before he went on to study architecture there and the visual confidence of an artist can be felt behind his drawings. Indeed some of them have a free-flowing ease which makes them appear much more facile and instantaneous than they are: in reality many studies occur which use xerox, model building, photography and sketch in alternation before the design is resolved and the free-hand perspective is made. The results show a resolution of parts, curve answering curve, asymmetrical volume balancing a column rhythm, that is comparable to the Ronchamp of Le Corbusier or the finely tuned harmonies of Michael Graves. The sophistication is quite remarkable in an architect so young. (Smith, born in 1948, started producing his eclectic projects in 1975 at the age of twenty-seven which is old for a Renaissance artist/architect, but young for one trained today in the university system).

The early projects such as the Doric House and Paulownia House show his interest in attaching giant porticos, the *Serliana* once again, to very modest, vernacular shacks conceived with the most inexpensive technology. One can criticize these works for lacking maturity, for being exaggerated jokes – for instance the Paulownia entrance is only half a *Serliana*, the other half is reflected by mirror. As in so much American historicism the classical portico shouts at you rather than lets you enter unobtrusively. Yet these overstatements are probably the result of youth and the fact that the projects are still unbuilt, exaggerations which would tend to go away when the building is detailed.

A more recent scheme, the Richard and Sheila Long House, is more subtle in its blend of historical quotes. As the aerial perspective shows, the house picks up the curves of the landscape, rather the way the Rococo church *Die Wies* picks up the undulations of the surrounding mountains. Two terrace views, two ovals, organize north and south elevations, while a third curve, that of the entrance drive way, determines the west front. Thus three curves determine a pinwheel or modified Y plan, which rotates around the family dining-room.

Approaching through the west entry, an egg-shape broken off axis, one reaches the foyer/stairs, another oval which forces movement in a counter direction. Then one is turned again toward the south terrace.

> From mid-point in the foyer the vista through the serpentine hall reveals half building, half landscape. I hope that one's vision, while walking through the hall, will be like a pan-in [during a] film. At one point the door frame will be revealed, then [the view] will pan-out to only landscape. I began the bedroom plan

as a simplified version of Dientzenhofer's St. Xavier. The phallic allusion became apparent later, and in this case appropriate to exploit? My objection to Tigerman's Daisy House is that it expresses a single idea – it seems obsessive.[11]

Personally, I find Tigerman's symbolism only explicit in plan, but the importance of this quote is that it shows Smith's interest in merging historical allusions with other things – the landscape, a filmic procession and the content of the bedroom. This is an accomplished eclecticism and one which uses previous solutions as a method of creativity. Like Graves' use of historical fragments they provide a test, or question, for the new function. Here, for instance, Kilian Ignaz Dientzenhofer's church plan, a dumb bell shape which mediates between a centralized and longitudinal plan, places entrance and study area on the axes which previously were given to narthex and altar. There is no question of sacrilege here because the allusion is implicit, as is that of the phallic symbol. And the treatment of the ceiling, rather than merging grandiloquent vaults, is a modest, even gentle, rise and fall.

It is one of Smith's great strengths that he can design beautiful curves without falling into the twin dangers of bathos and cliché. So much Post-Modernism is calculatedly ugly and ill-proportioned: Robert Venturi enjoys a dislocation in scales and Robert Stern gets a similar pleasure by distorting his mouldings, placing windows in disproportion to the cornice etc. Thomas Gordon Smith, who obviously has learned from these architects, nevertheless strives after a unification and resolution of parts in his work. This, inevitably, is like the Baroque response to Mannerist distortion and disunity. The south view of the Long House shows a gentle swell of curves up to the edge of the semi-enclosed terrace; then they cascade down in easy sweeps. An S-curve is answered by three U-curves; the bedroom door is answered by the gable window; the split, Michelangelesque pediments are also in counterpoint. The beauty of this antiphony is quite equivalent to that of the best Picturesque or Neo-Queen Anne design.

Actually many of Smith's design ideas spring from San Francisco architects, and the more general Bay Area tradition. He wrote a historical study while at Berkeley on John Hudson Thomas and he has studied the work of Bernard Maybeck, so naturally one can see a plethora of references to these two eclectics. From Hudson Thomas comes the picturesque massing and disjunction of large framed openings, the giant curves, and from Maybeck comes the overhanging eaves and emphasis on giant porticoes. All this architecture shares something with the Californian bungalow tradition which it helped create; in particular the emphasis on cheap, decorative construction and the superimposition of aedicular entrances. It is not surprising then to find the Matthews Street House a mixture of the bungalow and Maybeck portico, of the explicit symbol of a classical entrance *and* the cheap stucco box. These contradictions are a very deep part of the Bay Area tradition.

The plan, on a tight street lot of 130 × 30 feet, shows a sophisticated use of layered space, layered at right angles to the central axis. Since one side of the lot borders the adjoining house, Smith closes off this view and orients the secondary axis to one side, the south. This asymmetrical symmetry then is felt in other places. It pushes the major axis slightly to the left of centre of the lot, which then allows other spaces, or rooms, on the right side. In elevation this produces the staggered

THOMAS GORDON SMITH, *Richard and Sheila Long House*, Carson City, Nevada, 1977, project. The broken curve, the semi-form, the elliptical usage (in both senses of the word) relate this to Baroque architecture, but the materials are local and informal.

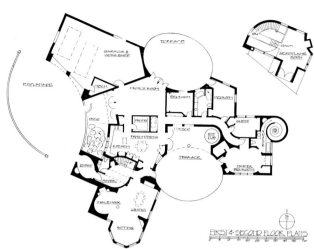

Long House, plan, shows again the mixture of Baroque semi-forms – twisted ovals, dumb-bells, volutes – and vernacular motifs. The basic Y shape pivots around the family dining-room. Several pure shapes are half enclosed and half open thus mediating space.

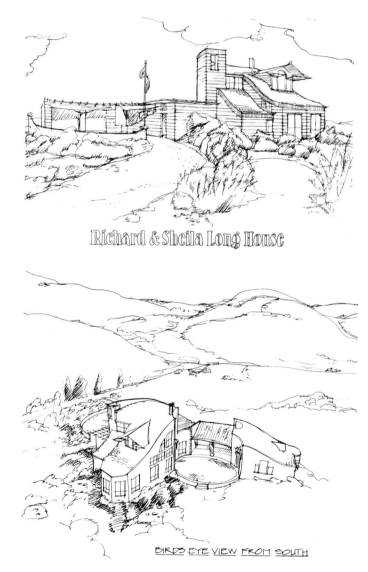

THOMAS GORDON SMITH, *Richard and Sheila Long House*, Carson City, Nevada, 1977, project. Baroque semi-curves pick up the rolling landscape and open the home out to views. Outdoor oval terraces are sheltered from the strong winds and sun. A mixture of informal, rambling skyline and formal motifs such as the gable, *Serliana* and pedimented door.

Long House, perspective of south terrace, 1978. Forms in easy-going counterpart, rise up and fall to either side of an informal portico with its massive single column. Michelangelesque pediments in green articulate formal points, while the smooth S-curve rises up to allow more space and light in the public area. Shingle decoration is painted following Bernard Maybeck's usage.

Long House, master bedroom towards south. A symmetry focusing on the bed produces the image of a face. The swell of the roof and odd skylights add a certain quizzical charm to the implicit metaphors.

27

THOMAS GORDON SMITH, *Matthews Street House*, coloured perspective, 1978. A formal classical front and an informal, green stucco
behind, staggered in plan to the right. The public area is picked out in
pinks, reds, blues and golds, reminiscent of Greek colourings, while the
flat green shades recall the pastel colours of the surrounding houses.
Significant points are highlit in red.

rhythm A/A' characteristic of the bungalow, but also an
asymmetrical wall-plus-column set against two columns.
A walk through this shifted symmetry is a varied experience. First the outdoor round terrace with its bed of
strongly coloured foxgloves, then the Doric portico set at
right angles to movement, then four more slots of space
at right angles to the axial approach, the largest one of
which, a demi-oval, is the sitting area of the living room.
Beyond this are three more spaces, shifted now slightly
to the right and centre of the lot – the kitchen space
below the private bedrooms. The cut-away aerial perspective shows the resolution of these spaces and the
complex geometrical patterns, which include an eclectic
mixture of diagonal floor tiles, Solomonic columns, sash
windows staggered up the wall and Japanese figural
shapes.

All in all the eclecticism is quite masterful, even if a bit
overpowering. As the coloured perspective shows there
is a basic division between the grand public space and
the modest private realm behind. Each realm receives its
appropriate symbolism, and the irony of the shifted
symmetry is indicated by the free-standing, displaced
Corinthian column banished way out in the garden,
where ruins are conventionally placed. One may object to
the exaggeration of historical references, but as mentioned there are reasons for this including the local
context of exaggerated bungalow design.

* * *

THOMAS GORDON SMITH, *Matthews Street House*, Michelangelo
and Dientzenhofer motifs combined with the San Francisco painted-
house vernacular.

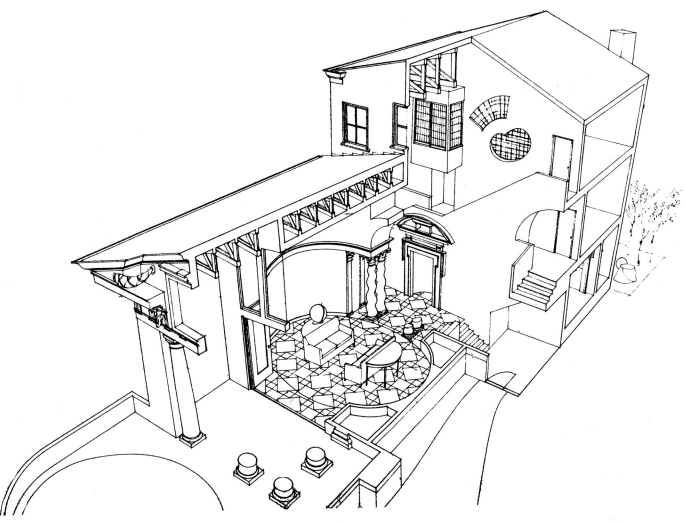

Matthews Street House, aerial perspective, 1978, showing the resolution of various sources – Maybeck, Bay Area, Michelangelo, Baroque and Japanese. Note the tiny scale, seemingly large because of the historical references.

Matthews Street House, plan. A central axis shifted slightly to north of the lot, allows a spatial development and orientation to the south. Basically the eye is led westward in a sequence of several spaces opening south. The shifted axis is common to eighteenth-century French hôtels, Lutyens and now Post-Modernists.

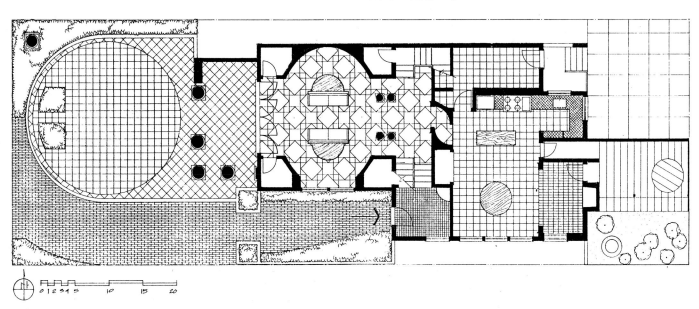

RICARDO BOFILL and OFFICE, *Xanadu*, Calpe, Spain, 1967. 'Baroque Modern' mixture of ascending curves, pan-tiles and semi-circles set against cantilevers and hyperbolic paraboloids in this collection of seventeen seaside apartments.

In conclusion, one should reiterate that there are real philosophical and social issues which divide Late-Modernists and Post-Modernists, and they focus over the basic issue of architecture as communication. Late-Modernists stress the aesthetic aspect of the architectural language, whereas Post-Modernists, in an attempt to say more and say it coherently, stress the conventional aspects. Each school has a certain validity and acts as a challenge to the other. The perennial truth of Late-Modernists, that beauty can result from technical perfection and that the means of architecture are also, partly, its ends, remains a challenge to Post-Modernists whose handling of new technologies tends to be rudimentary. Their counter-claim that architecture is a social art which communicates in a conventional code has, however, wider validity because it encompasses the technical and aesthetic codes within its framework. For such reasons I suspect that a future architecture will evolve out of Post-Modernism, but probably long after this name has been forgotten and a new label has been found. It is also likely that Late-Modernism and Post-Modernism will evolve towards each other, as they continue to compete, and approach some amalgam that might be termed 'Baroque Modern' (or is it 'Modern Baroque'?). But enough of labels.

1.3 THE RHETORIC OF LATE-MODERNISM – A PICTORIAL ESSAY

The following pictorial essay is an attempt to illustrate some rhetorical figures that are the basis for classifying Late-Modern architecture, below. Every architectural language has its own peculiar rhetoric which the historian and critic must define. To do this he might borrow terms from many sources not only from music, art and literary criticism. Here semiotics and classical rhetoric have been added to this heterogeneous list. The use of an architec-

tural language has as much to do with counterpoint as perspective, synecdoche as proportion and thus any extensive appreciation of a building will naturally make use of these various terms.

RICHARD MEIER, *Douglas House,* Harbour Springs, Michigan, 1971-3. The interpenetrating spatial levels and ship metaphor of Le Corbusier exaggerated and made into the subject of architecture. The subject of Late-Modernism is often Early-Modernism.

MODERN (1920–60)	LATE-MODERN (1960–)	POST-MODERN (1960–)
IDEOLOGICAL		
1 one international style, or 'no style'	unconscious style	double-coding of style
2 utopian and idealist	pragmatic	'popular' and pluralist
3 deterministic form, functional	loose fit	semiotic form
4 *Zeitgeist*	Late-Capitalist	traditions and choice
5 artist as prophet/healer	suppressed artist	artist/client
6 elitist/for 'everyman'	elitist professional	elitist and participative
7 wholistic, comprehensive redevelopment	wholistic	piecemeal
8 architect as saviour/doctor	architect provides service	architect as representative and activist
STYLISTIC		
9 'straightforwardness'	Supersensualism/Slick-Tech/High-Tech	hybrid expression
10 simplicity	complex simplicity – oxymoron, ambiguous reference	complexity
11 isotropic space (Chicago frame, Domino)	extreme isotropic space (open office planning, 'shed space') redundancy and flatness	variable space with surprises
12 abstract form	sculptural form, hyperbole, enigmatic form	conventional and abstract form
13 purist	extreme repetition and purist	eclectic
14 inarticulate 'dumb box'	extreme articulation	semiotic articulation
15 Machine Aesthetic, straightforward logic, circulation, mechanical, technology and structure	2nd Machine Aesthetic extreme logic, circulation, mechanical, technology and structure	variable mixed aesthetic depending on context; expression of content and semantic appropriateness towards function
16 anti-ornament	structure and construction as ornament	pro-organic and applied ornament
17 anti-representational	represent logic, circulation, mechanical, technology and structure frozen movement	pro-representation
18 anti-metaphor	anti-metaphor	pro-metaphor
19 anti-historical memory	anti-historical	pro-historical reference
20 anti-humour	unintended humour, malapropism	pro-humour
21 anti-symbolic	unintended symbolic	pro-symbolic
DESIGN IDEAS		
22 city in park	'monuments' in park	contextual urbanism and rehabilitation
23 functional separation	functions within a 'shed'	functional mixing
24 'skin and bones'	slick skin with Op effects wet look distortion, sfumato	'Mannerist and Baroque'
25 *Gesamtkunstwerk*	reductive, elliptical gridism 'irrational grid'	all rhetorical means
26 'volume not mass'	enclosed skin volumes, mass denied; 'all-over form' – synecdoche	skew space and extensions
27 slab, point block	extruded building, linearity	street building
28 transparency	literal transparency	ambiguity
29 asymmetry and 'regularity'	tends to symmetry and formal rotation, mirroring and series	tends to asymmetrical symmetry (Queen Anne Revival)
30 harmonious integration	packaged harmony, forced harmonization	collage/collision

CLASSIFYING MOVEMENTS ACCORDING TO THIRTY VARIABLES. Architectural historians usually classify movements according to a few stylistic categories, but here a more extended list of variables is used to bring out the complexity of the situation: the overlap, contradictions and differences among movements. Each variable may need a gloss to be fully understood. For instance the term 'utopian and idealist' in regard to architectural form, contains the notions that the Modern architect claimed to think out each design problem 'afresh' with regard to 'human needs' which generated a 'program' of 'functions' which was 'socially been assumed by a Modern architect, and many were enunciated by the theorists and propagandists. If one tried to list all of these notions the list would become impossibly large – in fact a book. So the chart is like any diagram, reductive.

The pictorial essay concentrates on *style* and *design ideas* since it would be vain to group visually according to *ideological* categories; but ideology is nonetheless important for understanding these movements. The order of the essay does not follow the order of the list and leaves out many categories, again for visual convenience and logic.

SUPERSENSUALISM, SLICK-TECH, SFUMATO

High and low versions of Slick-Tech architecture started in the mid sixties. Le Corbusier's last work with its high-gloss enamel panels and flat sheet steel and Hans Hollein's Candle Shop with its punched-out and warped use of polished aluminium established the style for architects and boutiques, but James Bond (given the Supersensualist title 'Kiss-Kiss-Bang-Bang' in Italy) defined the style for young executives and the Joint Chiefs of Staff. Hollein's work remains the most inventive and ironic in the genre as he incorporates veiled sexual meanings, and uses such rhetorical devices as oxymoron and sfumato (the 'soft/hardness' of the aluminium, the way it is treated as paper, the way the curve moves indistinctly from the flat plane, and light to darkness etc.) As can be seen in the boutiques on King's Road (GIRL, I-SPY, JUST LOOKING) Supersensualism is the natural style of narcissism because of its reflective and tactile qualities. Again the oxymoronic tricks of Hollein are used to good effect (metal as paper, logo as gate, inside as outside, manikin as person etc.)

(*below*) LE CORBUSIER, *Centre Le Corbusier*, Zurich, 1963-7;
(*bottom left*) HANS HOLLEIN, *Retti Candle Shop*, Vienna, 1965;
(*bottom right*) *Boutiques on King's Road*, London, 1968-70.

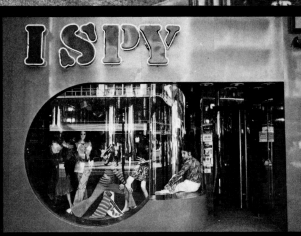

Wet-look distortion, synecdoche

The fantasy inherent in Slick-Tech revolves around the notion of
effortless mechanical control – which is well-illustrated by James
Stirling's giant executive toy produced for Olivetti. Like their sleekly
wrapped domestic equipment with its continuity of plastic over all parts,
the auditorium undulates in all-over GRP. This rhetorical device, synecdoche, a substitution of part for the whole or one element for others, is
coupled with a distortion of syntax (no usual joint, or gutter, between wall
and roof) and a dissonance of colour (cream clashing mushroom). Thus
an odd but interesting building. Note the gentle curved S-panels and their
resemblance to the 'soft-touch Divisumma 18 portable electric printing
calculator' as well as the classical cyma. On the inside panels placed
between Hollywood lighting fixtures can be raised or lowered to create
one of four possible conditions. This 'Yellow Submarine', with its Master
Control Room under the portholes, uses other explicit metaphors and
this places it on the road to Post-Modernism; whereas the Hyatt
Regency in Dallas seems to be unconscious in its imagery (the
animalistic head and tail, the Art Deco setbacks would seem to be
fortuitous). Both buildings emphasize the slippery wet-look and the
distortions caused by a reflective surface that is not entirely flat. This
produces highlights and again a sfumato which is not displeasing. The
Supersensualist fascination with gloss and reflection is
most apparent in the hotel – 'the largest glass
sculpture in the world' as one Texan
put it. Other images – 'a glittering
Xanadu', 'a pile of silver' – also focus
on the silver glass which, incidentally,
blinds rush-hour traffic when the sun
shines. Typically Bondian fantasies are
also served by this grand hotel: the 200
foot atrium highlights the space-capsule
elevators; the revolving restaurant, on its
560 foot tower, is surrounded by a network
of krypton bulbs (they last eleven years) which
can give Dallas, on occasion, two full moons
at night.

left) JAMES STIRLING, *Olivetti Training
School*, Haslemere, 1969-73;
above, right and below) WELTON
BECKETT ASSOCIATES, *Hyatt Regency Hotel*, Dallas, 1976-9.

SECOND MACHINE AESTHETIC AND METAPHOR

The qualities of the First Machine Aesthetic are taken much further towards an extreme emphasis on logic, circulation, mechanical equipment, technology and structure. The present aesthetic is lighter than the first, and also more flexible. Previous machinery tended to produce repetitive patterns; electronic and self-regulatory machinery is more capable of variation. Archigram, with its Walking City and 'robot' walls and chairs, stressed the dynamic part of this aesthetic, tying it inevitably with Supersensualism. The Pompidou Centre and Osaka Landmark Tower stemmed from the Archigram imagery, while the Japanese Metabolists and Viennese avant-garde developed their own brand of a changing, responsive architecture (the *Pulsating Yellow Heart* was a pneumatic structure that altered air pressure and acoustics as it changed).

A natural tendency of the Second Machine Aesthetic is towards the exoskeleton – bones, like an insect, on the outside

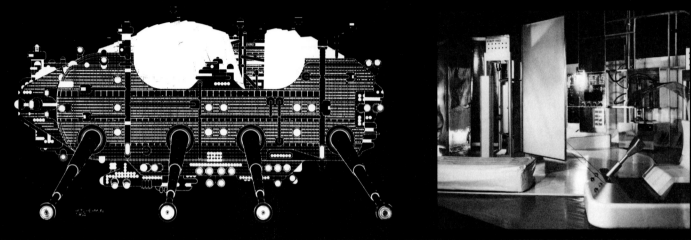

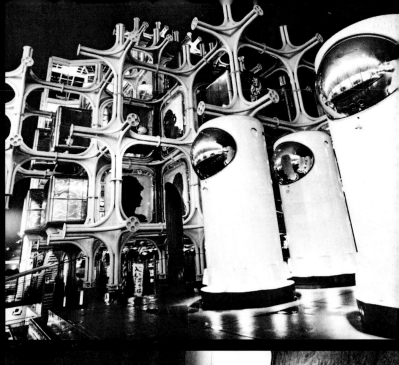

and circulation systems (of people and hot air) not far behind. Thus the 'skin and bones' of Mies becomes the 'bones, arteries and organs' of Rogers. In Kurokawa's case the 'bone and joint' have assumed primary place and the plug-in capsule is secondary. In all these cases there is an aggressive overarticulation, a hyperbole of strength, as if structure were more important than what it held, servant than served. Conceptually the buildings are all structure, and the function is merely tolerated. The visual results are thus often spiky and as complicated as the inside of a T.V. Metaphorically all these buildings tend towards 'the bug-eyed mechanical monster' of Science Fiction – not only the Walking City, but even the Takara Beautilion. Note, for instance, the fur-lined capsule, another theme of Sci Fi, which equates bodily parts with mechanical ones. A secondary metaphor, resulting from the space frame, is the notion of planes suspended in space and growing any-which-way they want, as if the structure were some kind of sea sponge. Bolt on a few more tubes and a new cell can spring out in any direction. Late-Modernism is thus not without some conscious metaphors, similes, but these tend to be closely allied to technology as mediated by Metabolic theory.

(opposite above) ARCHIGRAM, *Walking City,* 1964; and *Living 1990,* Harrods, London, 1967; *(opposite below)* RENZO PIANO & RICHARD ROGERS, *Pompidou Centre,* Paris, 1971-7; *(below)* KIYONARI KIKUTAKE, *Landmark Tower,* Osaka, 1970; *(above right and centre)* KISHO KUROKAWA, *Takara Beautilion* and *Expo Capsule,* Osaka,1970; *(below right)* HAUS RUCKER CO., *Pulsating Yellow Heart,* Vienna, 1968.

38

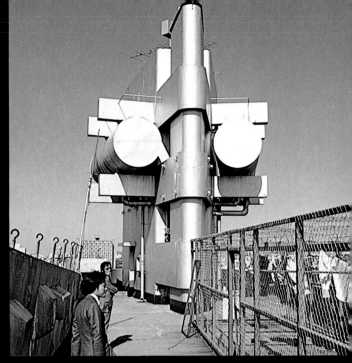

Hyperbole of the Second Machine Aesthetic

The syncopation of a rhythmical beat both horizontally and vertically, in the Sky Building and Pompidou Centre, ends in a striking rhetorical figure: a giant ship or sexual shape, or three exclamation points, and mechanical ducts. Rhythm contrasts with figure, a steady beat with a theme, and this binary opposition, as always, provides some drama. Without it, as in the Sports Club, the syncopations have no climax. Indeed the Pompidou Centre gains its power through contrast, as the glimpse between masonry Paris shows. Place it in suburbia, or repeat it, and its point would be lost (as are the countless 'Eiffel Towers').

The buildings opposite exaggerate their 'figures' even further to the point of architectural hyperbole. A balcony cantilevers way out over pine trees; a window rotates away from the wall cantilevers, and drops its glass; a box tumbles through the wall and roof and knocks a 'chicken coop' (chain link) askew. Colour in these cases, just underscores the hyperbole. The yellow sun sails accentuate the depth of the balcony; the red, green and white of the window set the forms in rotation; and the grey corrugation, red wood and silver pipe outline a trapezoid seen spiralling backwards.

In some of this play, or 'architecture about architecture', we have the autonomy that critics such as Manfredo Tafuri and Peter Eisenman see as typifying recent work. Such gratuitous expression has, however, characterized architecture of every period. Decorative flourishes, redundant structures, walls with no ostensible purpose have always been used as part of the expressive repertoire. What perhaps makes these expressive elements Late-Modern is their insistence on uselessness.

(*above and above left*) YOJI WATANABE, *Sky Building 3*, Tokyo 1967-9; (*left*) RENZO PIANO & RICHARD ROGERS, *Pompidou Centre*, Paris, 1971-7; (*below*) PIER BOTSCHI & DEREK WALKER, *Sports Club*, Woolverton, 1973; (*opposite above*) HELMUT SCHULITZ, *Architect's House*, Los Angeles, 1976-7 (*opposite, below left*) FRANK GEHRY, *Architect's House*, Santa Monica, 1978; (*opposite, below right*) MICHAEL GRAVES *Alexander House*, Princeton, 1971.

Frozen movement

A principle theme and then sign of the Second Machine Aesthetic is frozen movement, the movement of people or warm and cold air. The Metabolists based their city designs on tubes of moving vehicles, capsules and elevators, whereas the First Machine Aesthetic kept these systems in the background. Clearly the later emphasis was a response to the ideology of Late-Capitalism in an era, as it now appears, of energy surplus. What these giant icons of power will look like in thirty years is anyone's guess. Already Kenzo Tange's black monument to the elevator, with its atrophied offices, is a relic to the megastructure which never arrived and latched onto it. HHP's Health Center bends, smashes and snakes pipework through the structure and walls to have it emerge, rhetorically, as twin towers. Such an emphasis on coloured pipes might seem a theme of the First Machine Aesthetic, as indeed it is portrayed in the outsized tubes of, for instance, Fernand Léger's *L'Homme à la Pipe,* 1920. But the corresponding architecture of this period, Le Corbusier's Purism, never went to this extreme. Much of this architecture emphasizes the white and *black*

qualities of metalwork, here further enhanced by the black and white layout. Although there is colour in the Health Center, the exterior is sheathed in black reflecting glass intersected by white vertical bar joints. Tange's office tower mixes dark bronze with black steel and the VAB building and rocket continues the black and white opposition of such military graphics. Indeed, the Nazis conventionalized this opposition throughout their iconography because of its fundamentalist power. This rhetorical figure extends back to at least Boullée and his 'architecture of shadows' and white solids.

The Second Machine Aesthetic reaches the extreme of caged, ambiguous space on the interior of the VAB, 'the largest enclosed space in the world' – so big that it creates its own thunderstorms.

(*above left*) KENZO TANGE, *Shizuoka Press Office,* Tokyo 1967; (*above right and below*) HARDY, HOLZMAN, PFEIFFER *Occupational Health Center,* Columbus, Indiana, 1974-6; (*opposite and inset*) URBAHN, ROBERTS, SEELEY & MORAN *Vehicle Assembly Building,* Cape Kennedy, 1965.

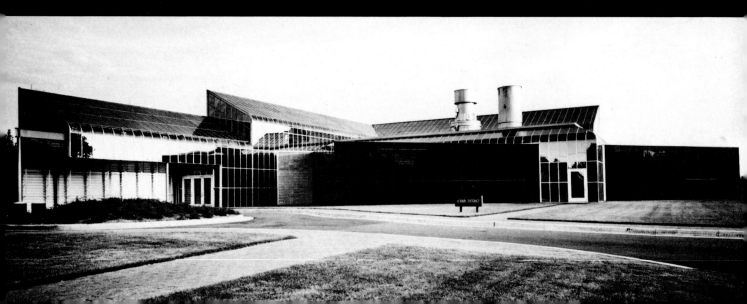

EXTREME ARTICULATION, SYNCOPATION, CONTRAST

Following on directly from the last work of Le Corbusier at La Tourette and Chandigarh was a style of architecture much more articulate than the International Style. For the white, planar skin volumes of the twenties, it substituted the three-dimensional facade, the *brise soleil*, the 'push-pull' of precast concrete elements, the expression of shuttering work in concrete, indeed the expression of all possible functions. This extreme articulation could, on occasion, enunciate more than one might want to know. The Boston City Hall expresses its council chamber, mayor's office, stairway, entrance, 'dentil frieze' of offices, brick podium, heating ducts, pour joints, shuttering marks, and 'problem of the corner' (or rather *'solution'*). The

Clark University Library expresses even more. This 'actio architecture' was, however, a welcome change from the 'dum box', the blank office block which had the temerity to expres just its vacuous self.

A primary means of articulation was the precast construc tional unit and its repetition between dark voids. By varying th size of the unit and the rhythm of voids quite a syncopate melody could be played as in the Boston City Hall. Here we fin a steady beat of top windows (a,b,a,b, etc.) amplified below i larger windows (A,B,A,B, etc.) while it both continues (on tw levels) and is interrupted (on one). This interrupted rhythm an fugal counterpoint were inspired by Stravinsky's music, among other sources. The clash of opposing themes, in all its sculptura weight, is reminiscent of Michelangelo. There are even Manne ist inversions at certain points: a stair hangs out over spac instead of resting on supports, and a concrete fascia makes tw right-angled turns to end up as an oversized balcony.

Extreme articulation is obviously an enjoyable exercise wit its suspensions and counterpoint, staccato and trills and shows Late-Modernism moving towards a Baroque *complexit* and nineteenth-century *contradiction*—these two keywords o a poetics not confined to Post-Modernism. One can even see operating on the planning level in a project by Denys Lasdu which sets zig-zag themes against saw-tooth themes, eac being a transformation of the other. Even the details pick up th staccato.

(*left*) KALLMANN, McKINNELL & KNOWLES, *Boston City Hall* 1964-9; (*below*) JOHN JOHANSEN, *Clark University Library* Worcester, Massachusetts, 1966-9; (*opposite, above left*) PAT RICK HODKINSON, *Foundling Estate,* London, 1968-74; (*oppo site, above right*) HOWELL, KILLICK, PARTRIDGE & AMIS *Weston Rise Housing Estate,* Islington, 1965-7; (*opposit. below*) DENYS LASDUN & PARTNERS, *University of Eas Anglia,* Norwich, 1964.

Forced harmonization

One problem that extreme articulation sets up in order to solv
is that of reducing multiplicity to unity, or of relating a set
multifarious parts to the whole. All aesthetic systems attem
this 'unity in variety', but extreme articulation pursues it with
vengeance because, as with Mannerist architecture, it ha
made the problem more difficult than it has to be in order
dramatize its final solution. (*Virtù* consists in the conquest
difficultà according to this sixteenth-century poetics.) We fir
then the emphasis on skill, ingenuity and overcoming difficul
combined with a scholastic device, when difficulty can't b
surmounted, of forced harmonization (*concordiae violentes*
Both complex harmony and forced harmony can be seen
these examples.

Le Corbusier's seminal use of the *brise soleil* in seve
variants both unifies them within a geometric figure ar
smashes them through each other. His Unité smoothes ove
these contrasts and produces syncopation as a result. Aldo Va
Eyck plays the game with two sizes of domed space (1:9) se
on two diagonals, while José Lluis Sert plays an even mor
complex game with (roughly) ten different formal elements ar
their variation in scale, colour and material. Certain overa
figures remain perceivable here (the stagger, the rectangula
reference plane) although violated in part.

Complex variation on a theme, from detail to room volume
inspires the work of three such different architects as Hertz
berger, Rudolph and Rosselli who achieve a kind of ornamenta
patterning with this method. Forced harmonization can be seer
literally, in Rosselli's rotated and collaged plans, derived fror
those of Frank Lloyd Wright.

(*above left*) LE CORBUSIER, *Algiers Skyscraper project*, 1939
42; and *Unité d'Habitation*, Marseille, 1947-52; (*left*) ALDO VAI
EYCK, *Children's Home*, Amsterdam, 1958-60; (*below*) JOS
LLUIS SERT & ASSOCIATES, *Boston University Comple*
1965-8; (*opposite above*) HERMAN HERTZBERGER, *Old Ag
People's Home*, Amsterdam, 1975; (*opposite, centre and righ*
ALBERTO ROSSELLI, *Lightscraper project*, 1965; (*opposite
bottom left*) PAUL RUDOLPH, *Arts & Humanities Building
Colgate University, Hamilton, 1963-4.

STRUCTURE/CONSTRUCTION AS ORNAMENT

Modern architecture expressed structure 'honestly'; Late-Modern architecture expresses it 'vehemently', and the same is true of construction. As a result both necessities approach the condition of ornament, although often at a gigantic scale. Stirling's work will set two basic constructional themes at 45 degrees to each other, or at some division of this number, producing as a result dissonant angles of 12¼ degrees. The Leicester building uses a constructional diagonal to finish off the top (avoiding direct light) and to produce a giant 'dentil frieze'. Lasdun repeats structural and constructional windows at such length that they induce the hypnotic effects of Op Art and Islamic ornament. Against this endless rhythm are set regular counterbeats, above and below, which indicate circulation and other functions.

John Portman's horizontal ornaments (the tiers of walkways) have become a cliché of Hyatt Hotels. They are made mildly interesting by setbacks which would have been still more interesting if the geometry wasn't entirely predictable. No surprisingly the greatest structural ornamentalists come from the Miesian School in Chicago. Helmut Jahn uses steel I-beams and triangular roof trusses with a precision and virtuosity that the master would have admired (while perhaps keeping reservations about the strong red, white and blue colouring). Very simple logical parts are taken to a Late-Modern extreme, repeated at length and given a separate colour to accentuate their difference (*the* truss, *the* curved glass panel, *the* translucent fibreglass panel, *the* white I-beam etc.).

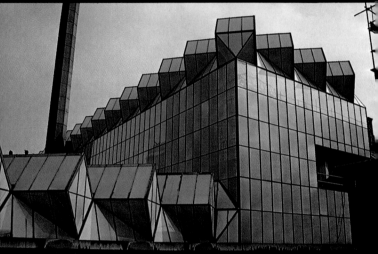

(opposite centre) JAMES STIRLING, *St. Andrews University*, 1959-63; and *Leicester University Engineering Building*, 1964 (with JAMES GOWAN); (opposite below) DENYS LASDUN, *Institute of Education and Law Building*, London, 1965 and 1973-8; (above) JOHN PORTMAN, *Hyatt Regency Hotel*, San Francisco, 1970-2; (right and below) HELMUT JAHN with C.F. MURPHY ASSOCIATES, *Saint Mary's Athletic Facility*, Notre Dame, Indiana, 1976-7; and *Bartle Exhibition Hall*, Kansas City, Missouri, 1977.

Ornament swallows the building

The development of ever increasing structural spans has led quite inevitably towards the point where the structure, and its constructional parts, eats up most of the building. This fetish for structure, of *pars pro toto,* is of course an effective rhetorical device of synecdoche. In one light the Gothic cathedral is nothing else (if we disregard the religion, liturgy and complex iconography) and its visual power results from the repetition of a single, structural bay.

For us it is inevitably the roof plane where these structural forces have the most freedom of expression, although illustrated here are two 'wall structures' which show that this plane too has possibilities. Craig Ellwood elides a roof structure with the wall, and then both of these parts with the continuation of the building. The result is conceptually a 'groundscraper', a linear skyscraper that has fallen on the ground. It's a 'bridge' as well, and these slightly perverse, implied metaphors *(cata-chresis)* no doubt add to its disturbing interest. About

Kurokawa's creeping and flying *(sic)* tetrahedra which raise and lower a black mushroom (auditorium), it is hard to find suitable, rhetorical categories with which to pin it, but perhaps *cacozelia* ('unhappy imitation') will do. Would a Modern architect have allowed himself such a conceit? Certainly Nervi tries to operate within structural necessity as narrowly defined, but even this can lead to highly metaphorical results, as in the Y-elements which seem to lean into the building with outstretched arms that hold back a flood.

(below left) PIER LUIGI NERVI, *Palazzetto dello Sport,* Rome, 1956-7; *(below right)* FREI OTTO, *West German Pavilion,* Montreal, 1967; *(bottom)* CRAIG ELLWOOD, *Art Center Coll-ege of Design,* Pasadena, 1974-6; *(opposite above)* KISHO KUROKAWA, *Toshiba I.H.I. Pavilion,* Osaka, 1970; and *Nitto Foods Plant,* Sagae, 1961; *(opposite below)* KENZO TANGE, *Theme Pavilion,* Osaka, 1970.

COMPLEX SIMPLICITY – OXYMORON

If Modern architecture tended to a distilled simplicity where many requirements were purified towards simple, regular shapes, then Late-Modernism, keeping this overall simplicity, allows it to become irregular and complex. The mixture 'complex simplicity' is itself a form of oxymoron, a slightly paradoxical juncture of opposed qualities. These may be, as in the buildings illustrated here, complicated plans unified by the simplicity of one or two materials; or perhaps a picturesque outline made up from regular, primary solids; or a simple monolithic image made complicated in its details. All of these latent contradictions exist to give interest to the work. They also keep it comprehensible.

For instance Roland Coate's and Eugene Kupper's houses have such complicated plans and volumetric shapes that they need a simple material to unify the variety. Coate uses grey concrete on almost every surface thus equating opposites (wall and roof, stair and bedroom), another oxymoronic trick. It produces a building that is an interpreter's delight (cave/house, German bunker/Aztec altar). The three concrete cylinders that press up, enigmatically, into nothing; are they totems, columns in search of a roof, fortified pillboxes or a place where a ritualized Californian sacrifice is performed?

The Nilsson House develops a complicated Post-Modern spatial sequence but pulls this together with a repetitive structural spine and constant use of painted stucco. The forms are basically simple (pitched roof, flat wall, void in shadow) but the composition is asymmetrical and relates to the slope of the hill. The complex space is layered at right angles to this slope, but as a series of simple parallel walls. The variety of window size is great, but the voids have a similar shape. Complex simplicity is a series of 'yes, but' statements.

(above right) RICARDO BOFILL and TALER, *Walden 7*, Barcelona, 1973-5; (right and below) ROLAND COATE, *Alexander House*, Montecito, 1972-4; (opposite) EUGENE KUPPER, *Nilsson House*, Los Angeles, 1976-9.

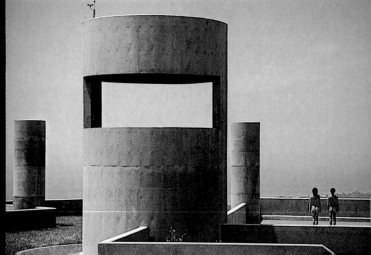

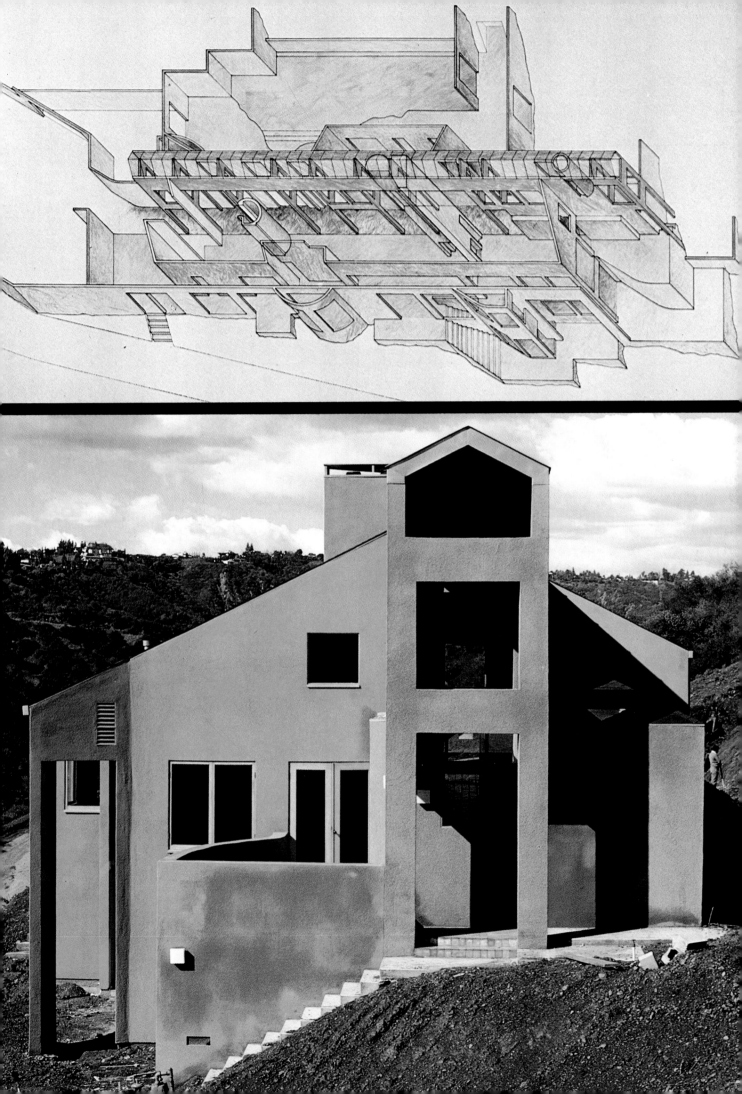

Ambiguous reference

A byproduct of complex simplicity is ambiguous reference. Such form often suggests more than it means because its complexity, unified around a simple theme, implies a strongly codified set of meanings, a conventionalized ritual, which may not exist in fact. This is most true of religious shrines, such as Ronchamp, but it also holds true for all such form in general. We could say that complex simplicity is the rhetorical figure of metaphysics; many of the buildings on these four pages look vaguely sacred in function. They elicit a reading of implicit codes. Thus James Stirling's Olivetti building has one end that implies a strict, hieratic function. Symmetrical sides slope up and then down to a suppressed centre, which in turn has circular apertures that reveal a further series of circular shapes. The extreme simplicity of outline and homogeneous material combined with the unusual shape and complex, but precise, detailing reinforce the hieratic reading. The implicit coding of Ronchamp is extremely varied, but focuses on the 'natural' signs of religion: here most evident (in addition to Le Corbusier's paintings on the windows) are metaphors of light and geometry, two traditional Christian signs. But these are supplemented by aberrant ones – 'Swiss cheese', 'fortress wall' and 'window/room' (each window becomes a virtual room). The plug-in units are certainly not religious in feeling but they nonetheless suggest a set of implied meanings which vary from fortified bastion to stacked bricks to prefab hilltown (the last of which was probably intended). Complex simplicity can produce marvellous malapropisms as we shall see.

(*left*) LE CORBUSIER, *Ronchamp Chapel*, 1950-5; (*below*) RICARDO BOFILL and TALER, *Valpineda Apartments*, Sitgus, 1967-8; (*opposite*) JAMES STIRLING, *Olivetti Training School*, Haslemere, 1969-73.

REDUCTIVE, ELLIPTICAL GRIDISM

The reduction of architecture to a few concerns obviously has a rhetorical power, the power of an unambiguous slogan. If this truism found expression in Mies' slogan 'less is more', then certain Late-Modernists have exaggerated this idea even further to 'less than less is more than more is nearly nothing'. Some Late-Modern buildings of Norman Foster simply try to disappear while others seek to reflect the environment. The power of these statements is not only what they say boldly, but also what they leave out. Slogan alternates with ellipsis, an overpowering, single image with an absence of signs, a silence. The duality – slogan/silence – is often built with the most neutral of forms, the grid.

Philip Johnson's twin towers in Houston illustrate these rhetorical figures: two trapezoidal, minimalist black wedges are placed ten feet apart on edge. A tension is inevitably created between the two sharp angles pointing, aggravatingly, towards each other (and ten feet apart for three hundred feet!). From some angles of view the diagonal chamfers of the roofs line up to produce a 'double-whole', one building out of two. This paradox is further heightened by another. The space between the two forms is itself a mirror image of the two wedges – a third building that isn't there. So the ellipsis suggests a positive presence, the silence another slogan (to Pennzoil). Add to these visual illusions the grey-bronze reflective glass and the way the surface changes with the changing light and one feels an aesthetic vertigo that is opposite to the stability of Miesian

0 30 60

skyscrapers. Where they were harmonious, Johnson's are dissonant; where they repeated a visual element to create order, Johnson multiplies the repetitions (between towers and space frame) to create optical vibrations. Although the Pennzoil is a simple building (or two) like Modern skyscrapers it is a complex simplicity, responding to the boring box with distortions, exaggerations and ellipses. Kurokawa responds to the boring box with the Big (boring) Box, an extreme example of reductivism. Here a scaleless, blank white structure hides the most extraordinary *mélange* of functions within, including a place to shoot ducks by laser gun. However, the promise of these functions is revealed by the rotating facade images and the single view in, which, because it is the only void in the

building, has an undeniable pull.

Slogan, and silence, can also be seen in the reductive images of Superstudio, their Continuous Monument, which started the Late-Modern fashion for gridism in such a humorous way.

(*opposite*) PHILIP JOHNSON & JOHN BURGEE, *Pennzoil Place,* Houston, 1974-6; (*below*) KISHO KUROKAWA, *Big Box,* Tokyo, 1974; (*bottom*) SUPERSTUDIO, *Continuous Monument,* 1969, as gridded space filling in canyon and as gridded verdure filling in the Golden Gate.

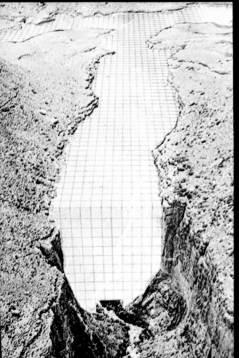

The 'irrational' grid

Modern architecture used the right angle and Cartesian, gridded space as a sign of reason and logic. The motive for this was as much conventional and conceptual as functional since other forms, including the hexagon, were proven to be more economic and pragmatic in certain respects. No matter, the grid was rational as a sign, and it could be clearly understood unlike the other, contending forms. From this conception, and Le Corbusier's Domino system, came the major syntactic feature of Modernism, a feature which Late-Modernism once again exaggerates and inverts in meaning. Grids are now applied as decoration, as they were by Pre-Modernists such as Otto Wagner; grids are used to confuse and disorient where previously they were used to order; grids are rotated, sliced, deformed and operated on until they lose all of their practical rationale. Clearly the grid, like the Doric column previously, has lost its primary function and become a symbol more than a pragmatic device, a symbol of 'irrational' rationalism, an oxy-moronic symbol.

Peter Eisenman makes an equation between all directions of the grid and thereby destroys this human coordinate system of up/down, left/right and back/front (they are all the same here). His House 10 not only does away with these usual signs, but the 'centre and heart' as well, becoming even more negatively a kind of non-totality where the four parts don't add up to a whole. The lying-down tower of glass and the glass window on the floor (under a cantilever) further the negative logic, while the omnipresent grid, which is felt in every detail, is so consistently fragmented that a delightful confusion, not order, results. This is Eisenman at his most nihilistic and ultralogical.

Kurokawa repeats the grid in plan, elevation, section, detail and city plan (the grid embraces the sidewalk); Isozaki also repeats the grid in section, plan, elevation and detail. He suspends two square parallelopipeds of grid over a (future) ivy covered base so that the gridded, die-cast aluminium panels, with their deeply grooved joints, will seem to float squarely. Floating grids for a museum. Hiromi Fujii takes this gridism to its irrational conclusion by telescoping grids inside each other again in plan, section, elevation, and window detail – so remorselessly that orientation is destroyed. The grid is rotated and spun through a mirror-reversal, and then so is the perceiver. This is the most extreme form of synecdoche we have seen, where part and whole are continuously reversible. His scheme, 'Simi-larity, Connotation, Junction' is, as Kenneth Frampton has shown, an example of pure logic on one level and cultural connotation on another. Toyo Ito shows the same mixture of logics in his PMT building which bends the applied grid thus, in a sense, denying its Cartesian absoluteness. It becomes a billboard, a mere screen rather than the hard, metal surface it is made from. Ito uses this paradox, like Hollein, with a subtle sfumato so the light and shadow, flat wall and bent wall, merge imperceptibly into each other. He also uses it to convey a metaphysical superficiality, a surface lightness and inconse-quentiality which he finds, and finds challenging, in the present consumer culture.

(opposite above) PETER EISENMAN, House 10, 1978; (oppo-site, below left) KISHO KUROKAWA, Fukuoka Bank Head Office, Tokyo, 1975; (opposite, below right) ARATA ISOZAKI, Kitakyushu Museum, 1974; (above right) HIROMI FUJII, Todoroki Residence, Box within a Box, 1976; (bottom) HIROMI FUJII, 'Similarity, Connotation, Junction'; (right) TOYO ITO, PMT building, Nagoya, 1978.

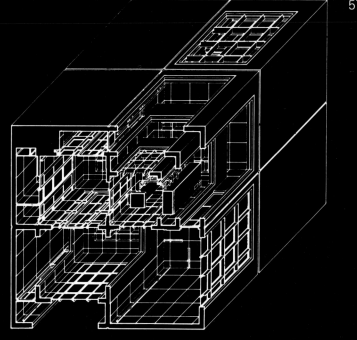

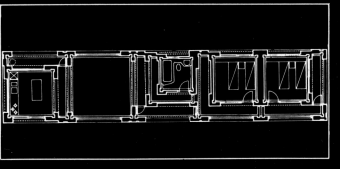

EXTREME ISOTROPIC SPACE – REDUNDANCY AND SIMPLICITY

A consequence of Le Corbusier's Domino system and the Chicago frame, the neutral grid of caged space, is the 'free plan' of Modernism. Exterior and interior walls are freed of their load-bearing role and thus movable partitions can articulate the interior without constraint. As structural spans become wider (over 100 metres of column-free space are now spanned in auditoria) and the structural supports are placed on the outside, a complete isotropic, sandwich space developed – the same in every direction. Superstudio and Archizoom, in the middle sixties, started to eulogize this spatial type as 'democratic', because of its sameness. The mammoth American department store, with its endlessly disappearing perspectives, became an ironic harbinger of an egalitarian society to come. Marxists could point to the 'cunning of reason' in history; that through crass economic pressures a new type of democratic space was naturally evolving right in the belly of Late-Capitalism (the Supermarket). Mies' endless, 'universal' space was becoming a reality, where ephemeral functions could come and go without messing up the absolute architecture above and below. The complete disjunction between pure architecture and pure commerce was thus achievable, with each realm given its complete autonomy.

When one sees the stunning results of Norman Foster all these wishes and ideas seem to have come true. Ethereal open space flows between a green ground (with its electrical outlets) and a baffled ceiling (with its mechanical and lighting grid). Open space shoots to the blue-tinged wall and beyond out into the view of the townscape, around pure white columns, across yellow bands of spotlit toilets, down the side of heating and cooling ducts to arrive at infinity. The wall disappears (or at least only thin glass fins remain as structure). The feeling of freedom and openness, like riding the freeways of Los Angeles, is conveyed. The space has an awesome grandeur, at once relaxing and sublime, comforting and endless, a modern equivalent to the wide-open prairie or the *parterres* of Versailles.

And yet one's enthusiasm for isotropic space is tempered by the fact that, on occasion, it can be excruciatingly boring, known at a glance, and the knowledge that it results quite logically from the most rapacious exploitation of real estate. The maximum coverage for the minimum expense is a dull sandwich. Perhaps this knowledge doesn't altogether kill our enjoyment of isotropic space, any more than the knowledge of Louis XIV's totalitarianism ruins our experience of Versailles; but it certainly dampens the enthusiasm. Extreme isotropic space thus comes as a *double-entendre*: the sign of the sublime and the rapacious. It also gains power through an effective use of two rhetorical devices – redundancy and simplicity.

The Wills Tobacco Factory, the largest column-free space in Europe when built (180 by 90 metres), shows the functional advantages of isotropic space: even light distribution, easy to clean, and complete flexibility to move machines and production lines around when the technology changes. At one point medieval banners were to fly over different work-stations to give a sense of place and identity. Helmut Jahn's Bartle Hall gives 60,000 square metres of column-free exhibition and meeting space (two city blocks). Again services occur on the

s and above in the triangular truss and below in the floor.
seats and trusses augment the feeling of infinity. The
pidou Centre with a clear span of 48 metres also features
giant truss, but this time as an elegantly polished silver zig-
with padded elbows. The conventions of Late-Modern
e are thus established: gridded, endless and isotropic, with
meter supports and services top and bottom. In this space
collage of changing activity.

osite below) NORMAN FOSTER, *Willis Faber Head Office,*
vich, 1972-6; (*right*) YRM with SOM (Chicago), *Wills*
acco Factory, Bristol, 1969-74; (*below*) HELMUT JAHN with
MURPHY, *Bartle Exhibition Hall,* Kansas City, Missouri,
7; (*bottom*) RENZO PIANO & RICHARD ROGERS, *Pom-*
u Centre, Paris, 1971-7.

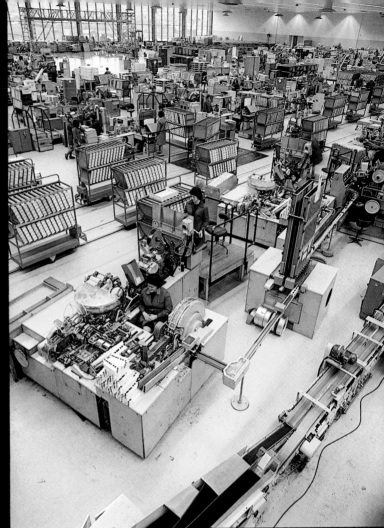

Flatness and surveillance

Extreme isotropic space becomes a metaphor for the horizon and by extension, the world. Louis XIV used an aspect of this space to regularize his court and extend his dominion over society and nature, equally. Corporations use this space in an analogous way, as a means of surveilling and controlling production and as a visual metaphor of power. Flat buildings sit on the ground like inevitable facts of nature, four square and immovable.

Foster's IBM is a black-tinted Rolls Royce of isotropic space which provides a democratic grid of equal squares to the employees. His inflatable office sets up a typical railroad perspective while his Olsen Office gives the 'office landscaping' normal to such schemes. Archizoom's 'No-Stop City' shows the randomized homogeneity of this space from a conceptual point of view: it's like wall-paper with patterns recurring on a statistical average. Foster's Ipswich building shows the drama of puncturing through the layers of isotropic space to reveal paper-thin trays of openness – and a mental diagram like Le Notre's gardens. The two remaining buildings, especially that by Farrell & Grimshaw, show the High-Tech expression common to isotropic space. Here we find those dazzling perspectives of mechanical control, layers upon layers of pipes, tubes, and moving energy, the light-webs and bright colours of services and trusses all threaded carefully through each other like a peasant rug.

(opposite, top left) ARCHIZOOM, 'No-Stop City', 1970; (opposite, centre left and right) NORMAN FOSTER, Computer Technology Ltd., London, 1970; and Olsen Links Office, Millwall, London, 1970; (opposite below) NORMAN FOSTER, IBM Head Office, Portsmouth, 1971; (below left) NORMAN FOSTER, Willis Faber Head Office, Ipswich, 1972-6; (below right) AHRENDS, BURTON & KORALEK, Habitat Warehouse and Showroom, Wallingford, 1973-4; (bottom) FARRELL & GRIMSHAW, Herman Miller Warehouse, Bath, 1977-8.

EXTREME REPETITION

Repetition is itself a rhetorical category which in language might result in alliteration and assonance. Architecturally analogous recurrences also occur which correspond to the repetition of an initial consonant (a marked structural member for instance) and the resemblance of proximal vowel sounds (the similar voids or 'back-ground' beween structural members). *Extreme* repetition is then just another Late-Modern exaggeration of an existing rhetorical device. Modern architecture justified repetition as a productive device, whereas now that it is exaggerated we can more clearly appreciate its persuasive power. The effect of extreme repetition may be monotony or a hypnotic trance:

positively it can elicit feelings of the sublime and the inevitable because it so incessantly returns to the same theme. A musical figure repeated at length, such as that in *Bolero*, acts not just as a form of mental torture but as a pacifier. Repetitive architecture can put you to sleep. Both Mussolini and Hitler used it as a form of thought control knowing that before people can be coerced they first have to be hypnotised and then bored. Too many curtain walls in New York seen in succession can cause the same kind of sickness that too many Bridget Rileys in London seen in succession have caused.

Philip Johnson's IDS Center staggers steel set-backs in

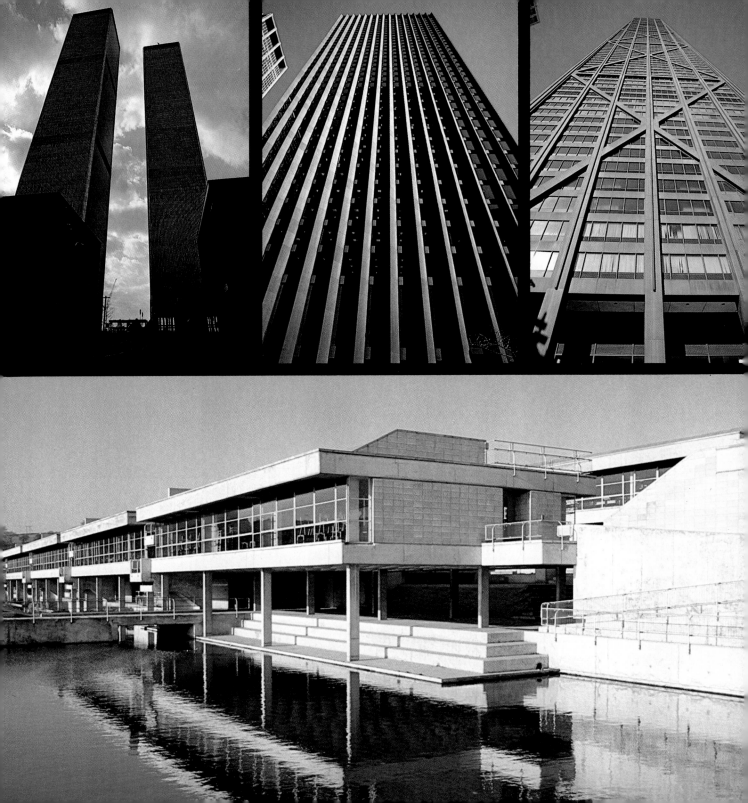

The sizzle of incessant space frames

The extreme repetition of a constructional element painted white becomes, like Late Gothic fretwork, a decoration that dissolves the scale of a large building. Geodesic structures often look like pine cones and pineapples, both conventional forms of decoration. The buildings which use this structure or space frame all over their surface elide the distinction between wall and roof, thus contradicting the basic convention of building which makes a visual and material separation between these two areas. This contradiction, and paradox, is further heightened by the same modular element appearing everywhere. The part becomes the whole, the whole the part – an example of both synecdoche and oxymoron. Another property of this extreme repetition is that it keeps the eye continuously on the move. One doesn't ordinarily focus on any single part for long because the optical buzz of attendant cues

stracts the eye, or tires the eye. Furthermore the equality of elements precludes a focus on one. Versailles, in so many ways the paradigm of extreme repetition, keeps the eye moving horizontally from column to column, from cone to cone.

(*opposite, above and below left*) PHILIP JOHNSON & JOHN BURGEE, *Garden Grove Community Church*, California, 1976-

80, and *Pennzoil Place*, Houston, 1974-6; (*opposite, below right*) ARUP ASSOCIATES, *Attenborough Building*, Leicester, 1970; (*below left*) BUCKMINSTER FULLER, *U.S. Pavilion*, Expo 67, Montreal, 1967; (*below right*) CESAR PELLI & GRUEN ASSOCIATES, *Pacific Design Center*, Los Angeles, 1975-6; (*bottom*) *Versailles*, LE NOTRE gardens, 1667+; LE VAU wings, 1661-5; HARDOUIN-MANSART centre, 1678+.

SLICK SKIN/OP EFFECTS

As the curtain wall continues to evolve towards 'less and less' (mullion) it approaches the ideal condition of a membrane, a surface that can flow easily around corners and over rooftops as if it were skin, or at least inflatable plastic. This diminishes the role of the four facades and the frontality inherent in most buildings. It tends to isolate the building as a free-standing sculpture and do away with all scaling devices – even the mullion disappears in the pure glass skin building. Furthermore it decreases the mass and weight while enhancing the volume and contour – the difference between a brick and a balloon. All these aesthetic effects are made possible by developments in stronger glass walls, thinner gaskets and various new means of assembly including small clips and glass structural fins. They lead to a Late-Modern curtain wall, the slick skin membrane which is quite different from the Modern one with its strong vertical divisions, its 'skin and *bones*'.

In England Norman Foster has pushed the technology furthest with his 'Big Black Piano' in Ipswich. The partially reflective black glass moves around the existing site-lines with a kidney or piano shape. From some angles the building reflects the environment, from others it is transparent and, depending on the light, opaque and translucent. Thus four visual conditions are provided with the same material with the added quality of sfumato – the gentle merging of one condition into the next. In Los Angeles the 'Silver' architects Anthony Lumsden and Cesar Pelli have developed the same four conditions of the slick skin playing on the resulting ambiguities sometimes for their semantic meanings.

Anthony Lumsden, for instance, has designed a bank which alludes to the silver standard and an area of investment where this bank's money is possibly headed. The oil-slick surface, the strong phallic rise of the shaft from a heavier base, and the ripples of one side suggest a series of meanings without naming them, like the symbolic poetry of the nineteenth century. Pelli's 'Blue Whale' is equally wide in its metaphorical overtones, some of which may be a fortuitous outcome of purely slick skin decisions. For Pelli's primary concern is with developing the inherent aesthetic characteristics of the membrane; above all its ambiguity and paradox.

The 'Blue Whale' is actually, with its metaphors and Mannerism, half a Post-Modern building. The Mannerism consists in setting up a series of expectancies in order to break them. For instance a linear, extruded shape would indicate the circulation takes place frontally and on an axis down the spine – but it actually occurs on the diagonal (see plan). The semi-cylinder protruding from one side and its circular platform would indicate a vertical circulation ramp. But actually vertical circulation is by escalator at right angles to these circles. This view also shows the typical mixture of transparency, reflection (and therefore a doubling of the cylinder), opacity and semi-transparency; in other words aesthetic, Mannerist ambiguities which support the semantic ones. It would be wrong to assert that Post-Modernism alone is Mannerist; indeed Late-Modernism, by its very definition an exaggeration of Modernism, is this, and almost all the thirty definers mentioned at the outset have a Mannerist component. The night view of the 'Blue Whale' shows how Mannerist the slick skin can be under varying conditions as it turns, chameleon-like, an orange, black and yellow.

(*above left*) NORMAN FOSTER, *Willis Faber Head Office*, Ipswich, 1972; (*left*) ANTHONY LUMSDEN, *Branch Bank Project*, Bumi Daya, 1976; (*opposite*) CESAR PELLI & GRUEN ASSOCIATES, *Pacific Design Center*, Los Angeles, 1975-6.

68   The all-over enigmatic form – synecdoche and oxymoron

If the slick skin tends towards a membrane, it also allows a single form to cover the entire building. Hence the enigmatic building, the result of a form repeated all over the surface, as if the architecture were a piece of sculpture. Le Corbusier's Philips Pavilion made from hyperbolic-paraboloids is enigmatic partly because of this synecdoche and also because it consists of a series of straight lines and distorted grids. We are accustomed to an orthogonal building resulting from these elements, so when we see them twisted the result looks like a building that has collapsed. In fact the hyperbolic-paraboloid is a strong structural shape. Thus is produced a double form of oxymoron: 'safe/unsafe', 'orthogonal/curved'. Late-Modernism developed such paradoxes from the later work of Le Corbusier.

In an entirely different way Norman Foster uses the all-over form to produce an enigma. When you drive up to the IBM building at Portsmouth it isn't there. All you find is a duplication of reality: two parking lots, two sets of trees, a symmetrical sky and yourself doubled – almost all of it disappearing to infinity. The building itself is absent, or at least subtracted of conventional signs: no doorway, no structure, no base, gutter and window (assuming it's all wall) or no wall (assuming it's all window). This is an architecture of 'absence' and abstinence whose signs of denial very much assert the missing parts. In a less reduced Modern building we might not notice the reduction; but when confronted with a rhetoric of absence we are forced to reassert the parts that have been purged. These enigmatic devices make the building a very strong image and then symbol of IBM: like a black Rolls Royce with tinted one-way glass the building invites and then holds off investigation. Like the 'black box' of computer technology it remains a compelling mystery of complex workings we are not meant to understand.

Arata Isozaki's museum uses the square all over at different scales and in different materials. This method he calls amplification (after one rhetorical term) as it is an expansion and transformation of a single idea. The most enigmatic part of the building is the entrance lobby where the square marches off in three or four directions and in the distance, in marble, gets larger as it recedes. This anti-perspective device, relating to M.C. Escher's impossible buildings, summarizes the grand enigma mentioned above of the 'irrational' grid (page 57).

(*left*) LE CORBUSIER, *Philips Pavilion*, Brussels, 1958; (*below*) NORMAN FOSTER, *IBM Head Office*, Portsmouth, 1971; (*opposite*) ARATA ISOZAKI, *Gunma Museum*, 1972-4.

ENCLOSED SKIN VOLUMES

The slick skin membrane allows, as we've seen, a greater scope for volumetric articulation than the previous curtain wall, an aspect which these skyscrapers share. Breaking down the apparent mass, density, weight of a fifty storey building is part of the motive. One way this is done is by destroying the four-square morphology, by adding extra facades, by making a facade of the corner and a broken one as Philip Johnson has done; or by fragmenting the facades vertically or in both planes. The latter building by Kevin Roche treats aluminium and green-tinted glass as if it were a light material, by folding it in and out and cantilevering large chunks of it. This is probably the most distorted 'skyscraper' to date and it represents a genre that should be given another metaphor ('skyholder'?). At the base the entrance flares out to welcome the user with its 'stiff upper lip'. (Late-Modernists are just beginning to articulate these traditional symbolic centres and the results are somewhat rigid). A distortion of scale is also created by the horizontal treatment of aluminium frame. The familiar floor to floor module is reduced to one-third its usual size, thus making the building both bigger in appearance and smaller in grain.

The 'skywedge' in Boston also uses the all-over slick skin module to break down the scale and weight. Its designer, Henry Cobb, describes a motive behind using reflective glass which is shared by all these architects. 'The reflective glass is very important. It's a contrast to the stoniness of the church. It emphasizes the disembodiment of the volume. It's very important to the principle of this building that you read it as a plane in space, not as a volume. What would be destructive is an obtrusive volume.' But the mirror-building has other important meanings. It fits into the environment by reflecting it. It provides a precious, sparkling quality akin to the use of gold and stained glass in previous periods. It works both literally and metaphorically as a sign of narcissism. Lastly it is oxymoronic in its very nature, providing the ultimate contradiction 'truth/falsity'. It holds 'a mirror up to nature' truthfully, but at the same time creates a *trompe l'oeil* and distortion.

(*below*) PHILIP JOHNSON & JOHN BURGEE, *IDS Center*, Minneapolis, 1972-5; (*opposite above*) KEVIN ROCHE & JOHN DINKELOO, *One UN Plaza*, New York, 1974-6; (*opposite, below left*) JOHN PORTMAN, *Bonaventure Hotel*, Los Angeles, 1974-6; (*opposite, below right*) HENRY COBB & I.M. PEI, *John Hancock Tower*, Boston, 1968 and 1973-7.

The undulating grid

Reduction and paradox are recurring themes of Late-Modernism which we've found in almost every definer of the style. Here we see the undulating grid used to reduce a building conceptually to a piece of domestic equipment, a paradox which is underlined by sfumato, highlights, and mirror images. Anthony Lumsden's project for the Beverly Hills Hotel expresses these qualities with the image of a typewriter. The 'roller' is here repeated seven times, merged each one with the next and set on a double stagger – both sideways and upwards.

The ends are given a neo-classical mullion pattern. The result, in the 'Silver Aesthetic', would have summarized the financial situation of Beverly Hills if only they had spent the money on it.

(*below left*) SUPERSTUDIO, *Istogrammi d'architettura*, 1969; (*below right and bottom*) ANTHONY LUMSDEN & DMJM, *Beverley Hills Hotel*, 1976; (*opposite and inset*) ANTHONY LUMSDEN & DMJM, *One Park Plaza*, Los Angeles, 1973; and *Manufacturers Bank*, Los Angeles, 1972-4.

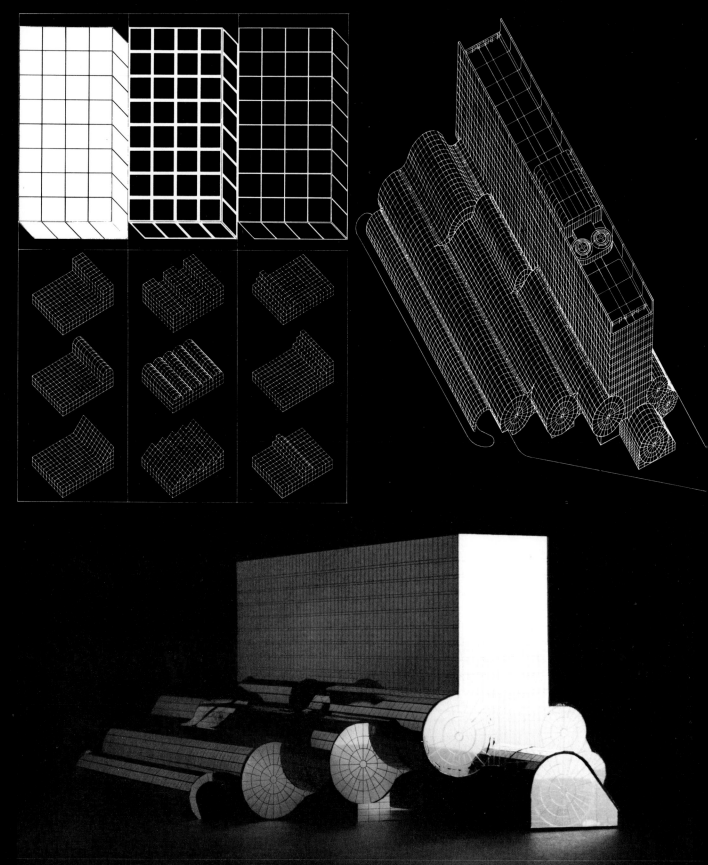

SCULPTURAL FORM AND HYPERBOLE

Following the lead of Le Corbusier's Ronchamp (1955) Post-Modernists started to develop a metaphorical architecture, while the Late-Modernists took off in a more purely sculptural direction. During the sixties they used reinforced concrete in a very expressive way and this trend has continued to develop into the seventies. Sometimes the results are overwrought and confusing; most often they make use of the rhetorical device hyperbole, extravagant forms meant to impress by their grand, overpowering sweep. One finds this sort of architecture at World Fairs, Olympic stadia, airports and city halls where the program demands a certain hyperbole. Kenzo Tange's buildings for the 1964 Olympics contrasts two sets of sweeping forms, hanging in a gentle catenary curve, with a taut tension member and then an emphatic concrete mast, smacked into the ground like an imperious exclamation point. This too is slightly curved in a 'Japanese' way, so the whole is an extravagant statement of national identity. Eero Saarinen's Dulles Airport is more confused in its historical reference having a 'Chinese pagoda' control tower, but equally dramatic in its use of curve and counterthrust. The rhetorical figure, developed from an earlier scheme of Le Corbusier, sets an inward hanging catenary curve against an outward pushing row of zoomorphic columns. The way these break through the roof plane and both push and hold reminds one of arms and heads and craning necks, clearly hyperbolic figures.

A more extreme use of a structural shape is I.M. Pei's upside

down pyramid in Dallas. This city hall also relates to earlier structures of Le Corbusier in reinforced concrete but treats the material with a hard, flat, precise surface more like steel than masonry. All sorts of extravagant figures are combined with this extraordinary shape: smooth glass walls incline on the same inward slope of the concrete giving a paradoxical identity to these two materials. Strong verticals smash through the slope to emerge on the roof and set up a basic antithesis to the horizontals. Then three different marching figures are juxtaposed – the stagger to one side mounting towards a heavy cantilever, and the two front diagonals, one in alternating bands, the other in indented blocks. All these create a predictable climax at the heavier cornice.

If Pei is here using form more as hyperbole than to communicate specific ideas or functions, this is also true of his Christian Science Church Center. This work has an excessive degree of drama, like St. Peter's, and functions in a comparable way to the Vatican for the Christian Scientists although at a lesser scale. Landscaping literally becomes part of the buildings. Water is treated as a flat, architectural plane to double the images, and extensive, linear forms are taken up in the Sunday School Building. This last has a huge double cornice surmounting a colonnade and flare, again all finished with a steel-like concrete. Precisionist concrete is the oxymoronic figure most identifiable with Pei.

Denys Lasdun also has developed the late style of Le Corbusier in a highly sculptural direction. His National Theatre achieves its fitting drama with a series of highly contrasting figures: four strong horizontals, earth-like strata for Lasdun, are punctured by three emphatic verticals, two of which merge at the top. This combination of smash and elision, of the dynamic and peaceful, is played in other keys. For instance flat, quiet walls are placed on a frontal axis to be offset by the buzz of coffers and lift shafts placed on the diagonal. All of these emphatic contrasts are made even richer by the overall *contrapposto*, the play of heavy forms placed in an asymmetrical, moving balance. It's a grand, abstract drama quite appropriate for England's national theatre.

(*opposite above*) KENZO TANGE, *National Gymnasium*, Tokyo, 1964; (*opposite below*) EERO SAARINEN, *Dulles Airport*, Chantilly, Washington D.C., 1962-4; (*above right*) DENYS LASDUN, *National Theatre*, London, 1964; (*right and below*) I.M. PEI, *Christian Science Church Center, Sunday School Building*, Boston, 1964 and 1971-3; and *Dallas City Hall*, 1966-78.

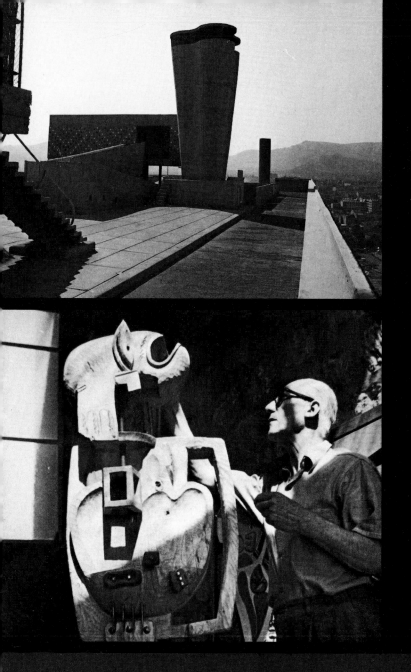

Enigmatic chiaroscuro

Part of Le Corbusier's late style was concerned with his 192[3] definition of architecture as the 'masterly, correct and magnificent play of masses brought together in light'. The masses became more massive, distorted and exaggerated after the War, achieving something of the *terribilità* of Michelangelo. Shapes are collaged into each other with great abruptness, tortured mouths gape upwards, kidney shaped funnels smash down into a base without any modulation, one sculptural object collides into the next without transitions, or mouldings. Much of this work has a tragic, painful dissonance about it and a swift movement from one object to the next *(epitrochasmus)*. In the hands of Philip Johnson this style inevitably becomes cooler, lighter and more serene, even surreal. His art museum in Texas also uses chiaroscuro in an enigmatic way. So pure, abrupt and dimensionless is the building in extreme light and shadow that people are needed to give it scale and to distinguish it from a cardboard model. Pafford Clay's collage of Le Corbusier's late work is a humorous and excessive rhetorical pile of architectural form divorced from conventional sense *(epitrochasmus* staggers, cantilevers, inverted pyramids, truncated rhythms, chiaroscuro, etc.). Marcel Breuer also uses the inverted pyramid, but with heavier simplicity. And he combines this with extremely distorted trapezoidal windows which are almost malapropistic ('learing bug-eyes' or 'mechanical pincers'). Oscar Niemeyer's church also has ludicrous associations ('roller coaster'), whereas Hans Scharoun's concert hall catches the metaphor of music with its trills and dissonance, counterpoint and syncopation. Finally Frank Lloyd Wright, in his late phase, produced some enigmatic forms with extreme chiaroscuro that oscillate between the sublime (pure form in asymmetrical balance) and the ridiculous (stacked ash trays).

(left and above left) LE CORBUSIER, *Unité d'Habitation,* Marseille, 1947-52; and (with SAVINA) *Sculpture on Wood,* 1926-42; *(below)* PHILIP JOHNSON & JOHN BURGEE, *Art Museum of South Texas,* Corpus Christie, 1970-2; *(opposite above)* PAFFORD CLAY, *California State College Theater,* San Francisco, 1974-6; and MARCEL BREUER, *Whitney Museum,* New York, 1963-6; *(opposite centre)* OSCAR NIEMEYER, *Church of São Francisco,* Pampulha, 1942-3; and HANS SCHAROUN, *Philharmonic Hall,* Berlin, 1956-63; *(opposite below)* FRANK LLOYD WRIGHT, *Guggenheim Museum,* New York, 1943-59

UNINTENDED HUMOUR – MALAPROPISM

Late-Modernism, like most periods of architecture, has no consciously sought architectural wit. Nonetheless there ar moments of humour, especially when the architect is deadl earnest and trying hard to make the great architectura statement. This loosens the critical faculties that usually bin him and something amazing issues forth. It may be 'Pereira' prick' rushing skywards from a heavily trussed base, o 'Bunshaft's donut and pill box' for the Hirschorn collection i Washington, or 'Bunshaft's travertine printer/calculator' for th LBJ library in Texas. This last also resembles an Egyptian tom (with its ramp and battered walls) and a portrait of the lat president in a grim mood. 'Watanabe's dragster' is clearly tryin to be funny with its extended exhaust pipes, captain's deck an upward tending balconies; Japanese have seen it as a 'rooste and a 'sinking ship'. Finally two great Late-Modern malaprop together at Yale, 'Saarinen's whale eating Johnson's tootsi rolls', quite conventional labels attached by the students. In a this work we have a combination of reduction and hyperbole two rhetorical devices, leading unwittingly to a thir malapropism, an endearing trait to have.

* * *

If we summarize the major rhetorical devices of Lat Modernism we find them focusing around a set of recurrin figures. Extreme repetition, with its attendant qualities o alliteration and assonance, sometimes leads to boredom, but is intended to produce feelings of awe and the sublim Repetition is mostly of structure as ornament. Extrem articulation, with its strong contrasts, forced harmonization and syncopations, sometimes produces verbosity but it i intended to enliven the surface of a building and communicat the complexity of functions within. Synecdoche, a substitutio of part for whole and whole for part, is evident in the all-over us of a single material and module. It is often combined wit reduction, ellipsis and oxymoron, the paradoxes which resu from the use of new materials ('transparent/opaque' glass) an new structures ('safe/unsafe' hyperbolic-paraboloids). Als sfumato, the indistinct movement from light to shadow, result from the new glass technologies and the slick skin plastics. Th new spatial type, extreme isotropic space, leads to a host o rhetorical qualities; redundancy, simplicity, ellipsis an reduction. Metaphor is sometimes intentional in the Secon Machine Aesthetic with its 'exoskeleton', its 'skin, bones an arteries'. Hyperbole and malapropism are at least implicit in th emphasis on sculptural form divorced from conventiona meaning.

If we attend to these major rhetorical devices within th language of Late-Modernism we can begin to understand it character: its relative autonomy and concern for purel architectural meanings, and its ambivalence with respect t Late-Capitalism and advanced technology.

(*left*) WILLIAM PEREIRA, *Transamerica Building*, San Francisco 1968-72; (*left and opposite, above left*) GORDON BUNSHAFT & SOM, *Hirschorn Museum*, Washington D.C., 1973; and *Lyndon Baines Johnson Library*, Austin, Texas, 1968-71; (*opposite above right*) YOJI WATANABE, *New Sky Building No. 5*, Tokyo 1971; (*opposite below*) EERO SAARINEN, *Ingalls Hockey Rink* 1957; and PHILIP JOHNSON, *Kline Science Center*, New Haven, 1964.

2. LATE-MODERN PRACTICE

2.1 JAMES STIRLING'S CORPORATE CULTURE MACHINE

This article, published in Architecture Plus, *March/April 1974, related to a metaphorical analysis I made of the building, part of which is included in the diagram below. As in so many buildings Stirling has eschewed conscious metaphor, except the reference to Olivetti machines, but the building is, as an exaggerated Late-Modern form, nevertheless highly metaphorical. By this time in his other projects, Stirling had started to move towards a Post-Modern contextualism where his buildings related to, rather than contrasted with, their context.*

In the late afternoon of June 21, 1973, four hundred British VIPs left Waterloo Station in a specially designed train for Haslemere, located in the stockbroker belt of England's rolling southland. They were not going to a Royal Garden Party, nor Ascot. They had been carefully selected for something else: to enjoy an evening, or 'happening' as it was contemporaneously called, the opening of the Olivetti Training Centre, and to take the message of cultivated excellence back to the rest of England. Olivetti's culture campaign had opened with a

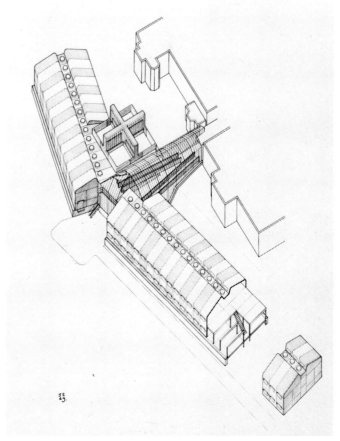

Olivetti Training Centre, Haslemere, 1969–72. Originally the wings were conceived as appearing like a marquee in alternating stripes of lime-green and violet, but after seventeen colour proposals refused by the local Planning Committee, the stripes ended up being mushroom versus Cotswold stone-plastic. (See colour plate page 34).

Multi-space/auditorium for lectures, exhibitions and teaching, with its four raisable walls. This 'executive toy' resembles the ultimate Olivetti automaton.

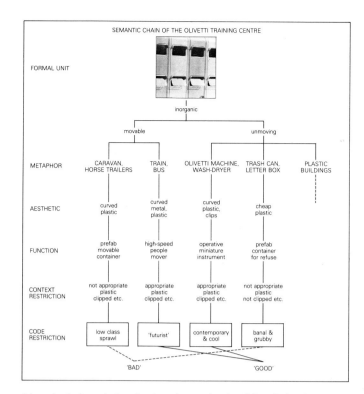

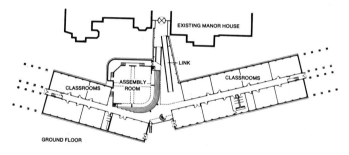

Metaphorical analysis of wing shows the implicit relation between metaphorical image and evaluation. Groups of students, in different countries, were shown slides of the wing and asked 'what does it look like?' The major answers and their semantic chains are mapped here. Surprisingly the metaphorical codes perceived were relatively similar in Norway, California and London.

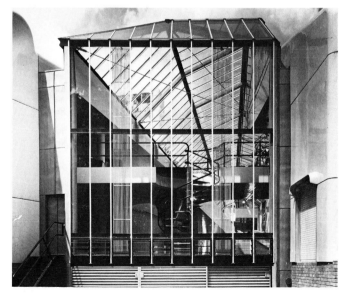

Plan of the new wing and its relation to the Edwardian mansion shows the picturesque layout and dissonance (22½° angles, collage of one system on another).

The glass link, framed between the two plastic wings.

Blitzkrieg, and exactly the right people from the arts, government and industry were there as front line troops. Yehudi Menuhin and Richard Hamilton of the Art Brigade; Directors and Chairmen of BBC, ICI, CBI and Barclays; Viscount Eccles, Paymaster General with Responsibility for the Arts (he exhorted British Industry to enter the fray); and many lesser recruits of the Culturati. They performed as predicted. BBC films, radio programmes, magazine articles and newspaper features followed – all free advertisement, unsolicited and graciously given to acknowledge quality.

Olivetti left nothing to chance. Like any forward looking country today, Olivetti knows that Culture Growth Stock is fast and safe in the seventies (a lesson it learned in the thirties); and, like a country, it is organized with Departments of External Relations, a Director of Cultural Relations, P.R. groups and so on. They designed this June 'happening' to promote their Corporate Image located midway between technology and art. Chefs from Harry's Bar in Venice were flown in to sing as they prepared their famous risottos, 'Bellini' drinks and 'Carpaccio' filettos. You couldn't buy a Carpaccio but, if male, were given a Henry Moore lithograph. (Wives got scarves. Has Olivetti's sociologist found Women's Lib less virile in England?) A music programme in the new auditorium included the Ambrosian Singers and a 'Divertimento for Olivetti machines,' composed and conducted by Tristram Cary. It wasn't quite Handel's 'Water Music' written for George I, or a Mozart opera commissioned by the Emperor Joseph II; but the idea was there. Following this was a Garden Supper Party with films by Ichikawa, lighting by 150 flickering torches, and a bonfire by tree trunks straight out of a Fellini or Antonioni. But the focus was the new Training Centre designed by James Stirling.

Part of this Training Centre resembles a blown-up piece of Olivetti equipment. Its rounded curves and slick surface recall the 'soft-touch Divisumma 18 portable electric printing calculator'. It doesn't have the 'rubber nipples', the new nice-feel keys of this computer; but it is vaguely sensual, especially around the auditorium which, in skin tones, slithers and undulates its way to the ground. You want to caress and fondle this auditorium – at least as much as you want to caress and fondle any Olivetti typewriter. In part, this metaphor is sustained by the unfamiliarity of the scale. Since there is no traditional eave, and the homogeneous plastic curves over roof and wall (thus getting rid of the usual separation, including even the gutter) the image of an integrated piece of domestic equipment is further enhanced.

From their ends, the two plastic wings look like railroad cars or Greyhound buses with their rounded windows and repetitive modules. This is the positive metaphor for those happy to see plastic extended to architecture. However, I've heard these wings condemned as 'clipped together caravans' (mobile homes are sometimes plastic in Britain), or 'stacked waste-bins' that have pivoting openings for refuse.

The four main elements of the new building smash into each other in a carefully careless way that is traditionally English. But they have a toughness and uncompromising quality – even a studied inelegance – which is not English at all. Had a Classicist designed it, there would be graceful separations between materials and spaces, doorways with mouldings and elegant junctures. Indeed, Stirling, with his commitment to the straightforward, has just let things happen. Or so it appears until one studies the repetition of 'awkwardness'. The glass link flares out from the Edwardian mansion at a dissonant angle and frames into the two plastic wings with even more disharmony. The cruciform auditorium bites into one wing leaving wedges of twenty-two degrees. If the wings are railroad cars, then what we see is a train accident.

Stirling might justify these angles for functional reasons since the existing trees, contours and expansion requirements all led to them. The plan is similar to the informal topological planning of the Brutalist movement for which growth was a prime consideration. But beyond this is Stirling's particular brandmark, a quality (that can be found in all his buildings) of dynamic dissonance. A comparable feeling in music would be the suspensions and tensions of Stravinsky; in painting, the distortions of Francis Bacon. The effect is tense, elastic and frightening. Perhaps also it communicates the moral commitment of functionalism: a stern asceticism and a preference for truth over beauty. Certainly none of Stirling's buildings are cute, comforting or sentimental; if they have elegance it is in their geometry and order and not in any provision of thick-pile carpets, symmetry or mouldings. The Modern Movement has, for the most part, spurned these values.

Rather, Stirling keeps his preference for cool surfaces, machine metaphors and vibrant colours. The fin-type radiators of the greenhouse are painted fluorescent lime-green; the ceilings of the corridors are also in high-gloss green; the outside plastic was meant to be in alternating bands of fluorescent violet and lime-green until the local Council forced them to be in creamy blancmange ('Fluorescent colours might frighten the birds').

This is really too bad, since the Training Centre is something of a recreation centre for upcoming Olivettians. Had the wings been in more vibrant colours they might have conveyed a more festive mood, that of impermanent marquees or tents located in a country park. This would have been appropriate to some of the functions located in the context of the existing Edwardian estate – a swimming pool, a sauna house, three tennis courts, a football pitch and bar – country club activities which provide an alternative to the teaching functions in the new building. The Centre as a whole really is a new building type: partly a training school for 150 students (sales and technical personnel, managers, even customers are trained about the new computers), partly a residence, and partly a country club. Perhaps one should think of it as a monastic university for business given over to pleasurable interludes.

To define this complex program, Stirling has adopted a characteristic articulation: the four main functional elements are given distinctive form. Two linear wings, that can be extended by adding new fibre-glass panels, contain the classrooms for sales and technical personnel. The panels, although prefabricated for ease of assembly, had in fact to be knocked into place by hand since the technology was relatively new to England. Another questioned feature: their repetitive nature masks the division into separate classrooms and the conventional structure underneath, which is a precast concrete frame. The other two elements are more radically new in construction and function. The central auditorium can be divided into smaller conference rooms – two, three or four – by automatically lowering partitions from the cruciform ceiling. This is very much the inhabitable Olivetti gadget: audio-visual rooms, fully air-conditioned, serviced and changeable at the press of a button, with

spot lights, black extract nozzles and fluorescent lime-green mushroom columns completing the image.

Finally the glazed gallery, a space which can be used for many activities. First of all, it is a marvellous circulation link between both wings and the mansion, a *trompe l'oeil* space which, because it flares out in three dimensions, seems twice as long one way as the other. It is the Spada Gallery of Borromini with a scissor ramp of Le

Interior of auditorium shows the supersensualism characteristic of the late sixties.

FRANCESCO BORROMINI, *Palazzo Spada*, illusionistic colonnade, Rome, 1635. This perspective appears four times its actual length because of foreshortening. Originally light filtered from above increased the depth and syncopation of columns.

Corbusier and glazing by Paxton – a kind of greenhouse ship's deck where grey flannel technicians can meet quietly and converse. The space is at once open to the outside wind, rain and natural elements and protected from them. Its spiky angles, filled with light and glistening metal, give momentary views of greenery.

During the musical opening, this space doubled as an extension of the auditorium, the ramps served as gal-

Glazed link flares in three dimensions creates perspective illusion (which is not however reinforced by the regular spacing of violet and lime-green structural and heating elements).

Control Room for the auditorium walls, lighting etc. and classroom corridor. The glossy surfaces, rubber floor and command module give this a typical Bondian flavour.

leries and the stairs as seats. Also the link can be used for exhibitions and, inevitably, for growing creepers and bougainvillea. On the outside sits a travelling crane which cleans the glass, a characteristic Stirling device that recalls his Constructivist sympathies and looks like a piece of space hardware. To put all this complex geometry together, or at least to achieve the intended dissonance, Stirling has once again made use of the axonometric technique which allows him to design in plan, section and elevation all at once. It makes the ideal view from which to see the building – a helicopter perching at 45 degrees to the southern wing.

No doubt this new Training Centre is well suited to its job. It looks unmistakably like a clip-together Olivetti machine, it extends the use of new technologies in an artful and unfamiliar way, and hence becomes a fitting symbol of the enlightened corporate policy of Olivetti. The firm stays just ahead of Fiat, Pirelli, IBM or other multinationals as a cultural patron. Probably the motives are mixed. Good art equals good business, and brings the immortality which Renaissance artists conferred upon the Medici. But there is also the recognition, stated by Adriano Olivetti, that the large firm should take responsibility for the social and cultural consequences which stem from its economic decisions. There are, however, some unintended consequences.

When you drive into this 42 acre estate, past exotic trees and rare horticultural species, and see this enclosed plastic tube extending away from the country house, you feel like an intruder at some secret government centre, some meritocratic 'think tank' where a super race is quietly planning out your future or perfecting a death ray. It could be the Hudson Institute or 007's nerve centre for counter-espionage. The subtle visual cues of landscape, Olivetti signs, tasteful lighting standards and blancmange plastic confuse the unwary visitor as to whether the complex is public or private. One expects another Olivetti showroom, or the public gesture which Adriano Olivetti intended for all his buildings, but then one finds the private school for the young elite. And private is the word. Unwary pilgrims are unceremoniously shown the door. Contrary to Olivetti's public spirit and policy elsewhere, the managers here are intent on keeping this new building to themselves.

2.2 STIRLING'S ST. ANDREWS DORMITORIES

This article, written in 1970, was the first time I explicitly raised the issue of metaphorical potency in architecture, and it led to a rather humorous and confusing exchange between James Stirling and myself (AAQ, Autumn 1972, Spring 1973). Later Stirling admitted under cross-examination that ship metaphors, although not intended, may have subconsciously influenced his design ('I was conceived on board a ship in New York harbour . . . . my father was a ship engineer,' etc.). The disdain for conscious metaphor mark this as a Modernist building, while its exaggerated emphasis on constructional technique make it Late-Modernist. This was one of the first applications of semiology to architecture in English.

'It looks like a great grey battleship' . . . . 'it looks like a concrete IBM card' . . . 'it looks like Op Art sugar cubes stacked at an angle' . . . 'in plan it looks like two power saws kissing (yes it does)' . . . IT LOOKS LIKE . . . Why does a Stirling building always have to look like something other than what it 'really' is? Why can't journalists (and even real people) just say: 'It looks like Andrew Melville Hall, a prefabricated concrete residence for 250 students at St. Andrews University in Scotland'? Why must any building always be seen in terms of metaphors that refer to additional things which are, by definition, alien to the 'real' building?

In trying to clarify several such issues of significance in architecture, I will make use of concepts developed in semiology – the theory of signs – and apply them to Stirling's Melville Hall.

The first concept – metaphor/context – concerns the two complementary ways a form gains meaning: either by being associated with other metaphors, e.g. battleship, aircraft carrier, etc., or by being in contrast with the surrounding context.

In trying to work out the most plausible meanings of Melville Hall, we would look for corresponding relations between the metaphors and context. Thus, in addition to the metaphors listed at the beginning, we might find further associations – the concrete setbacks of each room bear a vague resemblance to the crenelations of Scottish baronial castles while the orientation of every element toward the North Sea, including the gun-like extract hoods, reinforces the idea of military defence.

However, what about the more purely architectural metaphors? The building has been compared to the sloping underbelly of Le Corbusier's La Tourette, the collective housing schemes of Constructivists such as Ginzburg, and a skyscraper which has met a 'fate worse than death', that is a 'fallen groundscraper'.

As in most of Stirling's recent work, people see the Hall as some kind of nautical image, even though Stirling denies that metaphors, any metaphors, play a role in his design – which is more concerned with technical and functional aspects. 'Ships don't interest me much, nor am I very influenced by particular buildings of other architects, or associations.' The fact that people continually find marine metaphors where they were never explicitly intended is probably due to Stirling's consistent use of steel railings and concrete decks; in any case his buildings are highly expressive of various things.

End of accommodation wing showing extracts pointing out to sea.

The particular question for the whole building is 'how plausible are the various marine metaphors?' Certainly they gain strength by their interrelation – deck with railing, porthole and exhaust stacks – and by their placement in context – over a *sea* of grass, moored to the *dock* of the hill, looking out over the North Sea. So one may claim their priority over the competing metaphors of 'groundscraper' and 'Op Art sugar cubes' etc. without, however, excluding the latter.

The general question we might ask of any architecture is whether every form has a content and function and vice-versa. By carrying out a quite laborious and detailed analysis (see the diagrams) we may determine how articulate the architecture is and what meanings are either acknowledged, suppressed or redundant. Perhaps it should be emphasised here that complete equality between *form*, *content* and *function* does not imply anything more than an utterly straightforward building. On the contrary, as we shall see, evaluation consists in determining the *appropriateness* and *expressiveness* of the meanings as well as the *choice* of whether relations between areas should be shown or denied.

One further point to be emphasized: I have divided up the analysis into three distinct visual parts because these seem to correspond to an experience of approaching the complex from the side. Other approaches would yield other subdivisions, but the relations would probably be much the same. In the tables that follow, a *contradiction* is indicated by a (#), an *imbalance* by a (+), and an *equality* by no sign. The further relations to form are, it must be noted, *not* indicated.

Several conclusions can be seen from this table. First, as in 9, when there is an equality between content and function, we can say that the form *denotes* this function

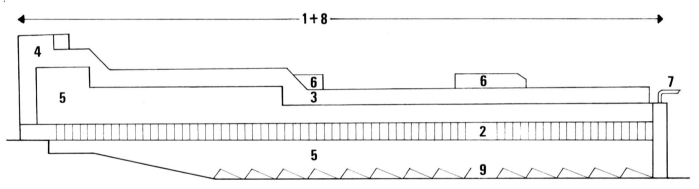

Inner face of the right accommodation wing.

	FORM	CONTENT	ACTUAL FUNCTION
1	linear form	mass-production line, circulation, orientation, open society (+)	mass-production units, circulation, orientation
2	linear glass wall	walkway, communal area	walkway, communal area snack area (+)
3	linear concrete wall	parapet, transition to sky (+)	parapet, windshield (+)
4	concrete volume	stairway, structure	stairway, structure, mechanical (+)
5	pre-cast walls	bedrooms, 'all the same' (#)	bedrooms, different interiors (#)
6	glass sheds	greenhouses? (#)	stairway exits (+)
7	metal funnel	extract, gun (+)	extract
8	descending shape	view, terrace	view, terrace, site economy (+)
9	canted base	basement, transition to ground	basement, transition to ground
10			actual organization into staff, student groups (+)

without any ambiguity. Second, the actual functions usually tend to be greater than both the forms and their connotations, or metaphors. This is to be expected since forms often work in more ways than are immediately apprehensible.

Last, we see in some of the contradictions and imbalances the way in which the building sometimes does not communicate the actual functions. For instance, in 5, the identical precast walls suggest that all the spaces behind are the same, whereas in fact they contain different functions in terms of use and sex (of the students). No doubt Stirling felt that a common exterior was more economical and egalitarian.

The same is true of 10 where the official and *ad hoc* organization of the residence is not expressed (beyond the fact that the wardens occupy the 'highest points' with their terraces). On the interior, each room is more personalized in ways which do reflect the different life styles of the transient residents.

Thus if we can see here good reason for some of the suppression and contradiction in meaning, the same is not so true of the central element of the building.

What I find questionable here (1,2) is that the centre and symbolic 'heart' of the whole scheme, the more formal communal area, is low in *Gestalt* and much less expressive than the wings. It is rather as if Stirling had no great interest or faith in the traditional, formal rooms of the community – such as the dining-room on the second floor – so that he merely packaged them in a prosaic outline of ambiguous glass (ambiguous in the sense that the uniform glass plane equates functions of different importance and partially allows the functions to be seen). This interpretation is reinforced by 2, the low level of the central element in comparison to the higher wings.

On the other hand, the suppression of this element in favour of the linear promenade deck (4,5) turns out to be a particularly brilliant inversion, because the real life of the community goes on between this promenade deck and the outside surrounded green slope. The amount of actual functions which occur here – varying from football to guitar playing and most important, let us admit, 'display and courting between students' – completely outdistances the visible meanings. One really has to see these various activities burgeoning on a warm spring day to fully appreciate the success of this 'major socializing element'. Students are forever looking back and forth from deck to slope and adopting all sorts of familiar poses for those down below on the ground.

If the central element shows both an inversion of expected meaning and the presence of unexpected functions, the bedroom units carry through this same imbalance and contradiction except without any of the drawbacks.

I have already mentioned the contradiction between a repeated, 'democratic' unit and the variety of social structures behind it (1) but perhaps the greater surprise is the way in which the precast unit carries all sorts of connotations and actual functions beyond the immediately obvious ones (indicated by the large amount of + signs). Thus the inverted T shape with its ribbed diagonals and smooth edges (2,3,4) suggests the individualiza-

Central element of the building from seaward.

The promenade deck.

	FORM	CONTENT	ACTUAL FUNCTION
1	central element	the symbolic 'heart'	dining rooms (+), 2 common rooms (+), walkway (+)
2	low centre, high wings	insignificant (#) mannerist (#)	formal community (#)
3	concrete volumes	rooms, stairway	rooms, stairway
4	linear glass walls	walkway, communal area	walkway, communal area, an entrance (+) display area (+)
5	green slope	sitting, sunning	sitting, sunning, games (+), display (+)

tion of each room marked also by an elegant border, but in fact the inverted T was also created for functional reasons.

First of all, it is a structural wall system, rare in England, but common in Russia, which achieves great economies and precision because it is manufactured in a factory; second, its edges are smooth so that the walls can be handled without chipping the ribs. Thus we find that delightful ambiguity common to architecture which has been worked through on so many levels of meaning that we are led from one interpretation to the next without apparent end.

To summarize, the St. Andrews residence shows an attention to significance on different levels which goes beyond the usual oversimplifications of today. In fact it

The bedroom units.

	FORM	CONTENT	ACTUAL FUNCTION
1	repeated units	'all the same', (democratic) (#)	different life styles etc. (#)
2	shape (inverted T)	one room	one room, innovating precast structure (+)
3	ribbed concrete	scale, identity of room, corduroy (+)	actual handling of concrete (+)
4	smooth edges	elegant transition (+)	actual handling of concrete (+)
5	big windows	view	fantastic view (+)
6	small windows	view	sun (+), view blocked to next window (#)
7	setbacks	view, crenellations (+), saw teeth (+), nervous (+)	fantastic view (+)

seems to me reminiscent of the Heroic Period of the twenties when form had a functional and social intention indicative of a new society to come, except, alas, it is here without the faith in the formal institutions of men that inspired the twenties. We can find this social pessimism explicitly stated in Stirling's writing and it no doubt helps to explain his curious inversion of the private sphere over the public, of making the informal activities twice as significant as the formal. But as far as the other internal meanings are concerned, St. Andrews shows a high degree of relations between the three areas, whether they are equalities or contradictions, as well as a high degree of coherent, metaphorical expressiveness.

2.3 THE SUPERSENSUALISTS I & II

These two related essays, published in Architectural Design *in 1971–2, were an attempt to celebrate and criticize, at the same time, an emergent design sensibility which was then relatively unknown outside of Italy. The show at the Museum of Modern Art, 'Italy – the New Domestic Landscape' (1972), changed all that, for New Yorkers at least. These Italian designers are typical Late-Modernists in their extreme emphasis on anonymity and repetition, but the attention to metaphor and irony place them on the road to Post-Modernism.*

THE SUPERSENSUALISTS I

'Yum, yum, yum, – slurp. It's so beautiful it's killing me'. 'It's so luscious I could eat it.' In Pier Pasolini's *Porcile (Pigsty)* a young, passionless scion, son of a big German industrialist, has daily orgies in a pigsty (because he cannot love *homo sapiens*) which culminate in himself as the main course for their (the pigs') evening swill. Do not ask why a juicy haut-bourgeois adolescent should provide nourishment for swine.

> Pasolini: Just at this moment (in the film) the son goes off as usual to the pigsty and sees Spinoza in a vision. Spinoza explains his life to him and tells him that his love for the pigs is equivalent to an affirmation of the existence of God and leaves him.[1]

So there. Frederico Fellini's *8½* opens with Marcello Mastroianni caught in a suffocating traffic jam of super technology and he escapes from his hermetically-sealed car to float up out into thin air like a kite – tied by the leg – until he is brought down eventually by the command of a passing horse-back rider who happens to be galloping along on a beach. What else?

No one, to my knowledge, has ever explored the relations, which no doubt do exist, between sensual love, metaphysical angst, beauty, advanced technology and (perhaps) Marxism before the recent generation of Italian designers and film-makers insinuated themselves on the scene. During the last ten years, since at least *Dolce Vita*, in the architecture schools of Italy, the film studios of Rome, the futuristic shops such as M-Design, Stil-Novo, O-Luce (O Luce, Che Bello!), the dripping, glossy pages of *Domus*, a veritable *Zeitgeist* has emerged which portrays a common sensibility, but – and this is the point of insinuation – with no explicit philosophy or exponent of the movement. In fact the philosophies which the Supersensualists do indulge in are likely to be regarded as nonsensical, hilarious or simply deranged by those outside of the movement.[2] Almost anyone outside of Italy is bound to find the equation of Catholicism and Marxism on a *sensual* level an impossibility. Who still believes that miracles are a normal part of everyday urban life? When in Pasolini's *Theorem*, the respectable capitalist father goes into a crowded railway station at rush hour, drops all his clothes to the ground and then walks naked through the streets into an arid, grey-green desert, almost everyone is tempted to regard it as an elaborate, surrealist joke – not a believable miracle which portrays the ultimate gratuitousness of reality. For that matter, the major axioms of *Theorem* are all incredible paradoxes.

GAE AULENTI, *House for an art lover*, Milan, 1969–70. Like Art Nouveau commissions for the same sort of patron seventy years previously, this work mixes art and life to the point where they are indistinguishable. The ambiguities are further enhanced by the ambiguity of space and highly reflective surface. Noland, Judd, Nolde, Lichtenstein and Segal, among others, find a home here. A bronze Magritte *La Folie des Grandeurs*, 1967 telescopes its torso out of the high altar in the 'bathroom'. Similar themes and treatment might be found in Hoffman's Palais Stoclet, but without such a slick coating of hedonistic self-indulgence.

Opposite

HANS HOLLEIN, *Schullin Jewellery Shop*, Vienna, 1972-4. This exquisite, tiny shop, a blown up jewel itself, highlights the mechanical ducts and bulbs with a glistening gold colour and sensual, lip-like folds which spill down into the doorway. The folds then cut through the top of the door and flatten out becoming geological strata surrounding the glass (river). The strong contrasts between masonry rustication and fissure are repeated in the interior as contrasts beween velvet and glistening metal, rectangles and curves. This Slick-Tech solution begins to address the issue of content in architecture, but it is before Hollein's more clearly Post-Modern buildings.

Christ (Terence Stamp) liberates a whole family of Milanese *borghese* by administering his divine member to everyone including the chambermaid. The logic of this theorem – existential transformation through ineffable sexual gratification – is seen through to its bitter-sweet end.

Pushing a bizarre proposition, or paradox, to its extreme conclusion is a normal practice of the Super-sensualists. Superstudio, led by the Florentine Adolfo Natalini, has designed the Continuous Monument which is 'a single piece of architecture to be extended over the whole world'.[3] In this case the screwball logic consists in a mixture of 'total urbanization' which is clearly totalitarian in essence and an absolute egalitarianism – since everyone has exactly the same room, or the same white square for every function. The motivation is metaphysical and sensual in origin: the Continuous Monument's 'static perfection moves the world through the love that it creates', through 'serenity and calm' and through 'sweet tyranny' (*sic*).

Their 'Project for a Monument to the Partisans of the Resistance' is a rounded version of the Continuous Monument being composed from the ubiquitous white squares and primary 'elements' of architectural construction (girders, arches) which look as if they were lifted from Plato's ideal Architectural Workshop (or at least August Choisy). An up-to-date version of well-dressed 'Resisters' is collaged onto the drawing giving it that ambiguous quality found in *Theorem* and *Pigsty* of the very wealthy engaged in left-wing politics (in fact they can be counted on to spout Marxist slogans as they step into their Lamborghini Espada). In a typical triumph of form over content, or the Continuous Monument over

Opposite, above
SUPERSTUDIO, *Continuous Monument*, 1969, a 'model for total urbanization' returns man-made form in its pure prismatic quality to a state of icy nature. One view shows the Continuous Monument on its way curving around the world touching Lower Manhattan; the other is an extension of the New York building envelopes.

Opposite, below
GRUPPO STRUM (Ceretti, Derossi & Rosso), *Pratone* ('Big Meadow'), Milan, 1970. These architect/designers created a few paradoxical 'chairs' and 'beds' from new materials such as polyurethane which became one thing when sat or fallen on and another enigmatic thing when left lying about the house. This 'Big Meadow' is a typical 'edible' object meant at once to satiate and disturb a consumer society.

ARCHIZOOM, *Dream bed, Naufragio di Rose*, 1968, with pure architectural elements, Bob Dylan, their lightning-flash symbol and veined marble, all enclosed in a de Chirico like space.

SUPERSTUDIO, *Project for a Memorial Park and Monument to the Partisans of the Resistance*, Modena, 1970.

SUPERSTUDIO, table lamp, 1970.

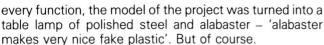

Cimitero Monumentale, Milan.

every function, the model of the project was turned into a table lamp of polished steel and alabaster – 'alabaster makes very nice fake plastic'. But of course.

Archizoom Associati,[4] another Florentine group of designers, has been mining the same metaphysical territory of enclosed, hermetically-sealed environments: 'dream beds', desert landscapes (why do deserts always appear?) and the 'Residential Park, a No-Stop City, a Climatic Universal System' which is their answer to the Continuous Monument as it extends over the surface of the world. Again, fascination results from watching a certain trend or social tendency become extrapolated to its extreme and absurd conclusion. If Terence Stamp can redeem the Milanese through fornication then suburban sprawl can be analysed into its logical sub-sets and spread equally, and beautifully, over the whole globe. The justification is, as usual, a pure form of garbled Marxism.

> The metropolis ceases to be a 'place' [and] becomes a 'condition'; in fact it is just this condition which is made to circulate uniformly, through Consumer Products, in the social phenomenon. The future dimension of the metropolis coincides with that of the market itself . . . Production and Consumption possess one and the same ideology, which is that of

Programming. Both hypothesize a social and physical reality completely continuous and undifferentiated . . .Therefore, the problem becomes that of freeing mankind from architecture in so much as it is a formal structure. Nowadays the only possible utopia is quantitative. . .[5]

As in Pasolini's reflection on his work, rational arguments, bits of science and sociology are abstracted from their systematic context, grasped as sensual images and blown up to the level of a miraculous fantasy. It is a total inversion of the science we are used to comprehending for its sanity and sweet reasonableness. Whereas most people are habituated to accepting death as a rational necessity for evolution, love as functionally justified for the survival of the species and conflict as the engine of social change – the Supersensualists grasp all these cosmic forces and invert their utilitarian bases or explanations. After all, from an individual, human point of view they are gratuitous and absurd. No one really wants to die, even if it is in some large sense functionally necessary. For a country which has just experienced the 'Economic Miracle', and partially jumped from a peasant economy to an advanced industrial state, every fact of life is likely to be just as fantastic and miraculous.

THE SUPERSENSUALISTS II: DEATH

Every now and then one steps into an odd environment and has a sudden flash of insight. The mathematician Henri Poincaré stepped on to a bus in Coutances and suddenly solved the problem of Fuchsian functions. Reyner Banham stepped, with a movie camera, into a southern Illinoian swimming pool and saw the point of lightweight technology, cleanliness, etc. St. Paul on the road to Damascus . . . When I walked into the Cimitero Monumentale in Milan I suddenly understood a whole area of architectural endeavour. I realized what motivated the ideal cities of the Renaissance, the utopian plans of Le Corbusier, the beautiful elevations and perspectives which every architect aspires to build. Eternity. The idea that much architecture intends to be eternal occurred to me in the 'Monumental Cemetery' of Milan and the thought that therefore this architecture had to be for the dead quickly followed. It was beautiful, more beautiful than a rendering, well-kept up and open on all sides so that one could study it like a jewel. Every style was represented from Lombardy Gothic to Saarinen orange-peel, from Art Deco to Mussolini modern. No living city had seen such a rich texture of perfected monuments. It took a cemetery to realize the age-old architectural dream of everything in its place and a place for everything, and the harmony and stillness, only broken by the occasional grave-keeper, whispered out the long suspected truth – 'perfect architecture is only for the dead'.

Back in the living, bungled centre of Milan, the architect Ettore Sottsass Jr. spoke of the omnipresence of death. His friend, the designer Joe Colombo, had just died; a close relative had committed suicide; he had himself barely escaped death twice. First in a concentration camp, second in the early sixties when Adriano Olivetti had flown him to the States for treatment of an 'incurable disease' (as far as the Italian doctors knew). 'We flirt with death', Sottsass said of the Italian designers and one can find this flirtation in his own ceramics and terracotta vases which are like so many superclean tombstones. Their high gloss finish and precision geometry make them final statements in the art of the reliquary even though they are intended as ash-trays or fruit dishes or vases in the house. Their status as consumer objects to be worshipped, fondled, loved is beyond compare. Yet Sottsass was sceptical. 'I can't get rid of the love of objects; I'm trying hard.' He had just contributed to an edition of the Milanese magazine *IN*, edited by Superstudio and Archizoom, with the overall theme 'The Destruction of the Object'. 'I'm from the older generation and I find objects are very important for the control of our life, because they concentrate meanings. The problem is to make a new symbol or image with objects and transform their function.'

The attempt to Destroy the Object is all the rage in Milan and Florence. The next two issues of *IN* will be titled 'The Elimination of the City' and 'The Disappearance of Work' following on from Superstudio and Archizoom's philosophy that the collapse of 'formal structures' accompanies the liberation of men. They speak of the 'elimination of fetishism and semantic redundancy'. One is reminded of Le Corbusier's 'vacuum-cleaning' period of Modern architecture. All the results of this purgation, like Le Corbusier's, turn into new objects of worship: fantastically sensual pieces of metaphysical furniture sold to the *borghese* of Milan through one of the many outlets: Poltronova, Cassina,

Knoll International, etc. For instance the 'Mies' chair of Archizoom presents the metaphysical problem of sitting down with utmost elegant wit. One sees a flat, dark slab leaning down between two chromium triangles. With its headrest and position, one thinks it's an operating table tilted towards the end so as to more easily push off the recently departed. But then if one dares lie on this table, the dark slab of elastic suddenly gives way under the bottom and the chrome bars turn into armrests. The overall triangular geometry is even more simplified than a chair by Mies. It is one of the strangest propositions in modern furniture, having all sorts of funereal overtones. In fact the metaphors of death pervade much of Archizoom's work, from their 'dream beds' which resemble sacrificial altars to their 'gazebi' and enclosed 'meditation centre', which resemble areas set apart for mourning and remembrance. Behind these early works is perhaps the subconscious attempt to destroy fetishism for objects, by taking it to the ultimate limit. At any rate Archizoom speaks of creating a 'closed basin', a semi-enclosed world, where the normal meanings of objects are either contradicted or pushed to absurdity.

ARCHIZOOM, *'Mies' chair*, 1968.

ARCHIZOOM, *Dream bed, Rosa d'Arabia*, 1968.

ARCHIZOOM, *Gazebo-Meditation Centre*, 1968.

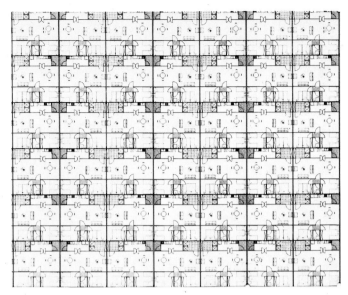

ARCHIZOOM, *Typological Plan.*

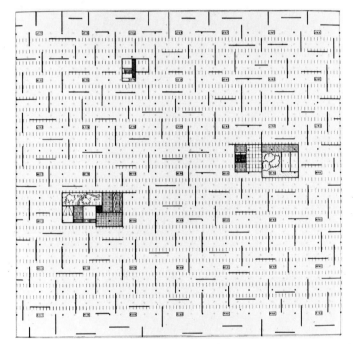

ARCHIZOOM, *No-Stop City – Residential Wood*, 1970.

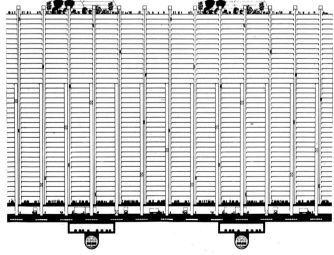

ARCHIZOOM, *Homogeneous Living Diagram.*

More recently they have done the same with the whole city and once again the results resemble the static perfection of the graveyard.[6] They have evolved what they call the 'No-Stop City, a Climatic Universal System' which can be spread homogeneously around the world resolving the contradictions between city and country in an even mixture of both. Elevators, beds, dining tables, rivers and trees are evenly distributed in a perfected plan that recalls the Ville Radieuse. As with Le Corbusier this ideal plan is the *termination* of a process, an industrial process most of all. Instead of taking the Futurist point that technology is in a constant state of compromising change – always scrapping, always innovating, never finished, never perfect – Archizoom freezes a certain stage of development and re-arranges the results in a radical way. All the elevators and spiral staircases are normal and standardized, without a history. The implication in 'No-Stop City' is that technology stopped and was perfected about 1925. And yet like Le Corbusier, the philosophy which underlies this is not just the culmination of development (i.e., death), but the process itself. In their explanation, Archizoom justifies 'No-Stop City' as a logical development of the urban and social process. Their ideas are partly based on the Marxist dialectic and current views of the post-industrial society. Hence they speak of the old bourgeois city, which is now superseded, as a collecting point of capital which reflects even in its pyramidal skyline the accumulation of wealth toward the centre. In opposition to this visual pyramid they place a 'two-dimensional net' of services and communication or a gigantic, homogeneous and endless structure. Their point is that the urban realm has become itself the market mechanism and this mechanism is now based on information technologies which decentralize and equalize the market in every point of the world.

. . .now the use of electronic media takes the place of the direct urban praxis: artificial inducements to consumption allow a much deeper infiltration into the social structure than did the (bourgeois) city's weak channels of information. The metropolis ceases to be a 'place', to become a condition: in fact it is just this condition which is made to circulate uniformly, through Consumer Products, in the social phenomenon. The future dimension of the metropolis coincides with the market itself.

Their view of the market mechanism can be termed idealistic, non-Marxist and based on the belief in the 'managerial revolution', because they think that with the market's proper management all conflicts can be resolved.

Production and consumption possess one and the same ideology, which is that of programming. Both hypothesize a social and physical reality completely continuous and undifferentiated. No other realities exist. The factory and the supermarket become the specimen models of the future city . . . the house becomes a well-equipped parking lot . . . Thus [architecture] mediates between the contradictory forces of public and private: now, however, this conflict is no longer left on the speculative level of existential consciousness.

Why not? Because now-

Economic Planning, by organizing the whole of society productively, eliminates the conflict, considers the contradiction fictitious and takes any strictly individual datum as experimental . . . Nowadays the only possible utopia is quantitative. Social conflict is no longer going through the phase of confrontation of alternative models, but is in that of dialectical negotiation between a balanced development of the system and the growing cost of the labour force . . . quantitative language replaces qualitative, thus becoming the only scientific means of approach to the undifferentiated stratification of production and hence of reality.

Perhaps the nicest thing about these arguments and the 'No-Stop City' is that they both take certain omnipresent truths to the extreme and thereby clarify their nature. Of course no present post-industrial society resembles the ideal of scientific managers making just rational decisions which eliminate social conflicts, but this ideology pervades both Russian and American State capitalism and it is pleasant to see it laid bare in its pure, absurd form. This is the ideology of technocrats, planners, bureaucrats, social engineers, the men of 'think tanks' and latter-day Saint Simonians such as Buckminster Fuller. Happily, Archizoom has pushed the assumptions to the point where one can see how they're both wrong and poetic at the same time. For if the market mechanism were perfectly regulated and 'isotropic', then it might result in the 'quantitative utopia' represented by the 'No-Stop City'. However, the obvious mistakes in the assumptions are 1: that the managerial revolution has occurred, 2: that any living city could result in the static, dead perfection which they represent, and 3: that a quantitative utopia could give any significance or meaning to life – or for that matter death.

The whole question of the significance of death has begun to preoccupy similar kinds of architects in different countries. Hans Hollein, a great influence on Archizoom, Superstudio and Sottsass, designed an exhibition 'Death' in 1970 which developed a rather new attitude towards its significance. He constructed an archaeological site and gave participants shovels to dig up the various remnants of the present: smashed Coke bottles, golf clubs and so on. As well as this, he placed the accoutrements of dying nearby – a sterile white hospital bed, screen, and garments to dress the corpse. Part of the virtue of this approach is that it gets the living involved in a process with the dead; either discovering their remains or seeing how we treat people in their last moments. In a way this involvement is an alternative to the pathos connected with the usual forms of memorialization.

ARCHIZOOM, *Homogeneous Residential Structures.*

ARCHIZOOM, *No-Stop Interior Landscape.*

HANS HOLLEIN, *Exhibition Death*, 1970.

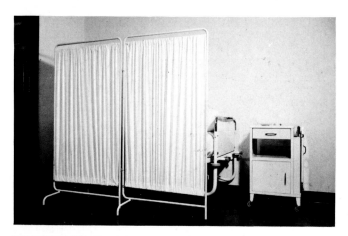

HANS HOLLEIN, *Death Bed in a Corridor*.

It was a feeling of pathos which pervaded the gigantic mortuary of the Cimitero Monumentale. There, the remains of the deceased are packed in an endless gridiron, or No-Stop Grave Yard. Many of the memorial plaques have photos and small descriptions which are meant to remind close relatives and friends of the particular significance of the departed.

Yet an air of hopeless mockery pervades the mortuary. Each remembrance is private and hence doomed to extinction in a short time. Each grave is overwhelmed by the presence of too many others. Like a telephone book, or New York's vast slab-heap of memorials, the omnipresence of numbers robs the significance of any one. Sottsass commented on this irony: 'People are buried in monuments to be remembered. A single monument is effective, but in a graveyard there are no memories, no people.'

Perhaps a reason for this situation is the Christian idea of the individual soul inhabiting eternity. If one believes in an individual after-life, then it makes sense to memorialize every person, although presumably God, being infinitely non-forgetful, would not need to be reminded of each soul. Yet these beliefs in eternal afterlife have eroded to the point where, most obviously, the individual graves have become kitsch reminders to and for the living. If this is true, it would seem inevitable that the pagan idea of immortality replace the Christian idea of eternity and that architecture, which crystallizes memory, would follow this change. Instead of representing a perfected process like 'No-Stop City', it would accentuate the individual act which stands out from this process. It would seek to memorialize that which is public and can be shared within society, giving to perishable human action that only kind of immortality open to it: the ability to be remembered by the living as a unique occurrence in a mass of expectedness.

HANS HOLLEIN, *Richard Feigen Gallery*, New York, 1969–71, exterior and interior. Juxtaposing a blank white surface with highly sensuous columns is a trademark which Hollein has picked up from his compatriot Adolf Loos. The traditional theme of 'paired columns' is given an ironic twist by being placed 'in' the entrance to reappear inside as an implicit sensuous sign of breasts or buttocks.

2.4 THE PLURALISM OF JAPANESE ARCHITECTURE

This essay, written in 1976, was intended as an additional one to Modern Movements in Architecture, *but it was published only in the French and Japanese translations of that book.*

The Japanese have built many interesting buildings in the last fifteen years, and if any country can claim to dominate the scene of Late-Modernism it is Japan. Inevitably it is also starting to produce Post-Modern works, one of which is illustrated on pages 24–5.

Recent Japanese architecture has expanded the languages of Modern architecture and opened up routes to the past and tradition which were previously cut off. Because of this it is likely that Japan will become a model to follow and influences will flow in a reverse direction, from East to West, as they did in 1890 and 1930. In many ways the Japanese architectural culture is like that of the Italian Renaissance: full of creative individuals who are competing among themselves, sometimes quarrelling, but actually building.

In Europe they compete, and quarrel, but for the most part don't build. In differing ways one individual and a group react against previous architects, so there is the constant dialectic going on which is the mark of health in any live culture. I have distinguished here five different positions in this dialectic even though from a distant, Western position they might all seem variations on the same theme. Before we look at them a major question has to be asked, a rhetorical question critics and visitors always seem to put.

Why was Modern architecture accepted?

Various reasons have been put forward for the acceptance of Modern architecture in Japan. The most popular explanation is that it was nothing new. The traditional architecture of Shinto and Katsura were themselves 'modern'; they used materials in a natural, unfinished state, they emphasized joints, construction and geometry; even at Katsura the delicate asymmetries were carried through in black and white. The whole 'International Style' was there for four hundred years

Katsura Imperial Villa, Kyoto, 1615–1624. View of *engawa*, the inbetween space, under the eaves. The black and white architecture set against an informal, natural landscape and on top of unfinished, natural elements (rocks) was also a key image of the International Style and one celebrated by Walter Gropius among others.

including standardization, flexibility, modular co-ordination, grid planning and the cherished value of anonymity.

Whereas the West had to overturn its tradition to become Modern, the Japanese simply revived parts of theirs. And this brings out a fundamental difference between the two cultures which has perplexed both sides. The West often proceeds by revolution, by a battle between generations which is supposed to regenerate the best in the past, whereas Japan proceeds by confrontation between past and future, East and West. Confrontation may be considered a kind of inclusivism and this may stem from Buddhism. For essential to Buddhism is toleration and inclusion of other faiths and customs, whereas Christianity, and its sects, are forever trying to become purified. Thus when Buddhist thought and Japanese architecture combine extremely varied material, they seem incongruous and unbelievable to a Westerner.

I will not forget my first impression of Tokyo with its thirty storey glass and steel buildings next to one storey Shinto shrines – golf on the rooftop and traditional garden on the ground. Mixed-up uses everywhere. Of course it's amusing and makes more sense to the city than functional purification, but what surprised me was that it could be practised everywhere with nonchalance. When Westerners practise complexity and contradiction they are self-conscious and like Robert Venturi write a book about it,[1] whereas in Japan it is a habit of mind and everyday experience. The West preaches eclecticism and syncretism now, whereas for the Japanese they have been a commonplace. This is one distinctive value which I think will influence the West in the future, but it led a Japanese friend of mine to give another reason for the easy acceptance of Modern architecture. He said 'We're so confused, we'll accept anything, and Modern architecture was just one more of the many styles we imported here along with Louis XVI'. Between eclecticism and confusion there is a fine line to be drawn, but whatever the cause turns out to be (and there are obviously many) they have led to a volume of creative architecture that is quite unique.

I. Late Le Corbusier and sculptural Modernism

With the upturn in the economy in the 1950s (due in part to the Korean War) architects had an opportunity to build on a scale that was only equalled in America. Three architects emerged at this time who were recognized as undisputed leaders of the profession – Kunio Maekawa, Junzo Sakakura and Kenzo Tange. The first two had trained with Le Corbusier in Paris, but all three were good friends of the master, and they saw him from time to time at CIAM meetings. Their friendship took on the aspect of a homage – their buildings are like versions of Le Corbusier's last works, and they're better in some respects. Le Corbusier never had the opportunity to use beautiful mathematical curves on the scale Tange did at the Olympic Games of 1964. Curve and counter curve sweeping to a strong bevelled mast – the whole complex was a beautiful reconciliation of the traditional and Modern language of form. There was something crude and heavy in this – indeed close up the gargantuan extract holes are blackened orifices – but it had the

KENZO TANGE, *National Gymnasium for the Olympic Games*, Tokyo, 1964. Two buildings in subtle counter-point are placed on a podium. The concrete masts, which hold the catenary and hyperbolic curves, end in the typical 'Japanese slant' which has become something of a cliché. Accentuated structural members and the slight, gentle curves are also traditional signs.

KENZO TANGE, *St. Mary's Cathedral*, Tokyo, 1964. The walls rise from a kite-shaped ground plan, they twist and culminate in a cruciform of light – an obvious, but effective use of the hyperbolic parabola. Again the use of slight curves and bevelled pylons recalls traditional language.

KENZO TANGE, *Competition Entry for a Sino-Japanese Cultural Centre*, 1943. Traditional forms used with great power and conviction.

KUNIO MAEKAWA, *Tokyo Metropolitan Festival Hall*, 1961. Bold shapes break out of a rectilinear volume in the typical Corbusian manner of 'compaction composition'. The precast panels with coarse gravel and tile paving are also Corbusian trademarks. This style spread through Japan in the sixties and found greatest use in the large number of cultural centres built at this time.

creative mixture of function and expression which characterized Le Corbusier's best works. Indeed Tange's St. Mary's Cathedral has the same mixture, and uses complex curves in an appropriate, symbolic way. The internal space soars up to a cruciform of light; the end pylons turn miraculously into walls and roof; the shapes are primitive religious gestures against the sky. It all vaguely recalls Torii gates and at the same time Christian cathedrals. But there is something strangely disquieting about these buildings, as there is of so much work in this tradition. It seems to stop at the level of a harmonious gesture and go no further: a few decisive shapes, several creative ideas and that is it. Unlike a late work of Le Corbusier, one can't go on discovering meaning after meaning – it is all over in a flash.

On the other hand, Kenzo Tange has a facility with

architectural form – a sensitivity to shape and proportion – which has always characterized the best Japanese architecture and which is known to the outside world as the typical Japanese touch. No designers in the West, with the possible exception of the Italians, can match this facility. While admired it is also looked upon with suspicion, and as if to confirm this suspicion, there is his design for a Sino-Japanese Cultural Centre of 1943 which is in the traditional style – apparently a compromise with nationalism. And yet even here there is a surprise for the Westerner who is well acquainted with such wartime compromises: the design actually has visual integrity. It is not a pastiche as, for instance, was Gropius' or Wright's work in a traditional style.

This ability to be both ancient and modern by turns, or in the same building, will always fascinate a Westerner because he finds it so difficult. The Western architect has recently returned to his classical tradition obliquely, with ironies and inversions, whereas an architect like Maekawa goes straight back to his. He may use the typical trabeated structure and tatami mat as he did in the Harumi apartments of 1958, or the gentle upturned eaves as he did in the Tokyo Metropolitan Festival Hall, 1961. This building has been called by Robin Boyd the first example of the 'New Japan Style': the traditional motifs are here transformed into a massive, concrete expressionism.[2] In a way it is characteristic of so much work in

JUNZO SAKAKURA, *Hotel Blue Sky*, 1971. The machine aesthetic orchestrated with tinted glass of many hues becomes a perfect symbol for this bathing resort.

the late Le Corbusier style. Built from monolithic and pre-cast concrete, sharply articulated into volumes which smash into each other, revealing sudden vistas and dramatic space – it could be in Chandigarh except for the upturned eaves and bevelled shapes. The effect is overpowering and quite acceptable in cultural centres, which can accommodate so much articulation. Each main function of the building breaks out of a rectilinear volume to proclaim its identity, but then recedes back into the whole. Recently Maekawa has left this rhetorical tradition and returned to a form of 'humanism', by which he means building in brick and emphasizing space rather than enclosure. The swing away from concrete gigantism has produced all sorts of symbolic reactions some of which will be discussed later.

The late Junzo Sakakura, another Corbusier disciple, produced several buildings which mix Modern and Japanese elements: his Museum of Modern Art at Kamakura 1951, is the classic Corbusian white box on black steel columns – except the columns rest in turn on traditional stone footings set in the pond, like stepping stones at Katsura. An even more subtle and striking mixture of traditions is his Hotel Blue Sky which combines a traditional cage of post and beam space, with tinted glass and voluptuous detailing.

It's almost the perfect expression of the structural, steel frame and glass panel and in this sense must be understood as classical Modern: its roots go back to the Chicago Frame of the 1870s. Yet other equally strong roots go back to the Shinden style of the Kamakura period with its overlapping rectangles of cage space. Both influences are there, but oddly enough the strongest feeling is that this building belongs to the Supersensualists.[3] It is witty, sensual and luxurious – altogether a pleasant surprise for an architect working in the Corbusier idiom. But again, this stylistic facility is a norm in Japan.

2. Metabolism, *engawa* and capsule architecture

A group of younger architects, some of whom were working in the Tange office in the late fifties, came together to start a self-conscious movement called

KIYONARI KIKUTAKE, *Marine Civilization Scheme*, 1960. Plug-in capsules on a cylindrical core resting on floating islands. The scheme is similar to Kurokawa's analogy with living plants called 'The Bamboo Type Community' (1959) which also consisted of circular towers hollowed out in the centre and capsules around them.

Metabolism. The name and philosophy were invented, almost as propaganda, for the World Design Conference held in Tokyo in 1960. Kisho Kurokawa was twenty-six and the other architects and critics, Kiyonari Kikutake, Fumihiko Maki, Masato Otaka, Noborii Kawazoe and Hirosha Asada were in their early thirties. They had studied the politics of European avant-garde movements and were determined to fashion an 'ism' which would compete with those of the West.

Strangely, they were aided in this essentially elitist activity by Japanese industry which was, at the same time, aggressively trying to invade Western markets. The World Design Conference would, it was hoped, unify the various professions responsible for Japanese trade and give them a single style, and co-ordination identifiable to the outside world. The Chamber of Commerce sponsored the affair.

Kurokawa and the others met every two weeks at night to discuss such designs as Kikutake's project 'City over the Sea', a series of gigantic cylinders located on what they called 'artificial land'. Since eighty per cent of Japan is mountainous, the Metabolists and others have often designed megastructures which move into the sea. From such utopian schemes developed the notion of the city as an organism which changes at various rates. Since Kikutake had studied to be a doctor before he became an architect, the word 'metabolism' came up in his mind to signify this philosophy. Kurokawa gives another account: he says they first evolved their designs of plug-in

KIYONARI KIKUTAKE, *Sky House*, Tokyo 1958. Four external pylons hold a square room in the shape of a sandwich. Services are not clustered in the centre, as with CIAM practice, but dispersed to the periphery of the open space so they can be easily removed and updated. 'Movenettes' they were called – mass produced WC units, kitchen etc.

KIYONARI KIKUTAKE, *Administration Building for the Izumo Shrine*, Izumo, 1963. Narrow horizontal slits create a Modern screen of concrete and let in very delicate light. The office is suspended inside the main space to be changed when obsolete – without disrupting the space.

buildings and megastructures and then consulted a dictionary for inspiration.

The philosophy has proved as multifarious as its origins. Kikutake said to me that 'Metabolism means many different things. For Kurokawa it means the coexistence of various elements whereas for me it means that which remains unchanged when change occurs.' For Kawazoe it meant 'the constant renewing in all nature – animals and plants, living organisms and the natural environment . . .'

At any rate, Metabolism became an extended biological analogy meant to replace the mechanical analogy of orthodox Modern architecture: functional separation, machine metaphors, rigid geometry and permanence were ruled out, in theory. Actually, in practice, these aspects were still accentuated as can be seen in the mechanistic imagery of their buildings at Expo 70. But the Metabolists compared buildings and cities to an energy process found in all of life; the cycles of change and the constant renewal of organic tissue. In a sense this philosophy was simply Taoism and Buddhism in modern dress – the incessant change of the former, and the idea of reincarnation of the latter. Indeed the word almost sounds like 'Metabuddhism'.

Kikutake first gave expression to these growing and changing ideas with his Sky House, built for himself in 1958. It's basically like a living sandwich skewered at four points high above the ground – 'in the sky'. 'Equipment' is dispersed around the open plan in 'movenettes', so

that it can be moved and replaced. Extreme visual separation (of the building parts) results from this philosophy and one can see this in Kikutake's next important building for the Izumo Shrine. The wall (which is conceptually a roof – these shrines always emphasize the roof) is separated from the ridge beam which is visually separated from the structural pylons. The stairs, porches, offices and plumbing are also pulled apart to allow harmonious change. And yet, here is a major paradox: the whole image *looks* much more permanent than the typical Izumo Shrine, which was built in wood and rebuilt on the average of every fifty years. One would like to know how much these elements have actually been changed since it was built in 1963. As with so much Metabolist architecture the emphasis on change has actually rationalized a monumentality that appears to be inflexible.

Nevertheless, as a monument the building is impressive. It again manages to be typically Japanese without being too explicit. The strong roof form has always been the major sign of Japanese building since the first Shinto temple, but here it's not quite a roof (nor a wall). The ridge beam projections are like typical wooden projections on Shinto shrines, but here they're much too long. Repetitions of rhythmical construction, Torii gates, battered walls – all the motifs found in this building – echo traditional signs, and appropriately so since it's a very traditional building task.

Basic to Metabolism has been a distinction between long-term support structures and short-term movable units. This distinction results in either the plug-in system of capsules (the 'Mova Block' design of Kikutake), or the 'artificial land' with various Sky Houses placed upon it. Kikutake refined these ideas in a series of articles and designs on mass housing in 1971. They led him to a notion which Kurokawa was also working on at the time – *engawa*, the space between buildings – or for Kikutake the semi-public space.

The idea of semi-public space ultimately grew out of Team Ten and Van Eyck's notion of the 'inbetween space', and research which was going on in New York City under Oscar Newman. Newman was to publish *Defensible Space* in 1972 which showed the relation between crime, vandalism and too much open, public space. The implications were Capitalist: everyone should own his house and privatize his area. The architectural answer was to break down mass housing into smaller domains and provide them with semi-public space which could be surveyed, controlled and looked after by the inhabitants. Kikutake and Kurokawa seem to have arrived at similar conclusions at about the same time – a good example of the way different traditions can produce similar solutions simultaneously.

Kikutake worked out a series of prototypes for mass housing which incorporated semi-public space. One type, the 'tiered, Kata, mass-housing' was built in Mishima Pasadena Town. It has a series of walkways and ramps overlooked by gardens and service courts. The idea, as with Newman and Team Ten, is to give a sense of communal living and identity through controlled, shared ownership. Dwellings are broken down into comprehensible scale and some are given room for future expansion or change (again 'movenettes' are provided). Ideally, Kikutake would like the room units to be capsules which could be expanded or reduced in size, and he envisioned a 'set of instructions' for rebuilding, following the example of rebuilding Shinto shrines.

KIYONARI KIKUTAKE, *Mishima Pasadena Town*, 1975. 'Tiered Kata mass-housing' recedes up the south side of a hill receiving full sunlight. The semi-public space of horizontal passages and vertical stairways and ramps is looked over by gardens, service courts and living rooms. The most private bedrooms are at the back.

KISHO KUROKAWA, *Odakyu Drive-In*, Otome, 1969. White, steel-pipe, space-frame supports a brown restaurant capsule and 'open air beer hall' below a red tent. White joints punctuate the air like little explosions. The extraordinary image is quite appropriate for roadside architecture.

KIYONARI KIKUTAKE, *Tokoen Hotel*, Kaike, 1964. Four different formal systems articulate the contents within – an eclectic facility which Western architects can barely approach. Interior rooms have traditional shoji, tatami and tokonoma and the handling of the concrete structure is reminiscent of traditional wood building.

Perhaps his most convincing building to date is the Tokoen Hotel finished in 1964. It shows the characteristic facility in handling different formal languages including the traditional. Four different styles are used to give a dynamic expression of the various contents within the building. A hyperbolic parabola for the roof-top restaurant is set off against two floors of bedrooms, a vertical circulation tower and communal spaces (articulated in other ways). The slight curves, bracket construction and entrance gate all add a slight Japanese flavour which is never explicit, but just discernible. This subtle an eclecticism was rare in the West at the time and implied an accessibility to the past which was respectful and easy-going without being lax.

Kisho Kurokawa has designed equally articulate buildings which make use of different systems to designate different functions (and heighten them as well). His Odakyu Drive-In is in every way as convincing as Kikutake's Tokoen Hotel. Both buildings are important because they show that an architect can use a rich gamut of varied forms in a semantically coherent way. A charge against Modern architecture has always been that it was reductive, and used an impoverished, purist language. Both these buildings use a syncretic language in a fresh and significant way: for instance the joints at Odakyu, which eventually swallow the restaurant, are modern versions of traditional brackets – elaborate, decorative celebrations of a change of force. Such exaggeration, it could be argued, is appropriate here because roadside restaurants are conventionally brash and striking.

Also this building is one of the first convincing metabolic structures, inasmuch as the different functional cycles are clearly separated. The services, structure, tent and capsule can all be pulled apart or added to without disturbing the whole. Open flange ends at the joints imply growth and transformation, thus making it the first convincing image of Metabolism to be built.

It also illustrates another concept of Kurokawa's, what he calls, after Peter Smithson, 'antagonistic co-existence'. A large white joint occupies the centre of the restaurant – 'the restaurant is eating the joint', Kurokawa said to me, making a double pun. 'The conflict between two harmonious systems, the regular space and regular

KISHO KUROKAWA, *Fukuoka Bank*, Osaka, 1975, provides semi-public space and shelter for the community. People can pass through the space, unlike the Ford Foundation Building in New York, to which it is somewhat similar. A strict formality in grey, white and black is semantically appropriate to the function.

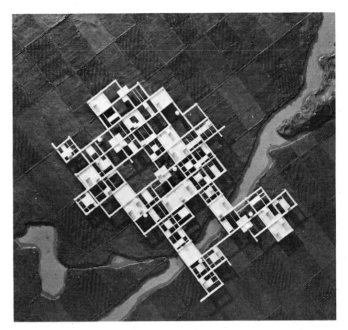

KISHO KUROKAWA, *Agricultural City*, 1960. Three functional levels – work place, social area and individual houses – are stacked on this infrastructure. The project was for an area of farmland periodically devastated by flooding.

structure, is unharmonious.' Antagonistic co-existence is very closely related to his favourite concept of *engawa*, which he uses to mean all sorts of things: the 'inbetween space', the semi-public space which he tries to include in all of his buildings, the verandah space between inside and outside as at the Katsura Imperial Villa, and the street space between two buildings. In fact, *engawa* can mean an empty space seen positively, as the interval between two columns, or as the positive silence between two musical sounds (as in Zen aesthetics).

All this stretching of words can be quite annoying and if we are to follow the Metabolist philosophy we have to be prepared for endless verbiage. Kurokawa has invented many neologisms to describe his architectural ideas. There is 'fibre form', 'urban connector', 'decimal system and street architecture', 'energy metabolism and infrastructuring'. These words point to a common meaning – basically the linear, street pattern which has *activities* that occur on it (not just a vehicular route). He has made this 'street architecture' the basis of his designs from the early Nishijin Labour Centre to the recent parliament building projected for Tanzania.

One of his earliest projects, the Agricultural City anticipates a structuring device of Shadrach Woods and Team Ten, the three-dimensional grid or web, which clusters activities along circulation routes and leaves open space between. In a way, this pattern is centuries old, going back to both Chinese and Greek prototypes, and Kurokawa's rationalization – 'the automotive traffic pattern becomes the primary infrastructure' – is hardly unique. But the low horizontal clustering of different activities was at the time an opposition to the dominant planning models of CIAM with their functional separation and towers set in a park.

Somewhat complementary to this was another set of distinctions – 'porous space', 'point stimulation', 'masterspacing', 'interiorization' and recently 'capsule architecture'. These sets of notions contrast with the 'street architecture', as the point contrasts with the line. 'Point stimulation' can be illustrated by the joints of the Odakyu Drive-In or Takara Beautilion. In each case an individual joint allows or 'stimulates' certain possibilities with an elegance that is complex and delightful. They have become a trademark of Kurokawa's style, perhaps his most recognizable detail.

If you blow the point up in size, you have the capsule, or what Kurokawa calls (after Buddhist notation) JIGA. It's a word signifying the self and identity; in architectural terms, say, the space for a tea ceremony.

> It's a space for individuality, for man to identify himself on an equal level with the cosmos . . . After the modernization of Japan, we lost JIGA. Therefore it was important for us Metabolists to rediscover it – in the new Japanese house. You know that when we tour foreign countries we always go in a group – because we have lost JIGA and we now have conformity. My capsule architecture is a metaphor of JIGA. At least on a spiritual level – whereas on a physical level the metaphor is a bird's nest, or as you say a washing machine.

The metaphors of these capsules *are* polyvalent. Some architects have criticized them as too restrictive and

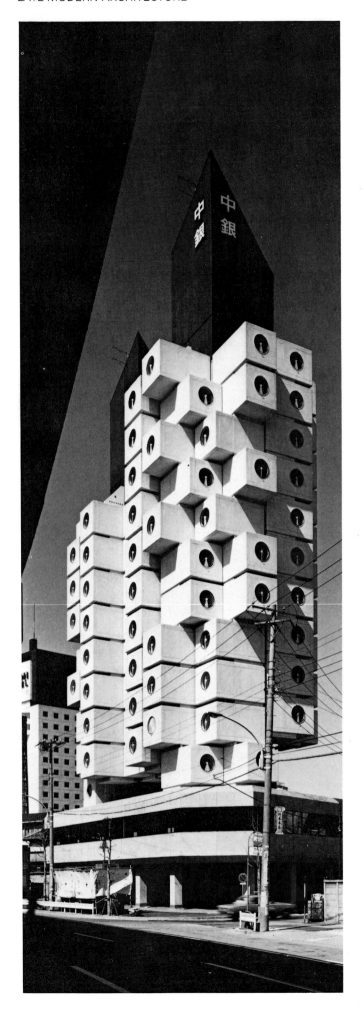

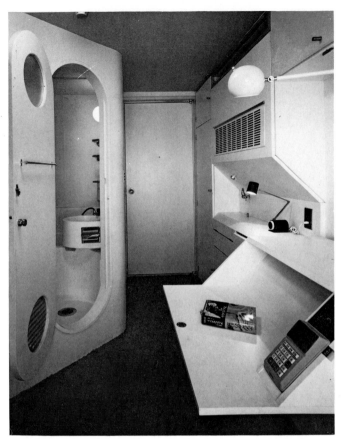

KISHO KUROKAWA, *Nakagin Apartment Tower*, Tokyo, 1972, suspends 140 rooms from two concrete cores. These steel boxes are modified shipping containers which contain bathrooms, stereo-tape decks, calculators and other amenities for the businessman or bachelor. 20% are used this way, 30% are owned by companies, 30% are privately owned (extensions to the family house) and the final 20% are used in miscellaneous ways – for work.

conformist, the very opposite of JIGA, and designed individual boxes as an alternative. It's an open question, however. A few such capsule towers in Nagoya, or the Shiga Prefecture, are individualized statements of identity, since they contrast with the traditional and recent environment. However compared with hand-built tea ceremony pavilions, the comparison Kurokawa makes, they do lack identity.

The Nakagin Tower is made up of asymmetrical and syncopated clusters of capsules so there is an air of individualism and, the old Zen notion, imperfection. The unfinished balance, according to Zen aesthetics, allows the imagination to complete the picture. We are back at the paradox that architectural Metabolism is really Japanese traditionalism in new clothes. The same might be said of the 'mixed systems' approach which underlies much of the capsule architecture. The fact that these systems are 'open', that they can accept other prefabricated technologies, parallels once again the open nature of Buddhism.[4]

Kurokawa has designed for himself one of the most striking examples of this openness, the Karuizawa Capsule House, with its corten-steel exterior and tea ceremony interior. Here the 'mixed system' might appear mixed-up – combining as it does such incongruous elements as precision steel boxes, space capsule windows, imitation wood, a touch of Western vulgarity and traditional order. Some architects are annoyed at this permissiveness, it seems to include too much, the kitsch of consumer architecture and the high seriousness of

TATSUHIKO NAKAJIMA and GAUS, *Kibogaoka Youth Castle*, Shiga Prefecture, 1973. Bedroom and bathroom capsules are suspended from a utility core. The main space shows the typical 'mixed systems' approach of combining various prefabricated, traditional and even Western elements (the Statue of David). A translucent roof, FRP (fibre reinforced plastic) shells bring light into the public baths while prepackaged HVAC units (heating, ventilating and air-conditioning) are clipped on pieces of sculpture.

Kabori Enshu, the tea master of the sixteenth century. This is the 'inclusive architecture' of Venturi and Moore, but at the same time it is more relaxed than their work.

Kurokawa's Big Box is another example of the easygoing mixture of opposite traditions. At first sight it is just an ordinary square building, oversized but not distinctive. Then one notices the variations, that part of the facade can rotate into one of three images, that bright red service units are attached to the side and that the inside contains all sorts of unlikely activities in different styles. These vary from an Italian Piazza in the Renaissance style to a modern discotheque. The relaxed, commercial motives are undisguised and it is such signs, coupled with Kurokawa's enormous success, that elicit the strong criticism from architects. Part of this can be attributed to professional jealousy, the competitive spirit which I mentioned at the outset, and one which is usual when so

KISHO KUROKAWA, *Karuizawa Capsule House*, 1972. The tea ceremony room is based on the designs of the tea master Kabori Masakazu (Kabori Enshù) – 4½ tatami mats. The use of imitation wood beams and a few Western forms shows the mixture of permissiveness and rigour which Westerners find so disarming.

KISHO KUROKAWA, *Big Box*, Tokyo, 1974, is rather like Cedric Price's Funpalace, a collection of urban amusements. Bowling, golf, swimming, athletics, shooting ducks by laser gun are some of the activities. The Italian piazza in the entrance is surrounded by four ethnic restaurants and contains, in the centre, a gigantic, plastic tree.

Opposite
KISHO KUROKAWA, *Takara Beautilion*, Expo 70, Osaka, 1970. An ultimate in Slick-Tech imagery and Metabolist theory, this building was put together and disassembled very quickly. Stainless steel capsules, 2.2 metres square, are plugged into a framework of steel pipes which have open flange ends to receive further growth.

many creative architects are working at the height of their careers. The Metabolist movement has broken up under this strain as each Metabolist has become successful and diverged in viewpoint. There hasn't been a general meeting since 1965; Maki and Kikutake last collaborated on the Peruvian housing competition in 1970, and they split with Kurokawa at this time because of a professional misunderstanding. But their design ideas had already separated by this point.

Fumihiko Maki has continued on his own to produce a peculiarly sensitive form of Metabolist architecture; one relying on his concept of 'group form', relating the space between buildings rather than necessarily using a single form language. Both Otaka and Maki will use various styles in a set of buildings on a podium, or 'artificial ground', which provides some of the unity, while repetition of similar volumes (group form) provides the rest. The sequencing of urban space and the intimate urban scale are very subtle and humane, although without great drama. They are reminiscent of Mediterranean hill towns and particularly the work of José Lluis Sert – not surprising since Maki worked at Harvard with him. There

FUMIHIKO MAKI, *Hillside Terrace Apartment*, Tokyo, 1969-74. A shopping mall below and apartments above. The pedestrian areas move from public to private in a very subtle way.

YOUJI WATANABE, *Sky Building No. 3*, Tokyo, 1971, metallic capsule units turn out to be painted and not capsules. Air-conditioning units are exaggerated as clip-on elements and the roofscape watertanks are streamlined because Watanabe was 'influenced by the desire to recreate the marine architecture of the Navy'. 'Airstream' caravans also appear to be stacked.

Opposite
ARATA ISOZAKI, *Gunma Museum*, 1974. The neutral grid repeated at many different scales, from the overall plan to the smallest detail. Actually Isozaki chose the neutrality, of silver aluminium and square, to signify a twilight architecture of greyness. At dawn or dusk it merges with an industrial landscape and signifies, for him, a type of metaphysical nullity. The 'smash joint', the elision of opposite surfaces and directions without a transition or moulding is typical of Late-Modern detailing.

is however something impersonal and self-effacing in Maki's work, as if he were suspicious of architectural form and felt it presumptuous to design too hard, or impress the building with his own signature. Thus it ends up looking in the mainstream: honest, unassertive, sensitive but undramatic.

? The techno-aesthetic
By contrast, the work of Youji Watanabe seems dramatic, even melodramatic. Watanabe, very much the artist-architect, has recently looked to the Futurists and Archigram and he's given the world in his Sky Houses an image of technosophistication which is quite illusory and delightful. It's illusory because the buildings which

appear to be put together from mass produced, metallic elements are in fact often made of poured *in situ* concrete. It's delightful because various sorts of image are juxtaposed – those from the world of aerospace technology, naval warfare, transport service and amusement parks.

This metaphorical architecture improves on view when contrasted with the usual barracks of modern housing and one can only question its appropriateness, not its expressive force. The aesthetic codes of Japan are more permissive than those in Western countries, and Watanabe's fantasies should be appreciated for exploiting this freedom. The *abeku hoteru*, the love palaces such as Hotel Meguro Emperor in the form of a fairyland castle, are other buildings which exploit this potential. And there is a group of young architects, discussed below, who have made this their starting point and developed an autonomy of symbolism. Japan has been characterized by the semiologist Roland Barthes as 'the empire of signs' and one can see in such varied sign behaviour just how far this empire can go. I was continuously surprised in Tokyo by the communicative

SHOJI HAYASHI (?) and NIKKEN SEKKI, *All Japan Working Youths' Hall,* Tokyo, 1973. Two walls of steel and concrete support many activities between them. An auditorium for 2,400 at the bottom, several conference halls, a traditional garden on the sixteenth floor and hotel and restaurant near the top. The blank side walls give a mysterious air as if the building were a solar telescope or modern pyramid.

Hotel Meguro Emperor, Tokyo, 1971. Impressive stylistic melting pot mixes Late Disneyland with Ludwig II with rounded windows from the Age of Plastic.

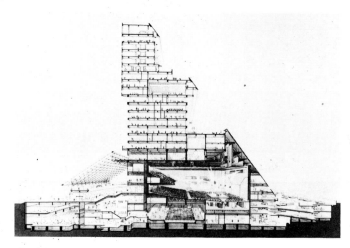

Complex section, showing many activities and roof terraces. On the interior of the entrance, a dappled light spills through the translucent marble and lean-to space frame.

building, whether it was a modest restaurant or an overly expressive department store.

One building that particularly stopped me was the All Japan Working Youths' Hall designed in the shape of a ski-jump – or is it a wedge of white, cream cheese? Perhaps it's a solar telescope or immaculate launching pad? The front entrance looks like an exploded entry to a xerox machine. All these images are carried through in the techno-aesthetic of shiny surfaces and precision engineering. It's a feat of rigour and detailing which could only be realized by a large building firm, the calibre of SOM – which is what Nikken Sekki is: one of the largest architectural firms in Japan and certainly the most sophisticated.

The interior of this huge building is carried through with a pristine, white smoothness, the mark of the International Style. The immense entry hall is an airy wedge of white marble which is filled by a dappled light that spills through the translucent marble roof and intricate space frame. One is prepared to enter the world of banking, or perhaps a prestigious company building for Olivetti. At least a Westerner associates these signs with business efficiency and power. How shocked then he is to find a series of cultural functions, the most incongruous of which are traditional wedding ceremonies. On one white floor (it could have been the Union Carbide Building in New York) were four or five weddings taking place simultaneously in different rooms, side by side. The

largest amphitheatre was devoted to post-nuptial, family photographs. It was bizarre enough to find such juxtapositions between old and new, work and ceremony, but what doubled the incongruity was the perfect dress of the participants, made up in ancient sartorial splendour. In New York one might find five marriages taking place on the eighteenth floor of the Union Carbide Building, but not the bride, groom and family all dressed in Regency clothes. This dualism, schizophrenic to a Westerner, is quite acceptable to Buddhist philosophy.

Such buildings and such incongruous imagery brings out in a vivid way the 'arbitrary nature' of the architectural sign, the fact that the relations between form and function are set by usage and custom. This fact allows a permissiveness of formal usage which has gone far in places like Los Angeles, but further in Tokyo. A busy street in Tokyo is a kaleidoscope of signs – the usual neon and billboards – but also images taken from different media and cultures. They compete for attention, for commercial reasons of course, but also because the Japanese have a strong tradition of rhetoric which accentuates differing kinds of signs, from Baroque to abstract, from explicit to implicit. There is a built-in eclecticism within the Japanese culture used as it is for absorbing and then perfecting outside sources of rhetoric.

4. Eclecticism and Neo-Mannerism
The work of Arata Isozaki embodies this proposition at its best. He is facile and creative with four or five different formal systems. His work in the early sixties was in the tradition of sculptural Modernism and it influenced the leader of the office where he worked, Kenzo Tange. Isozaki developed several utopian schemes making use of two traditional systems: the Japanese masagumi brackets and the Greek column and beam relationship. From these eclectic fragments he fashioned cities in the air, the gigantic Metabolist works that Tange was later to build in Yamanashi and Tokyo. But then he moved on to develop various styles of Le Corbusier, Wright, Mies and others.

He developed the spatial contrasts of Paul Rudolph in a library in his home town of Oita. Next he used the geometrical ordering of Jim Stirling on a bank in this same southern city. Following that at the 1970 Expo he mastered the Archigram vocabulary of robots and space technology, while soon after he was influenced by Superstudio and the Neo-Rationalists (the 'Five Architects') and their preoccupation with grid manipulation. No wonder that when Isozaki stated his eclectic method of design he said 'the visual vocabulary of contemporary achitecture has all been discovered'.[5] He might have added that he's perfected a lot of it.

Isozaki is frank about his revivalist position. In the same article he comes to rather disarming conclusions for a Modernist who is always 'trying to make it new', trying to evolve his own distinctive language separate from the pioneers.

> All that is left for us to do is to manipulate already existing multifarious and extremely accurately worked out visual vocabulary items ... mix in a disconnected fashion the many layers of historical fact, multiple styles, and regional visual vocabularies ...One may trace elements [in my buildings] borrowed from the works of many great architects: Le Corbusier's concrete, Mies van der Rohe's steel sashes, Nervi's precast concrete, Wright's sense of fluidity, Aalto's plastic surfaces ... Louis Kahn, Robert Venturi, Charles Moore, James Stirling.

It could almost be Philip Johnson describing his bag of sources (sourcery), but there's something obsessive and tempestuous in the creativity which isn't present in Johnson. Fierce turmoil is evident in Isozaki's work as if he's struggling to get rid of the influences he has done so much to master.

This is what makes his work Mannerist in the conventional sense of that term; he takes the traditional codes and exaggerates, inverts or contradicts them to increase their rhetorical power. The only obvious style not distorted is the traditional Japanese which remains missing from the repetoire. Isozaki confines his references to Western allusions just as he restricts semantic overtones to mechanistic and geometric metaphors. For this reason his various revivalisms are within the overall class of the techno-aesthetic.

Although he has written on Mannerist painting and has illustrated the article with sensual evocations of hands caressing the human torso, there is no clear indication of this erotic humanism in his architecture. It is transformed into the surface and section of his buildings. These have a sensual aspect, but they do not use warm materials and historical signs as would a more inclusive Mannerism: they are cold, mechanistic and high-gloss, speaking about the virtues of the hospital and laboratory, not the boudoir, library or home.

There are exceptions to this. The exterior of his Fukuoka-Sogo Bank Home Offices is certainly warm in surface: it's made from red, Swedish granite, polished or chipped at the base, and then ten storeys of red, Indian sandstone. But this is as close as he comes to using traditional materials in a friendly way. When speaking about this large bank he faces the important relation between 'control and violation' of this control – implying that he is giving us a humanist architecture.

> ...this is a conscious rejection of the universal space in favour of an aggregation of fragments ... such treatment concentrates on the characteristic nature of each isolated 'place', which is one of a number of

ARATA ISOZAKI, *Fukuoka-Sogo Bank*, Oita, 1966. Forty-five degree geometries and volumes reminiscent of Stirling discipline this building which, on the interior, is one of the first examples of Pop architecture.

ARATA ISOZAKI, *Fukuoka-Sogo Bank, Home Offices*, Fukuoka, 1972. Cylinder columns visually support a large beamlike structure which houses the space for computers – but the supports curve away from the beam denying their structural role, and are obviously too big. All very Mannerist.

ARATA ISOZAKI, *Ropponmatsu Branch Bank*, 1972, 'is in effect a simple, monotonous, aluminium-clad solid set in a disorderly town. The aluminium itself is light and of such a nature as to impose no specific, fixed meanings'. Except, of course, it looks like a good safe place to put your money. For more blank boxes see Miyawaki's work.

separated parts ... Such eccentric elements amount to a violation of a single-system control. Furthermore, each detail is constantly violating the control system.[6] This emphasis on identity and 'place' was common in the sixties but Isozaki, like Team Ten, articulates it with a restricted, Modern language of form. Although the areas of this building are different, they are all abstract and geometric. Thus identity, such as it exists, is only on the level of analogy and not within a historical code which the ordinary man knows. It is an elitist code, 'architects' architecture' and, not surprisingly, Isozaki is regarded among architects as the foremost creator within this code.

ARATA ISOZAKI, *Home Offices*, interior. Southeast end of the entrance hall with a favourite Isozaki detail – the extract guns. Polished chrome, polished white tile floor, a skylight picking out the overhead bridge – a dazzling, anonymous space.

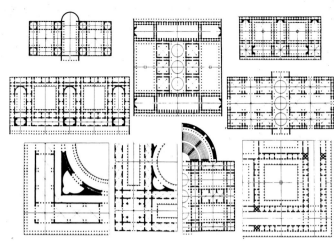

J. L. N. DURAND, examples of geometric composition from his course at the Ecole Polytechnique. Addition of units to a rectilinear plan with axes and cross-axes.

ARATA ISOZAKI, *Nagasumi Branch Bank*, 1972. The interior is an exquisite, almost Dada use of white and grey rectangles, the *grid appliqué*. Doors and railings are slightly out of phase and thus become extra significant. Isozaki has emphasized the nihilism: 'This building has almost no form; it is merely a grey expanse. The multi-level grid guides one's lines of sight but does not focus them on anything in particular. At first encounter, the vague grey expanse seems impossible to decipher and utterly odd.'

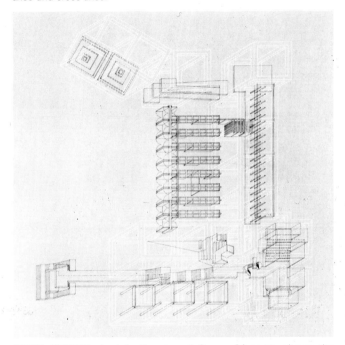

ARATA ISOZAKI, *Analytic Drawing of Gunma Museum*, shows the 'deep structure' of white cubes and the secondary 'surface structure' in black outline. One only perceives the surface, but *conceives* the basic rectangles – two of which deflect from the grid to receive accentuation.

His other bank buildings show an even more esoteric formal language: the Ropponmatsu Branch is a blank, aluminium box with the identifying logo 'Home Bank' etched in computer graphics. The image is a forceful statement of banking, security, safety deposit boxes and impenetrable bank vaults. But if this is appropriate symbolism, it appears quite fortuitous because Isozaki begins to use it in other contexts irrespective of content. In the Nagasumi Branch Bank it dissolves to become a white and grey grid of glass, a greenhouse for tropical plants, not a high-security bank. Like so many architects, Isozaki becomes momentarily obsessed by a formal idea (he calls it 'formalism') which he manipulates and develops for its own inherent logic, not the logic of the particular context. Hence his work is as arbitrary and removed from society as the universal Modern architecture he criticizes.

Recently his interest has moved to a method of design he calls 'amplification' – one of seven methods he characterises with his set of neologisms. The others are 'chess men', 'slicing', 'projection', 'packaging', 'trans-feral' and 'response'. 'Amplification' consists in taking a basic square unit and subdividing it so that 'entire surfaces [are] filled with an unbroken series of units. It will then become an empty frame composed of nothing but units.' 'Nothing but units'? This is the right-angled world of Modern architecture, the Rationalism formulated in 1800, and taught at the Ecole Polytechnique in Paris. But it is put to non-rational, indeed surreal ends, since the goals Isozaki seeks are not an increased efficiency and practicality, but rather a heightened perception of architectural elements.

Isozaki, like Superstudio and Peter Eisenman, plays with an orthogonal syntax until it has developed into a complicated and delightful game of caged space. In the Gunma Museum sudden views of cubic space explode as one walks through a sequence of rectilinear cut out, or punched through, walls. Sometimes, as in the glazed lobby, there are four spaces interpenetrating at once. A suggestion of space beyond, the conceptual layering of one cube on another, is achieved by allowing indirect light to be seen behind cut-outs – an old design idea of Le

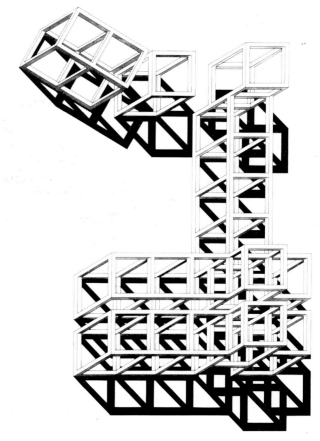

Gunma Museum. The aluminium rectangle on stilts is the focal point and houses the most important, permanent collection of art. Mechanistic metaphors abound – a launching pad, a box for robots – or a jewel box. Notice the way two square systems meet to produce the non-joint, a visual smash-together of two elements separated by a thin line. A new visual language.

Gunma Museum, basic structure.

Gunma Museum, entrance stairs.

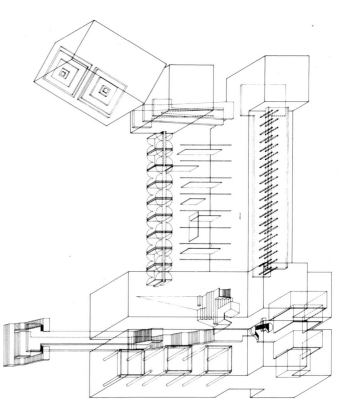

Gunma Museum, supplemental structure.

HIROMI FUJII, *Miyajima Residence*, Tokyo, 1973. Exquisite calm is achieved by the precise detailing and reductive aesthetic. One is reminded of Minimal Art and the ascetic spirituality of Wittgenstein's house.

Corbusier. To one side of the glazed lobby is a cubic restaurant propped up on round pillars, a room within a room.

One can fault this exciting spatial play on the level of semantics – it is clothed in mechanistic metaphors inappropriate to viewing some art – but it has the characteristic integrity of Modern Art. It is sculpture that follows its own internal logic wherever imagination takes it. Isozaki calls this allowing a method 'to develop autonomously', which of course means irrespective of social concerns, or popular codes. Another architect, Hiromi Fujii, has followed the same path remorselessly applying the grid all over a building. His houses, reputedly difficult to live in, are like Minimal Art – very clear propositions of simple construction rules and again, like Isozaki's Mannerism, an exaggeration of these rules. They seem to imply a strong religious ideology, something like a Shaker creed, while at the same time a self-denying nihilism. They speak of a pure, Platonic universe of the mind and also a petty, functional materialism. Perhaps this is where the contradictions inherent in Modern architecture have led the Late-Modernists, since one finds them repeated in Eisenman's, Rossi's, and the Neo-Rationalists' work.[7] In any case, to see where else the autonomy of architectural method can lead, we turn to a generation of architects just turning forty.

5. Autonomous symbolism & defensive architecture

During the last few years, since about 1968, there has been an increasing concern with an arbitrary symbolism cut off from any roots – whether they be historical, functional or social. This has been partly caused by international communications – the profusion of cultural alternatives conveyed mostly through the architectural magazines – also by the growing interest in signification, and the theory of how architecture communicates. I have already mentioned above a key rule of semiotics – the 'arbitrary nature of the architectural sign' – and it is not surprising that the knowledge of this rule has led to more and more arbitrary forms.

Once one knows that significant form is determined mostly by usage and very little by technology, function, economy (and all the fashionable 'determinisms' of the last hundred years), the door opens on a new territory. We become more free to choose the symbolism we want from the corpus of history, or from a corpus which can be invented. The constraints are mainly social; what the client and locale will accept. Thus we are faced with a rather unique existential question, at least unique in the degree to which it is explicit: what identity should we choose and construct?

Previously, traditions circumscribed this choice and enforced certain norms such as the Palladian villa, or in Japan the minka and shinden. Then with the rise of various determinisms, which justified Modern architecture, these traditions were undermined, until finally a point was reached where the basis of architecture had to be reconceived. It turned out to be not so much a 'natural' activity, as most theorists from Vitruvius to Le Corbusier had argued, but more of a cultural one.[8] The result of this insight is causing an upheaval in design theory and practice although few people are willing to admit that it is happening. They would prefer to have their choices circumscribed by tradition, technology or a socially acceptable determinism – any of which can make the architectural sign 'motivated' rather than 'arbitrary'.

There are however a minority of architects who have explored the potential freedom and designed buildings that are based on anthropomorphic images, pure syntactic structures or bizarre, non-architectural codes. Of course this existed previously; there has been the rare non-conformist architect such as Bruce Goff, and the short-lived movement of Fantastic Architecture, but there hadn't been whole neologistic groups of them in different countries – Archigram and ArchiteXt, Archizoom and Archibrain – who based their design on non-conventional codes.

By the 1970s we find young groups in several countries feeling their way along, tentatively, pushing the images of buildings in extraordinary directions. The 'Five Architects' in the USA go back to syntactic structures of the 1920s, the Austrian avant-garde goes forward to the space imagery of the 1980s. It doesn't matter functionally which direction in time and space they move because architecture is a 'non-critical' activity.[9] The technical and functional requirements are very loose and can be satisfied by rooms of many shapes and size. An important aspect of architecture that does remain, however, is the 'image of man' it projects, the way of life it promotes. But even these functions aren't altogether crucial because there are more potent sign systems which have comparable functions such as literature and cinema. Nonetheless architecture helps articulate daily life and it does this mostly in a cultural way. On the highest plane, it has the job of articulating the relations within a society and the relation of an individual to the rest of the world. Since these relations are now contested from all sides, both politically and metaphysically, it is not surprising that architecture has developed all sorts of personal imagery. While the results may not be as profound as previous architecture, rooted as it was confidently in an unquestioned tradition, at least they are scrupulously honest to the cultural *role* of architecture.

The area where individual expression can find its greatest autonomy is the small building, usually the house and most often the interior. One of the first buildings to exhibit symbolic autonomy was the 'House with Explosive Space' designed by Yasutaka Hayashi. The space explodes on the inside around tubes of three storey space while, on the outside, the tubes also appear to explode. In part the sinister image of the house is very compelling. It's both defensive like a castle and offensive like a battery of cannons. The free-standing villa no longer invites a peaceful discourse with its neighbours or the countryside, but becomes an aggressive image of hostility.

As the architect Miyawaki has pointed out, there is often good reason for this.[10] Urban life in Japan is beset with strife: noise, pollution, mixed land uses and terribly small building sites (on the average about 100 square metres in the cities). All these forces compel the single family house to become defensive – a cocoon, a shelter, an impenetrable barrier to the outside world in which the individual can, at best, find complete peace. The logic of

MONTA MOZUNA, *'Anti-Dwelling Box'* to dwell in, Hokkaido, 1971. Mozuna explores the ideas of duplication, of boxes within boxes, of the little house within the big house. This traditional notion, which can be found realized in little Japanese shrines, dolls' houses, Roman Temples and the aedicules of Gothic architecture, is taken by Mozuna to absurd lengths. Absurdity and paradox are quite conscious methods used by these designers to underscore the self-referential nature of architecture. It is architecture about the language of architecture.

YASUTAKA HAYASHI, *'House with Explosive Space'*, Tokyo, 1969, a cubic building with the *grid appliqué* and 100 round pipe 'windows'; entry from the centre below. The free-standing villa has lost its roof and doorway and become a disquieting metaphor. Is it a square leggo block exploded in size, or some apparatus waiting to be plugged into or attached?

TAKEFUMI AIDA, *'House like a Die'*, Kamo, 1973. Autonomous symbolism carried through with an assured absurdity. Aida has said: 'This house was created according to the system used in dice and says no more than that dice are dice.' Of course it says much more – to wit that one can find extraordinary connections between things which have ostensibly nothing in common, and that the architect should avoid suitable form.

the situation leads to Miyawaki's 'Primary Architecture', that is the simple box exterior often made from thick concrete, and the exuberant, spatially flowing interior where the owner can feel at home and protected. The outside proclaims identity and ownership (of a tiny building lot) while the inside proclaims warmth and humanity. Thus the movement towards 'interiorization' and its many devices: skylights instead of large picture windows, expensive interior furnishing instead of costly exterior, interior gardens and interior spatial dynamics. Usually these elements are present in all defensive architecture.

Takefumi Aida has taken the logic of the 'exploding house' a bit further in his 'House like a Die'. Now the cubic box on stilts has lost its gun holes and gained the marks of a die. Some god cast it on the side of a hill so that it landed with the unit one on the roof (a skylight) and the number six on the underside (the six columns). Einstein said 'I cannot believe that God plays dice with the world'. Aida appears to answer 'Since I'm not God, I will play dice with my architecture (and my clients)'. Einstein didn't believe causality and cosmic order were a matter of chance; Aida does – at least for architecture. The manifesto which accompanied this building stated the following propositions:

3. House like a Die expresses the independence of architecture and the multiple meanings of dice . . .

5. Dice have many associations: chance, gambling, suspicion, whiteness, cubical form and so on.

6. This is what I call architecture of the mask . . .

8. If the facade of the individual building is a mask, the city is an aggregation of various kinds of masks . . .

10. The idea of suitability of form – what is suitable to the residence, what is suitable to the kindergarten – has become well established, but it ought to be one of the aims of architecture to overthrow this concept.[11]

One can agree with many of these propositions. Architecture does have independent (arbitrary) meaning; it's symbolic function can be a mask, and the city is made up of people and buildings in symbolic clothing. But why should the symbolism, or mask, be unsuitable?

Here Aida provides a clue, although not a straightforward answer, to his paradox. He says, in a slightly different context, 'it is a way to expand the metaphysical meaning of architecture'. Presumably, as with recent art (Pop, Op, Minimal and Conceptual) we are to experience an exemplary metaphysical shock when conventional categories are so completely exploded. The tactic is similar to the unexpected kick from behind of the Zen master. Furthermore, Aida's metaphysics seem to be based on a personal type of nihilism, chance and absurdity. He has published in several issues of *ArchiteXt* (the loosely associated group magazine) a photo of himself sitting in worshipful pose in a blank space, lit dramatically from the side like a Mannerist subject in deep chiaroscuro. The implications are uncertain. Are we to worship him, a Buddha, extreme subjectivity, egoism, *what*? The members of ArchiteXt all place emphasis on their own personal image, and some of them find in exaggerated idiosyncracy the key to humanity, even the universal.

The architect must always make absolutely subjective judgements in relation to the architectural image that he wants to create. In short, as far as the architectural image is concerned, I intend to make my judgements as autocratic as I can.[12]

TAKEFUMI AIDA, *Nirvana House*, 1972. Another defensive, white box set in a hostile landscape. The purity of the facial statement is marred by the TV aerial, electric metres and telephone cables. Compare with the 'Face House'.

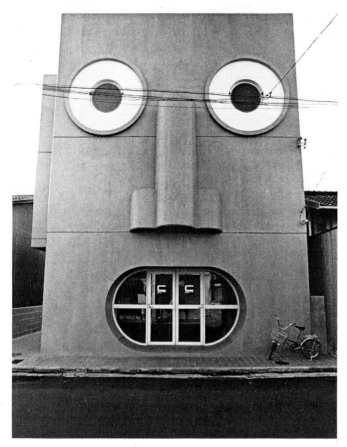

KAZUMASA YAMASHITA, *'Face House'*, Kyoto, 1974. What *has* happened to the tradition of 'saving face'? Entrance mouth, duct nose and pivoting window eyes – and where are the ears and hair? An attempt to metaphorize Modern architecture has reached a half-way house.

Aida wrote this in 1972 and Miyawaki wrote an article at the same time with much the same message: '*It all boils down to doing what you want; there is nothing else. . . I produce primary architecture. I am doing what I want to do.*'[13] The buildings which follow this egoism are often autocratic and utterly consistent to an idea. Aida has produced a kindergarten that is hidden behind slanted earth, because he wanted to make this building 'disappear', he wanted to 'abandon all of the images that are thought typical of this kind of school' and 'return architecture to the natural landscape'.[14] This idiosyncratic treatment is possible since architecture is a non-critical activity, and it doesn't matter what a building looks like as long as it can accommodate, in a very loose way, the various functions. If one objects that a kindergarten shouldn't look like the Treasury of Atreus at Mycennae (the school does resemble the entrance to a grave for Greek kings) then Aida says one has understood him perfectly. Architecture should look like what it shouldn't look like.

Two of his other buildings follow this logic, the Annihilation House and Nirvana House. They are white boxes, square in plan and symmetrical – attempts as Aida says to 'imprison function within innate forms', and basic

'ideas' about such forms. The Nirvana House is vaguely reminiscent of a face with two eyes, four nostrils and a doorway for a mouth. The idea that the house can resemble a face is an old one, particularly in the West, where it is said to humanize the dwelling.[15] For instance, the gables of Amsterdam look like so many Dutch burghers carrying on a humane dialogue, respecting each other's individuality while very much still forming a group.

Within such a context, it is hard to place Yamashita's 'Face House' because the image is quite mechanical and terrifying. The front door seems to be baring its teeth and screaming. Clearly it's a statement of individuality within the context of an anonymous and dull Modern architecture. Also it's another example of defensive architecture. But behind it lies the notion of autonomous symbolism. If houses happen to share formal properties with dice, they also do with facial structure, so, the argument might go, why not bring out these fortuitous similarities. They may be absurd, but then the world is constructed as to be often absurd. The examples of puns, double meanings, visual illusions, Modern Art and Modern architecture come to mind. The latter two often follow single ideas to the point of absurdity.

Yamashita has written to me 'My Way of Architecture', a letter which underscores the variability of his approach. He, like Saarinen, tries to treat each problem as unique.

> I like to design structures based on the requirements of their actual use and functions. I try to find out architectural expression in the form resulting from each condition proposed. Conditions differ . . . Therefore, it is quite natural that the solutions reached by the same architect differ completely according to each case.

He contrasts this inductive approach with the deductive work of the Metabolists.

> My way of architecture is completely different from that of Kurokawa or Kikutake. Their architecture is designed in order to express exactly the concept they have established . . . [They] set up a methodology of design, and design architecture in order to explain it clearly in architectural expression. They are eager to display a large megastructure even though it has no relationship to society, or even though it is technically too difficult and too expensive to employ such a structure . . . If there is any philosophy in my design [it is that] 'I don't have any physical solution (form) ready beforehand'. And I am not interested in pseudo-heroism, nor desire for self-glorification.[16]

A great paradox is present. Yamashita is here the typical functional architect, directly opposed to Aida's egoism and formalism, yet he has produced buildings which are similar, in which the form looks determined beforehand by a metaphysical conceit.

A case in point is his Dental Clinic. It is another box building on three sides which becomes a cascade on the fourth. The whole thing looks as if it has come out of a cookie mould. Alternating bands of beige and red brick remind one of an Italian campanile, and the polychromy of Sienna. Yet Yamashita has justified these forms on a functional level. The stepped appearance results, he says, from having the largest functional areas at the bottom and the smaller ones at the top. Thus he would appear to differ from Aida who wishes to deny functional determinism. The fact that opposite approaches can produce similar buildings is another striking example of the arbitrary nature of the architectural sign. Similar formal systems can have opposite meanings, because

KAZUMASA YAMASHITA, *Dental Clinic*, Hiratsuka, 1973. The iceburg principle of design where greater activity occurs at the base and less at the top. Parking, dental clinic, library, teaching space and mechanical equipment occur up the five levels. Yamashita worked in England in the sixties and the influence of Stirling and others is apparent here.

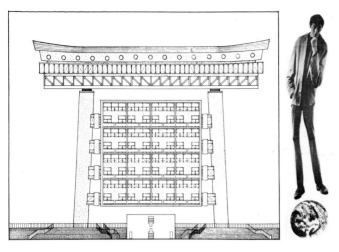

TAKEFUMI AIDA, *Torii Gate Housing*, 1970.

MINORU TAKEYAMA, *Surveying the World at His Feet*, 1970.

these are set by conventions and codes, sometimes private codes.

It would be wrong to look too hard for similarities where they are not intended to exist and ArchiteXt is itself an illustration of this point. The appellation refers not so much to the existence of a cohesive group as to a loose collection of individuals who happen to live near each other in Tokyo. Five architects in their late thirties came together in 1970 to found a 'magazine' which would disseminate their subjective philosophies. Perhaps the only common intention was for them to become, as they put it, 'a liberation front of Japanese culture by offering a spirited defense of experimental and sometimes unconventional architecture'.

They didn't publish group statements – in fact this occasional journal was simply the fortuitous encounter of five, different, poetic statements encased in a white envelope.

Minoru Takeyama has summarized the enterprise as 'discontinuous continuity' – a paradox with which the others might agree. They are Aida, Miyawaki, Takamitsu Azuma and Makoto Suzuki, a non-group group, a kind of parody of other architectural fellowships such as Archigram and Archizoom. Indeed many of their statements are satires of the architectural avant-garde.

Aida has designed a giant Torii Gate with space frame and plug-in housing a rather Post-Modern juxtaposition, while Takeyama satirizes Buckminster Fuller (and himself) in their shared pretensions to be universal men who wish to cover the earth with geodesic domes and tetrahedra. He shows pictures of the earth, taken from Apollo 10, becoming successively enclosed by white triangles and accompanies this with a dialogue which ends:
Charlie:
'Wrapping the earth? Are you trying to make a new planet?'
ArchiteXt:
'Certainly, Yes! Earthtecture! I've done a good job. I've erased pluralism and dualism from this globe...No Heaven and Hell, no black and white, no East and West,

no North and South, no mountain and sea, no Ying and Yang...no borders, no divisions, no geology,...no meteorology...ZZZZZZZZ...Monism now takes command here...'
Snoopy & Charlie: '...We are overcome!...'
This 'parody of Apollo 10' is really a parody on the whole Modernist commitment to total design. From the thirteenth-century notion of 'God the Architect of the Universe' to the twentieth-century inversion 'Architect the God of the Universal' – Fuller's 'Universal Architect' – there has been the extravagant idea that one man, or one style, or one culture can subsume everything. Takeyama satirizes this prevalent notion with an elongated photo of himself pondering the world at his feet, like Rodin's thinker. His architectural firm called United Actions is, like Kurokawa's, responsible for everything from the doorknob to world resources. This was at one time a Bauhaus doctrine, an Art Nouveau conceit, the secret dream of Le Corbursier and IBM. Total design and the *Gesamtkunstwerk* culminate in the statements of Hans Hollein that 'All is architecture'. 'We must design the total environment', say Schools of Environmental Design, 'to save it!'

One never knows with Takeyama and his United Actions whether this universalism is serious or not (and he may not know either).

Miyawaki has wrestled with this troublesome and attractive idea too. In one article he debates the role of the Modern architect and 'the designer who stands in for God'. If 'God is Dead', who else could succeed Him but a Modern architect? Miyawaki traces the idea (which comes from CIAM) that has resulted in the architect-hero, the leader of society like Kenzo Tange, who hopes to reform people through his buildings. Sadly, society pays little attention so the evangelist architect must end up preaching to other architects. Thus forms the little sect of Modernism, soon inflated with its own afflatus.

To deflate this sort of sect, Miyawaki proposes that the young architect give up the claim to universalism and concentrate on the small things he can master. Build with subjectivity.

> Finally, I have suddenly become aware that there is nothing else but primary forms. This is the egoism of the architect . . . What I want to do.[17]

I have already mentioned Miyawaki's analysis of the pressures on housing and one can see them best exemplified in his own 'Primary Achitecture' – the twenty or so box buildings he has designed as houses and banks.

One of his early buildings was the Blue Box House which perches precariously on the side of a hill, amidst urban sprawl and greenery. The outside primary forms exclude contact – except for a small porthole which commands a view of Mount Fujii. Also one corner of the pure form is violated to allow bamboo trees to penetrate up into an enclosed, interior garden. The interior spaces provide everything that the harsh exterior rejects: complex, flowing geometries, a traditional tatami room, lush furnishings and peaceful, controlled nature. A skylight illuminates the central stairwell which is designed in opposition to the grid. 'Since people rarely ever make right-angle turns, walls must not use them. Each movement vector has its own grade, and the planning of the house must reveal them with complete clarity.'

Miyawaki uses clear circulation as the organizing element in his Akita Sogo Bank. The 'interior street' is expressed on both ends of the primary form to become a sign of entry, and clarification of what happens inside.

MAYUMI MIYAWAKI, *Blue Box House*, Tokyo, 1971. Cantilevered from the side of a hill, this blue box allows the outside to come in through a small porthole in the child's bedroom, a skylight and hole into the garden. The living room has an L-shaped picture window.

The skylight which runs above it also accentuates this street. In writing about this building, Miyawaki wryly pointed out how his 'Primary Architecture' had become respectable by 1974. Big corporations were designing big boxes (Kurokawa was designing them too) and painting them in primary colours. His peculiar anti-fashion had itself become a fashion, something which led him to the point of rejecting it. But he decided instead to develop its potential further.

Miyawaki, like certain French architects, insists that architecture is a man-made, not natural, product and therefore something quite artificial. Since he is particularly attracted to the natural landscape and mountains of Japan, he is rather daunted by building anything which spoils or pollutes virgin territory. But, after debating the question, he decides (perhaps rather predictably) that if one is going to build in nature, then it is better to contrast the architecture with the setting than to submerge the building in verdure. His White Triangle Restaurant for instance is set off against a mountain peak, thereby focusing our attention on the essence of opposite qualities.

> The problem is how to put an artificial thing in a natural setting. Inevitably the piece of architecture exerts a polluting influence on the environment. We must try to find ways to minimize the pollution.[18]

This he does visually by lifting the triangle on columns and painting it a most unnatural white. Thus a clear, artificial product is opposed to untouched nature, and each extreme brings out the other. This binary symbolism is, as Miyawaki admits, only one possible approach, but of general importance is the fact that a commitment to symbolism underlies all his work. He has written on the unsatisfactory signification in American cities and proposed 'Primary Architecture' as a particular symbolic response to Japanese cities.[19] These striking primary forms give a strong identifying element to repetitive, grey streets. Also 'they make possible perception of the whole through observation of only a part; they allow the individual to grasp the entirety in an instantaneous glance'. Indeed, as he says, by standing out from the environment they become a stimulus for perception, and appreciation, of urban form. They define a location and place. Doubts remain as to their appropriateness for all urban buildings, but Miyawaki has applied them mostly to banks and houses where they have a certain suitability.

MAYUMI MIYAWAKI, *Akita Sogo Bank*, Honjo, 1973. A three storey space, punctuated by vermilion columns, is expressed on both entrances and becomes another example of 'street architecture'. The exterior is painted the colour of water iris, the city flower of Honjo, while vermilion posts are common to traditional temples. Miyawaki's traditional structural expression appears somewhat ironic, as do the time-capsule chairs.

MINORU TAKEYAMA, *Ni-Ban-Kahn II*, Tokyo, 1970. Blown up graphic devices advertise this collection of 14 bars in the bar area of Shinjuku Tokyo, where there are over 20,000. The glass wall becomes a gigantic beacon advertisement at night. This was the first time an architect had moved into such a commercial, down-market building task – and also one of the first convincing expressions of Pop architecture. The building has since been restyled by Takeyama in 1977.

MINORU TAKEYAMA, *Pepsi-Cola Factory*, Mikasa, 1972. Floodlit at night, a giant, sparkling Pepsi advertisement by the motorway. Takeyama talked the corporation into providing a public gallery above the factory floor area, so that the interesting automation process could be observed. The inward pitched roof funnels the snow and melts it.

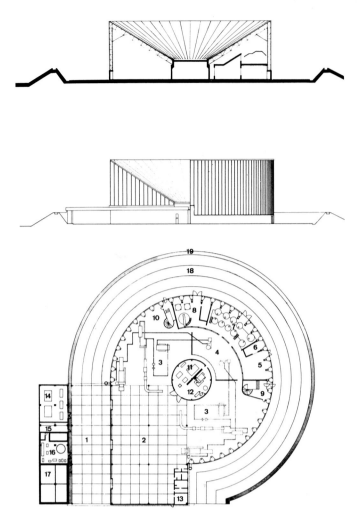

Minoru Takeyama's approach also emphasizes the autonomy of symbolism, but he is not limited to primary forms (although he favours them). His philosophy is more explicitly semiotic, so he will use a repetoire of signs, varying them to the situation at hand.

A case in point is his bar building Ni-Ban-Kahn II which was made from graphic codes (the number 2), popular codes (the bull's eye) and industrial codes (the red and white convention). He combined these with an exciting, fragmented geometry (the architects' code, or 'architects' architecture') to produce the first convincing example of Pop architecture to be built at this scale. It is actually popular, used for a popular pastime which city planners have notoriously overlooked, and exploded with Pop-up supergraphics and colour. In fact it reflects the actual living patterns of the area, and a land use which is not quite legal. In this sense it can be seen as a Japanese version of Street Art (wall paintings and graffiti) set against the bureaucratic planners who are trying to clear up this sort of thing. Takeyama said that after it was built he made elegant drawings and axonometrics so that architects could appreciate the building. This ironic inversion of customary practice shows how discontinuous is the popular code from the architects'.

Takeyama's next significant building was also a gigantic advertisement, this one for Pepsi-Cola. It sits, if that is the right word, in an open space not far from a motorway, so it is a conspicuous symbol of production. At first one is perplexed by the image. A primary form is cut away, three quarters of a circle, like Miyawaki's cut-out primary shapes. The building types it is reminiscent of are

engineering structures: a launching pad, bandstand or underside of a stadium – hardly anything to do with the production of Pepsi. In fact, Takeyama had to persuade the corporation to give up one year of advertisement to pay for the exquisite, lattice, space frame.

In a certain light the primary form is appropriate to Pepsi: it sparkles and bubbles when the light spills into the lattice structure by day and out at night. And the people of the area come into the stadium, sip free Pepsi and watch from their ring-side steps over the production below. Also, Pepsi-Cola cans are cylinders. So there *is* an appropriateness to the symbolism, however far-fetched. Yet really the form is autonomous and, like Ledoux's architecture, the unfolding of an absolute idea. In this case it is a cylinder modified by a pitched roof and space frame.

This idea is developed somewhat differently in the Beverly Tom Hotel. Again the cylinder has a chunk of 90 degrees sliced out of it and the lattice work is present: now an exquisite dome held together by large black ring-joints. But the articulation is more appropriate and understandable than the Pepsi building. Restaurant, bedroom, roof garden and service core each find expression. The overall symbol is of a masculine shape too obvious to mention (although Takeyama does point out that it comes from the Shinto sexual symbol 'Tenri' and he says it can be found everywhere in the building). One can object that hotels shouldn't be phallic and that this is just another advertisement of questionable shape. But Takeyama does give other justifications beside the sexual; he points to the similar cylindrical shapes in the nearby environs

MINORU TAKEYAMA and UNITED ACTIONS, *Axonometric of a lot in use*. *Ad hoc* modification of the urban system by the inhabitants – the black boxes can be turned into rooms. The planning ideas owe something to Chermayeff and Oscar Newman.

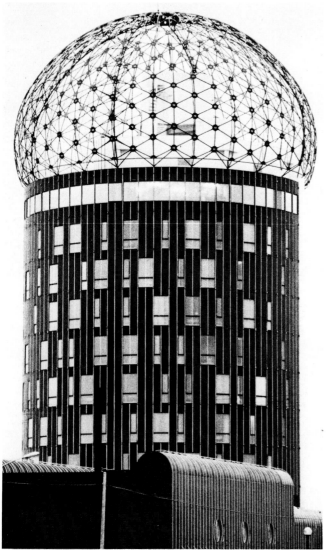

MINORU TAKEYAMA, *Beverly Tom Hotel*, Yomakomai, Hokkaido, 1973. About 80 hotel rooms are syncopated in the ¾ cylinder; a band signifies restaurant, a lattice dome the garden and the barely visible white structure is the service core: a semantically articulate architecture.

such as oil drums and silos. In any case, there are other equally plausible comparisons and the autonomy of architectual form allows us to make other interpretations.

In fact it is refreshing to find that Takeyama has mentioned a variety of interpretations; that some visitors find the building like a 'warehouse', the black painted walls without 'warmth' and the whole building with 'no sense of scale or sense of materials'.[20] Here we have, almost for the first time, an architect acknowledging a popular code and seeing the question of interpretation as legitimate even when it differs from his own. His may not be a full semiotic interpretation, but at least Takeyama is making a step towards seeing the *process* of signification as important – as legitimate as any one set of meanings we may give the building. As J. P. Bonta has argued, we are on the threshold of an era which finds this process a key to understanding how interpretations work and change.[21]

The combination of aesthetic invention and autonomous symbolism has led Takeyama to a new form of housing which is unrecognizable as a domestic function. His 'Connected House' looks more like a prestige factory with expensive air-conditioning units than what it is: a large, extended courtyard house with black box skylights. On a semantic level there is nothing left of the traditional house (no walls, doors, roofs in a normal sense) while much has been added which wasn't previously domestic: the heavy concrete shafts (which perversely house the equipment ducts).

It's again a compelling (and confusing) image which asks us to reassess our idea of the house. No longer a single box, but now some kind of collective fabric with a very close grain of protected courtyards and semi-public space. In a sense it is similar to the back alleys of Kyoto which are pedestrian paths onto which private rooms open. Takeyama has envisioned this system for an enclosed neighbourhood block. The idea is to establish

MINORU TAKEYAMA and UNITED ACTIONS, *Housing Collectivity in a Family Group*, 1974. A system of post and lintel frame is set off against a planning grid of courtyards, rooms and black box skylights. This home for three generations is zoned in terms of age groups. Another defensive building, it is sited near the factory owned by the family.

the semi-public space and territoriality which have been lost in the coarse grain of high-rise living.

The image is the happy jumble one associates with the typical Japanese city. It has always been a mystery to Westerners that Japanese streets are laid out on a rational grid plan yet ordinarily have no rational, consecutive numbering system. Furthermore, the standardization of parts coupled with flexible variation in use has also proved an enigma. Great trouble is taken to make the system efficient and rational and then, as if to protect the individual's freedom, it is systematically made impossible to decipher. I have heard it said that this *banchi* system of order (or disorder) allows one to avoid the draft, because he can move house faster than the mail can catch up with him.

No doubt there is a traditional Japanese love of the labyrinthine village. Houses are dark, entrances are hidden, ownership is ambiguous – all the village signs are a complex maze known only to the inhabitants. In this way the urban mystery reflects the well known ambiguities of the Japanese language. They both protect the individual by allowing him to use, from a variety of meanings, the ones he needs for the occasion. They also make life more enjoyable (and a little slower).

*   *   *

The variety of architectural positions current in Japan leads to a confusion which might be questioned if not deplored; but it also sustains a dynamic architectural culture which absorbs new ideas and transforms them. Perfection is traded in this situation for creativity, classical harmony for variety and stability for change. Given this dynamism it is quite likely that, as the dialectic continues to develop between the five major positions, there will be further interactions and new regroupings. The basic antimony between Late-Modern and Post-Modern architecture is bound to lessen as each side borrows from the other. A convergence of these two major approaches is even possible given the eclectic and inclusive philosophy so prevalent in Japan.

2.5 IRRATIONAL RATIONALISM – THE RATS SINCE 1960

The irreverence of this piece, published in A & U in 1977, might be misunderstood. Largely it is directed against the doctrinaire, monotonous, even morbid, aspects of the Rationalists. I would not change this ironic doubt, but were I to rewrite the text today certain aspects, mentioned positively in the text, would be highlighted and developed: the historicism and urban contextualism. These have been key for a development of Post-Modernism. Much of the overemphasis on grids, repetition and restricted logic characterizes Late-Modernism, but no architectural movement is without its excesses. Since this article Michael Graves has become considerably more Post-Modern and incorporated into his work traditional elements and ones with a local reference.

Philosophical antecedents

The philosophical problems with Rationalism have long been known, especially in the Anglo-Saxon world. Hence its recent re-emergence as an architectural movement is apt to raise eyebrows. Can these designers really propose a return to principles we know to be questionable and furthermore ones which have had such a deleterious effect in this century? (Abstract form, endless right angles, and architectural 'truths' which are supposedly universal).

The answer to this question is by no means clear. On the one hand, the architects (known affectionately as 'Rats' since at least 1975) share some of the defects of the Rationalist philosophy – dogmatism, elitism, reductivism – but, on the other hand, they have given this philosophy a new twist so that it often appears ambiguous, surreal and sensible by turns. Like any architectural movement it is made from a heterogeneous corpus of styles and ideas which are only loosely grouped around a common banner. No doubt, some of these architects wish the movement had a different slogan and pennant under which they could fight. A name, a tag, influences the way people look at architecture which is why I propose, half-ironically, the prefix 'irrational'. This Rationalism has always been, in part.

As a philosophy, stemming from Plato, Descartes in his more Jesuitical moments and Kant, Rationalism emphasizes truths known intuitively to the mind, without any reliance on experience. The *a priori* truths of mathematics, the categorical truths of space, time and causality don't, it was argued, depend on knowing anything about the external world. These self-evident propositions ($2+2 = 4$, the laws of geometry and logic) could generate a whole series of deductive truths as long as correct reasoning was followed.

By the same token, Rationalist architects would generate wholly consistent and 'true' buildings if they followed certain general principles in a rational way. The Abbé Laugier said 'if the problem is well stated, the solution will be indicated', a slogan Le Corbusier and other French architects liked to quote. Laugier hoped to generate truthful architecture from the elements of a primitive hut built out of wood. 'Let us never lose sight of our little hut', he needn't have urged. The next 150 years were spent looking at primitivist construction, designing primitive huts in first year studies at the Bauhaus and in woodlands away from the city.

SOUTH WEST ELEVATION   NORTH ELEVATION

SIR THOMAS TRESHAM, *The Triangular Lodge*, Rushton, 1595. With certain historical licence I illustrate this essay in Catholic symbolism as a Rationalist building. Like other buildings of its time, it is an absolutely clear geometric expression of a single idea, in this case the Trinity. Rationalist architecture makes a virtue of reducing form to the expression of a powerful idea which is held dogmatically – witness Boullée, Ledoux, Le Corbusier and Aldo Rossi. Here three triangular gables on each of three sides surround a central triangular chimney. The windows are built from trefoils, so is the door-head with its inscription announcing the theme *tres testimonium dant*. Three floors, countless plays on the owner's name (*tres*-ham) and various other hermeneutic symbols of the banished Roman Catholic mass made this a sermon of high treason. Rationalist buildings are often just as symbolic and geometric.

'An architect must be able to justify by reason every-thing he does', Laugier also averred, and it was this proposition which really proved so fatal to the Rational-ists. Their assumed truths, like the primitive hut or the grid used for all planning, have always seemed embarras-singly absurd. How could one possibly base a sophisti-cated urban architecture on such simplistic notions? The successive attempts by Rationalists to find new, indubit-able propositions were equally bizarre. An eighteenth-century architect wrote 'Gothic architecture improved' and tried to do just that by rationally turning the Gothic pier into a Classical Order. Another eighteenth-century Rationalist sought the 'Natural Model' for architecture and inevitably came up with man's ancestor, monkey-man, living in caves. In the twentieth century the same pursuit continued as architecture would be indubitably founded on the firm rock of function, logic, economy and structural determinants. All these vain attempts were motivated by the search for *certainty*. And here we have a deep, underlying psychological motive which runs through all the Rationalists, no matter what their particu-lar truth happens to be.

Before discussing the Rats, I should like to mention the pitfalls of the basic philosophy. In architecture, as indeed most science, it is clear Rationalism won't take one very far since a large part of its creation and realization consists in endless empirical data. Interviewing clients, using material at hand, modifying design endlessly according to *ad hoc*, contingent requirements – Rational-ist architects have always proven themselves weak on these things. In general they are hostile towards public opinion and contemptuous of anything that would dis-prove their basic assumption. In short they are 'fact-proof', hermetically sealed off from the pollution of reality like a good air-conditioned building. These architects might be called 'reinforced dogmatists'. Their ideology continually reinforces the evidence to which they attend thus strengthening their original belief, much the way reinforced concrete gets stronger and stronger if heated and battered.

Admitting all this quite candidly and, unlike their predecessors of the 1930s, the Rats are disarmingly frank, they might point out the following virtues in their position. It is clear, consistent and unlike other architec-ture, quite passionate and convincing. If architecture is an art that should move and persuade us, then Rationalism is the best style. It is not botched and bungled by petty requirements. It can be quick and decisive, cutting through all the indecision and fog of more democratic design. Finally, in a Rationalist Age, the Age of Science, when all positions are unprovable, it becomes the most credible. People, especially leaders of a field and academics, are most credulous towards anything offered up as rational.

This last argument, however pragmatic, is tasteless and needn't be dwelt upon. The devastating critique of Rationalism is quite enough, and it has been made by Karl Popper.[1] Basically the critique shows that no propositions are self-evident and unquestionable. Contrary to what the Rationalists contend, science develops by subjecting its 'truths', or hypotheses, to constant criticism, or refuta-tion, and it is this continual process of conjecture and refutation which eliminates errors. The Rationalists rarely, if ever, try to refute their own theories; they wouldn't, for instance, conduct market research on one of their housing estates, because its truth lies outside society and everyday experience. They have no use for

Popper's *Critical Rationalism*, or what is now called the 'sophisticated form of "falsificationism"'. This latter kind of Rationalism tries to falsify its truths and tentatively keep only those which have withstood this test. Rational-ist architects have not been prepared to do this.

Hence the Rats are doomed to a kind of beautiful irrationalism, the lyrical and clear expression of proposi-tions which are often as unlikely as Laugier's 'primitive hut'. The beautiful style, which has been going on since at least Boullée and Ledoux, appeals particularly to an elite – a small but coherent group of architects and critics. They have, in this century, produced the supreme expres-sions of organization that appeal to the mind: the sublime idealism of Leonidov's structures, the grand organiza-tional sweep of Tony Garnier's Ideal Industrial City where every function has a logical place, the well-ordered, and well-scrubbed housing blocks of J.J.P. Oud, almost all the work of Le Corbusier and some of that of Nervi – these are the triumphs of *the style that appeals to thought*. If the Irrational Rationalists have a justification, it isn't in either their truths or their method, but in their ability to make diagrams of ideas exact and exciting.

Many of the themes and problems of recent Rational-ism were worked out by the Italian architects in the twenties and thirties. Guiseppe Terragni and the MIAR (*Movimento Italiano per l'Architettura Razionale*, 1927) stated the abstract qualities to be sought: 'The desire for *sincerity*, *order*, *logic* and *clarity* above all, these are the *true* qualities of the *new* way of *thinking*' (my emphasis). The 'call to order' is a recurrent call: Paul Valéry made it in his dialogue on *Eupalinos or the architect*, an article which Le Corbusier and other Rationalist architects continually cited. The desire to put architecture 'in order' corresponded quite directly to attempts to order the political universe in the twenties, so it was not surprising that the MIAR often looked to Fascism to give the lead. In fact several Rationalist exhibitions and manifestoes were explicitly dedicated to Mussolini, and Terragni's best work – the Novocomun and Casa del Fascio – were implicated in reactionary politics. This sad and confusing connection of Italian Rationalism with Fascism has been well documented by Giulia Veronesi and Leonardo Benevolo and I will not dwell on it except to point out the psychological connection.[2]

Rationalism has *sometimes* proven weak on totalitar-ianism because they both emphasize order, certainty and clarity, and they both tend to look to a classical past for inspiration. These common tendencies don't of course mean that Rationalist or Neo-Classical architecture is 'Fascist', but it does mean that in our century they have *tended* to go hand in hand. This connection poses a great semantic problem for architects such as Aldo Rossi, because try as they might to dissociate themselves from Fascist architecture of the thirties, their style is histori-cally tied to it. We know that one dimension of architec-tural meaning is always historical association, and no one can escape this. All the Rationalists try to resemanticize their style, but they are only partly successful. There is always a tinge about it of Mussolini's Third Rome.

Universals and right angles

The Rationalist architecture of the early sixties was carried on by Mies Van der Rohe, Matthias Ungers and his students in Berlin, James Stirling and Louis Kahn. At least, in retrospect, these seem to be the major expo-nents of ideas and a style that was later to be named in the 1973 exhibition 'Architettura Razionale'.[3] This exhibi-

LOUIS KAHN, *Dacca Assembly Building*, office corridors, Bangla Desh, 1962–8. 'Cardboard architecture' stems from the drawing method of Palladio and his representation of flat, masonry surfaces ruptured by black, geometric holes. A dramatic style of building, reminiscent of Roman massiveness, looks best in sharp sunlight. Otherwise drab.

tion took place at the 15th Milan Triennale, forty years after the last exhibition with this name.

Mies' work put forward the notion 'of universal space', a neutral, flexible sandwich of space with movable elements that could supposedly incorporate all functions. It also promoted the ubiquitous right angle, a natural result of post and beam construction.

The underlying notion which justifies this, the *a priori* truth of the right angle, is not just based on constructional truth – on vertical loads and horizontal surfaces – it also is one of the ordering systems most easily grasped by the mind and hence claims a certain psychological universality. Furthermore it is simple. For these sorts of reasons Louis Kahn often started his design with a square plan – what he called the preform or FORM. He would then look for circumstances in the particular brief which distorted this Platonic form – what he called DESIGN. Thus any of his buildings would be a mixture of Rationalist forms (triangles and circles were added) with empirical twists and turns. The particular style he used to represent these buildings in model form was very reminiscent of Palladio's drawings, those flat, smooth surfaces punctuated by dark square holes. Kahn's models looked like Palladio's farmhouses, and they were so starkly seductive that the style of 'cardboard architecture' was formed, influencing greatly the whole Philadelphia School and the New York Five. Even Robert Venturi whose later work was in an empirical style, whatever was the local vernacular, practised cardboard architecture.

Another great influence of the early sixties was Hadrian's Villa, an example for urban planning which fascinated not only Kahn, but Colin Rowe, Vincent Scully and Matthias Ungers. Projects began appearing by 1963 which showed the mixture of varied and clashing geometries of this Roman villa.

Hadrian had done in the second century what modern planners could do now: use a limited repetoire of six or eight geometric units and their extensions and then smash them together in a 'juxtaposed manner' (a favourite phrase of the time). Colin Rowe was later to write a book around this compelling image and method, which he called 'Collage City' and 'Collision City'.[4] Part utopian and absolutist and part historical and accidental, Collage City, like Hadrian's Villa, could incorporate anything into its pattern without being destroyed, because its pattern was already rich and fragmented, *but* geometric. It is

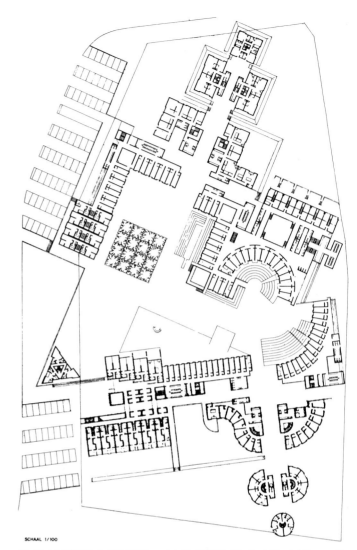

SCHAAL 1/100

O. M. UNGERS, J. SAVADE and J. F. GEIST, *Student Hostel Competition*, 1963. Like Hadrian's Villa, a series of different unit shapes are repeated on a series of axes that cross and sometimes collide. Multiple geometries, dissonant angles and a subtle *public* order emerge.

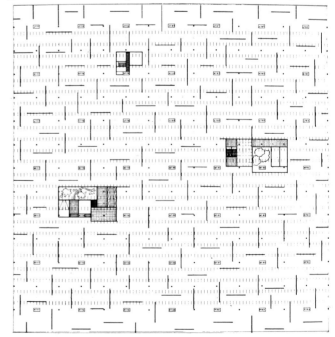

ARCHIZOOM, 'Homogeneous Living Diagram' *No-Stop City, A Climatic Universal System*, 1970. An endless Cartesian space with recurrent partitions, columns and services. The models of supermarket and parking lot are used with a mixture of irony and love. Isotropic space is at once the death and resurrection of architecture.

ALDO ROSSI, *Residential Unit in the Gallaretese Quarter*, Milan, 1969–70. A long residence – 182 metres long – has a 'portico' entrance repeated infinitely at its base, and then long corridors above. The stark black and white photos again remind one of Palladio and 'cardboard architecture' – indeed the reality looks like a model.

ALDO ROSSI, *Project for the Modena Cemetery*, 1971. Along the four massive walls and under them is the columbaria; in the centre, stepped shapes are the ossuaries; in the green patches the burial ground. The cone represents the common grave while the sacred cube is for the war dead and partisans. The symbolism is as strong in its own way as Thomas Tresham's triangle.

worth emphasizing that Rowe's approach was much more universal than Mies' and other Rationalists' because it was made from a richer repetoire of primary elements and more open to distortion and accepting new uses.

The work of Archizoom and Superstudio in the late sixties took the collage approach and streamlined it back in the direction of Mies. Back was the ubiquitous grid; in fact, 'No-Stop City' and the Continuous Monument were three-dimensional gridded space that was to zoom around the whole world, uniting all activities in a common white rectangle. Superstudio spoke, with barely discernible irony, of the 'sweet tyranny' this would induce in people admiring the grids. Archizoom spoke about 'isotropic space', homogeneous sandwiched space which would be well serviced like a supermarket and just about as neutral and boring. They considered this a subversive proposition to a consumer society – taking its ultimate building type and the pressures towards conformity to their absurd extremes. Rationalists have always loved an argument pushed to absurdity, especially if it starts from a self-evident truth.

Reduction to archetypes
About 1968, Aldo Rossi's projects started to have a great influence in Italy, and elsewhere in the student design world. In a sense they had a profound impact for precisely the reason that the schemes of Archizoom, Superstudio and the New Brutalists did: for pushing the

nihilism of consumer society so far that it actually became poetic. This paradox of meaning though anti-meaning is underlined by all critics of Rossi whether they praise or attack him. They all respond to the ambiguity of portraying death, silence and alienation with such ruthless consistency and remorseless repetition that these primary meanings are partly transformed.[5]

The experience of the Modern architect in Italy has always been closely associated with death. Several Rationalists were killed in concentration camps, others designed monuments to patriots, so it is not surprising that mortuary themes and death-camp overtones constantly inform their work. One of Rossi's most important schemes, the project for the Modena Cemetery, 1971, is next to the Lager of Fossoli, a place of commemoration for those who died under Fascism – and this cemetery has a sanctuary for the war dead and the partisans. It's a cube with black square windows opening onto a void – sort of mass housing for the dead, in a de Chirico style (even with a pitch black shadow drawn in the empty piazza). Endless straight lines and repeated arcades enclose this sacred image of stillness. A squat cone juts up on the main axis, reminiscent of death-camp chimneys, but this awkward cone is not for 'the final solution' – it's a monument to 'the common grave'. The fury that such ambiguous images can inspire in people should be compared with the anger that Lena Wertmuller's *Seven Beauties* generated. She also used the images of an extermination camp for their ambiguous beauty, and like Rossi, is inspired by a kind of metaphysical gloom.

Rossi's images are not necessarily pessimistic, although they have been compared even by favourable critics such as Vittorio Savi to mental hospitals; Rossi himself is inspired by galleries, arcades, silos, factories and farmhouses in the Lombard countryside. In his additions to the working class area in Milan, the Gallaretese neighbourhood, he has produced a Modern version of the traditional tenement corridor, which, he says 'signifies a life-style bathed in everyday occurrences, domestic intimacy, and varied personal relationships'.[6] The only problem with this characterization is that few people would see it; most would compare it with engineering works, tunnels or roadworks, as Rossi has admitted in the same article quoted above. Or they might say it signifies 'barracks', 'social deprivation' and *l'homme machine'*. In point of fact Rossi's language is so reduced in signification that it is read in diametrically opposite ways: by the elite, by critics such as Manfredo Tafuri, as 'emptied sacredness', as 'a discourse on itself', and by the public or hostile critics as 'quasi-Fascist' and 'cemeteries and prisons'.

Tafuri answers these critics with a kind of miraculous escape clause contending that Rossi can arise above historical associations, like an architectural superman, because his architecture is autonomous, free from contamination.

> . . .the sacred precision of his geometric block (the Gallaratese) is held above ideology and above all utopian proposals for 'a new lifestyle'.

or

> . . .The accusations of Fascism hurled at Rossi mean little, since his attempts at the recovery of an historicizing form exclude verbalizations of its content and any compromise with the real.[7]

How does Rossi manage this disappearing act, this superhuman feat which has eluded every other architect? By using a 'syntax of empty signs', by 'the law of exclusion', by reducing the classical language of architecture even beyond the purity of Fascist Stripped-Classicism.

Such extreme nudity ravages the mind of certain critics and makes them suspend their usual scepticism in a conversion that can only be termed religious: 'emptied sacredness', they aver.

Well, it may be too obvious to mention, but Rossi's forms *are* bivalent: sacred and all too real, sublime and prison-like, heaven and the concentration camp, and I don't see any point in denying both aspects since Rossi himself so clearly plays on both sets of meaning. This duality of extremes is slightly titillating, if not provocative, and I personally find his work full of a terrifying loneliness and claustrophobia which is not undesirable in a painting. Some of his best architecture is painting. The same is true of another Rationalist, Massimo Scolari, who also claims the 'autonomy of architecture' from ideology and historical contamination.

Such autonomy is possible only under extreme and artificial conditions: when the perceiver abstracts himself in time and space from a building, brackets off its

contextual setting and concentrates on the distortions of the language itself. Within these limits he can experience the building as a unique aesthetic act, an act which furthermore just refers to itself, or to its own internal relations (void against curved barrel vault etc.). It is this kind of meaning towards which Rossi and Scolari aspire, hence their celebration of the monument as the most architectural of building types.

> Distributive indifference belongs to architecture . . . the architecture of maximum precision – i.e., that of monuments – offers potentially the maximum freedom.[8]

We are thus back in the Surrealist world of Mies where any function can be poured into the same, semantic form.

Historicist Rationalism

The one area where the Rationalists aren't altogether irrational is in their treatment of urban form. Several of them, particularly two brothers from Luxembourg, Robert and Leon Krier, have mounted well observed attacks on the devastation of city fabric. They criticize all the forces, whether economic or ideological, which have destroyed the texture of cities and they have proposed quite elegant alternatives which patch it up or create new wholes.

> The debate which both Robert Krier and myself want to raise with our projects is that of the urban morphology as against the zoning of the planners. The restoration of precise forms of urban space as against the wasteland which is created by zoning. The design of urban spaces, both traffic and pedestrian, linear and focal, is on the one hand a method which is general enough to allow flexibility and change and on the other hand precise enough to create both spatial and built continuity within the city.[10]

Basically the Krier brothers follow Camillo Sitte's notions of articulating continuous urban space as a negative volume that flows and pulsates and reaches a crescendo around public buildings. This as against functional separation and the forces that tend to make each building a freestanding, embarrassed monument. At Echternach Leon Krier inserts a traditional arcade and circus, using the existing morphology of the eighteenth century to create an identifiable spine to the town and a culmination of the entrance route on the existing abbey. Height, scale, silhouette, building material is all compatible with the existing fabric, although accentuated to give a new emphasis to the public realm. Leon Krier uses the traditional aerial perspective of tourist maps to stitch these forms together. The image which results is reminiscent of eighteenth-century Bath and it is with such master builders as the Woods that the Krier brothers bear comparison. They are inheritors of a great tradition which was broken in the twentieth century by, among others, the previous Rationalists.

Leon Krier's competition entry for the Royal Mint Square Housing, 1974, is, in my view, the most sympathetic urban scheme of the Rationalists. It preserves traditional London street patterns and a few existing buildings, and incorporates those elements in a new pattern which cuts diagonally through the block. Thus two triangular courts and a central avenue are created which remain free from motor traffic; and the public realm is very subtly introduced in the form of arcades and a public square in the centre. Krier introduces several touches reminiscent of Le Corbusier and his *objects à*

MASSIMO SCOLARI, *Architectural Landscape*, 1975. Like 'Collage City' a set of fragments from utopia. The wall, the nineteenth-century tube bridge, the girder support 'an impossible' cupola in a still landscape. M. C. Escher is just as much an influence here as de Chirico.

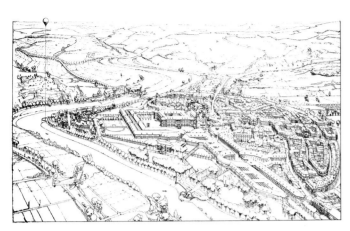

LEON KRIER, *High School at Echternach*, 1970. Krier takes this mediaeval and Baroque city and accentuates its fabric sympathetically as shown by this tourist perspective. The existing Baroque school is doubled and a glazed corridor is placed between the two halves. Then this Baroque facade is varied to form a main entrance boulevard that focuses on the existing church (which is transformed into a community house). Sportsground, park and a circus are added. Note the quaint 1920s technology, the bi-plane and balloon monument to Leonidov – typical Rat symbols.

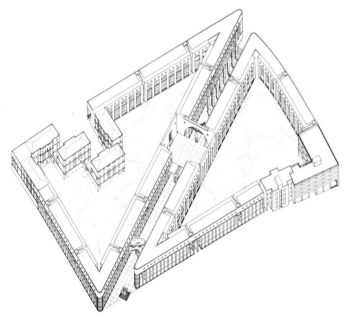

LEON KRIER, *Royal Mint Square Housing project*, 1974. A very sympathetic bit of city stitching and patchwork that nevertheless has a grand urban scale reminiscent of Bath. A diagonal route bisects the site, saving several existing buildings, keeping the street fabric and creating green triangular courts. A 'public room' with entrance portico on one side and gate to a car park on the other is in the centre of the pedestrian way. Various 'poetic' elements are placed along this route such as the cypress trees and 4 telephone booths.

ROBERT KRIER, *Siemer House*, Warmbronn near Stuttgart, 1968–73. Near symmetry and the black/white stucco style of the twenties is given an Expressionist twist. Skylights and geometry interplay very nicely with the slanted ground-form.

réaction poétique: a set of four telephone booths grouped together as a raised altar, existing trees, a gate and portico entrance to the 'public room' and a row of cypress trees. These elements are set along the avenue to punctuate its otherwise rather repetitive syntax. Like all the Rats, Krier is obsessed by long, linear site-lines as if the city should afford endless opportunities for target practice.

Both Kriers extend their historicism to all periods including the recent past, so their buildings tend to be ironic juxtapositions of various references rather like the collage cities already discussed. The work of Le Cor-busier, James Stirling, Palladio, Leonidov and de Chirico is incorporated or transformed in fragments to provide hermeneutic texts for the initiates to decipher. In-group jokes (a head-waiter serving up Le Corbusier's head, like Holofernes, while James Stirling scratches his head in consternation) as well as barely disguised Communist slogans decorate their public realms. Robert Krier, in his Siemer House near Stuttgart plays with Expressionism and the black and white architecture of the twenties. Black edged skylights and black voids punctuate white stucco cubes with a nearly complete symmetry. The Rats have reintroduced symmetry ironically, along with the

RICARDO BOFILL and OFFICE, *Concrete Factory Converted into Architect's Office*, Barcelona, 1972–6. Grand vistas of space opening out to the horizon, the sea, the mountains and architecture. This is that nineteenth-century theme *The Architect's Dream* finally realized.

white International Style that had previously banished it.

The most successful historicist, at least in terms of public recognition, is Ricardo Bofill and his group from Barcelona (Giscard d'Estaing described him as 'the finest architect in the world' and Bofill is not even French). They have produced housing in a variety of historical styles varying from neo-Gaudíesque through neo-vernacular to neo-Gothic (housing in the shape of a cathedral – what occupies the high altar? Nothing). Bofill and his partners have consciously embraced the Rationalist position, so that now one can speak of a Paris–Rome axis to the movement that includes peripheral centres in Berlin, Barcelona, London and New York.

For Bofill the Rationalist historicism means the free use of endless Roman arches, peppered with a few columns, Gothic windows and cypress trees. At Walden 7 (a hill of housing satirizing the dystopia of B. F. Skinner) Bofill has used a very intricate geometry at a vast scale to induce true basic responses: claustrophobia on the inside and agoraphobia on the outside. When one is on the 18th floor, on one of the bridges overlooking a fountain at ground level, and the wind is whistling through a twelve storey opening cut into the hill, then vertigo is the proper response. Bofill has proven popular because he makes picturesque use of the Rationalist style, always varying the surface and usually painting it a strong colour; so his work contrasts strongly with the grey mass housing it is meant to supplant.

Very often Piranesi's prison sketches are invoked as a source of Rationalist poetics, and with Bofill more than

RICARDO BOFILL, *Walden 7*, Barcelona, 1972–5. A man-made hill of twenty storeys with twelve storey holes punched through it and precipitous bridges across the open courts within. The red tile and repeated curves set up a very sensual rhythm.

the others, you feel you are back in this delightful madhouse of the eighteenth century. Appropriately his office is moving into one of these phobic buildings, a converted concrete factory that already is *The Architect's Dream* come true (endless vistas of pure form, grand space and cypresses, cypresses, cypresses on the roof!).

In America, Rationalist historicism got a champagne breakfast with Arthur Drexler's exhibition at the Museum of Modern Art entitled 'The Architecture of the Ecole des Beaux-Arts' (October 1975 – January 1976). Here was MOMA, the mother of the International Style in the USA, almost polemicizing a return to all the bad old virtues of the nineteenth century: ornament instead of pseudo-functionalism; urbanism and public buildings instead of mass housing; axes and heavy arcades and even heavier cornices as against airy transparencies; a love of detail, colour and history instead of the eternal, black and white present. Such were the implied alternatives. Unfortunately as a coherent polemic Drexler's exhibition never finally took a stand and engaged the present; as it might have done if put on by a Krier or Rossi. But it gave a good indication of which way the wind was blowing up Fifth Avenue, from the IAUS to the MOMA.

Architecture about itself

The acronym IAUS refers to the Institute for Architecture and Urban Studies, an institute run more or less by Peter Eisenman which has been a centre for Rat study for five years. Not only do many of the New York Five meet there, but also Rem Koolhaas, Mario Gandelsonas and Kenneth Frampton, all sometime-Rats, work there. The house magazine, *Oppositions*, always carries one or two articles on international Rationalism by Manfredo Tafuri, Colin Rowe and others.

Eisenman's work, when it is not called Rationalist, is termed 'White' (which it almost always is when not black); 'Structuralist' (concerned with the relation between deep structural grids and surface structural representation); 'cardboard' (not only looking like this homogeneous crudboard, but also like a model); 'virtual' (in the sense of conceptual rather than just perceptual); and 'Corbusian' (actually more like Terragni). There are many labels under which a discussion of Eisenman's work can proceed and all of them are esoteric. He claims to be an elitist, indeed an anti-populist, making architecture more complicated than it has to be in order to engage the mind (and torture it into submission).

His logical diagrams of the way the building is 'generated' (key word borrowed from Chomsky) would please any scholastic; they're more complex than the generation of rib mouldings from fan vaulting. And he presents the finished building as an illustration of the generation! Yes, the buildings are *about* the making of architecture, a process not a result. That is they represent on the surface very hard to perceive transformations which the interior geometry has undergone.

Ideally speaking, Eisenman would like to show the several arbitrary *rules* which have determined the building: the moving of volumes about on the diagonal, the rotation and inversion of lines and planes, the layering of space and so forth. In short only the *syntactical* elements are represented (or 'marked' in Eisenmanese). The basic marking is that of the surface structure which represents two or three different deep structures (grids, rotated and sheered grids). The basic problem is that no one, even Colin Rowe who has greatly influenced this process, can actually understand the markings. They are too ambig-

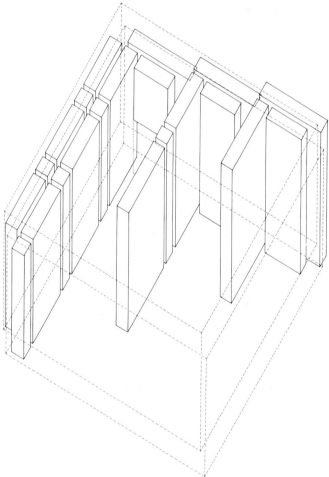

PETER EISENMAN, *House II*, an example of 'cardboard architecture' finished in 1969 for Mr. and Mrs. Richard Falk, Hardwick, Vermont. A structural square grid and a virtual grid interact along with a series of logical (but arbitrary) rules: diagonal sheer, inversion of themes, gradation of partition size, graded ascension of floor levels from one side to the other. Some of these rules are 'marked' on the outside for those who care to read the building with the transformational diagram in their hand.

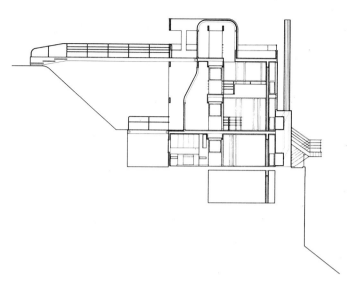

RICHARD MEIER, *Douglas House*, Harbour Springs, Michigan, 1971–3. Using a Corbusian syntax of independent structural frame, entrance ramp, and double height space, this building like Eisenman's represents layered space on its facade. Mullion lines take up, for instance, balcony points and column lines. Meier has given a bent wall on the entrance side which allows space to flow vertically and sideways across four levels – outdoing Corb at his own game.

uous, and coded with too many possible referents to choose between several readings. Thus the glass bead game, which is seductive to play in the case of an architect like Palladio, is ultimately frustrating. Rationalism pushed into a reductive corner proves once again irrational. To say this, however, is not to condemn it as expression. Eisenman's houses actually absorb a lot of *semantic* content – they are experienced as elaborate structural symphonies, as the white, light-filled architecture of Le Corbusier and Mykonos, as playful games, of nonsense poetry. One client fell in love with his structuralist game even though a transformation in the rules drove a column smack through his marital bed. Another client hated the transformations and lived in the basement before he moved out (a mathematician who *understood* Chomsky). No matter, Eisenman goes on and on with his logical convolutions until they dazzle the mind through sheer excess. As William Blake said of methodologists 'if the fool would persist in his folly he would become wise' (*Proverbs from Hell*), incidentally.

On this score, Richard Meier isn't quite as wise, or excessive, as Eisenman and his buildings are really just about some schemes Le Corbusier left unfinished or never bothered to fully work out. Meier, one of the Five (along with Michael Graves, John Hejduk, Charles Gwathmey and Eisenman) confines himself to the early twenties syntax of Le Corbusier before it became more curvilinear and Brutalist. As he says of his Smith house, it is Le Corbusier's Citrohan on one side, Maison Domino the other and, one might add, a collage of what's left over in between. The emphasis, again, is on layered space, and distorting syntax, or architecture which is making a comment on previous architecture, and the surprising fact is, given the rarity of this game, that it is neither pastiche, nor uncreative. Meier actually continues the

Corb tradition, even if he bends it in the direction of *House Beautiful* and the Jet Set. Like many of the Five he has found clients among the *nouveaux riches*; white Rationalist architecture in America is, semantically speaking, the counterpart of the Neo-Classical style. You don't ask for a Palladian villa now, but a Corbusian one.

Meier has recounted, apparently with a straight face, how the Douglasses wanted another 'Smith House' like the one they saw in *House Beautiful*.[11] After persuading them to have a new improved model, Meier found the local citizenry wouldn't accept anything but wood finish. He tried 'thirty different shades of white-grey and buff coloured paint – in an effort to resolve this issue'. But the answer was 'no'. The Douglasses built their white jewel elsewhere.

If Eisenman's architecture is about a logical design process, then Michael Graves' is about certain architectural elements – particularly doors and points of entry.[12] He 'foregrounds' these elements, calls attention to them by dislocating them from their habitual context. For instance in the Hanselmann House, the public entrance is raised, pulled away from the main body of the house and given an extra articulation of columns, thus creating a screen, or billboard effect. Key to Graves is the opposition between 'sacred and profane' space and the transition between them particularly pronounced in Baroque church architecture. The Hanselmann House has some of this quality.

You approach the frontal planes directly on axis, and the procession towards the more private areas is articulated by a series of implied and real planes set at right angles to your movement. This layering of tight space was a theme of Corbusier's Garches as Rowe pointed out (in an essay that influenced all the Five's buildings[13]). Graves, however, plays the game quite differently. By

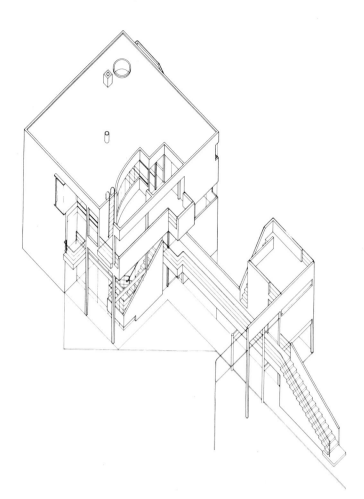

MICHAEL GRAVES, *Hanselmann House*, Fort Wayne, Indiana, 1967–8, axonometric. The entrance from the southeast is up some stairs, over a bridge to the middle of the house. The gate of columns and entablature, if built, would have given a pronounced sacred feeling to entry – in effect a double doorway – the first one a public symbol of the second.

Hanselmann House, actual state. The layering of space, set at right angles to the approach, becomes tighter and tighter as you reach the entrance. You have to cross a series of 'marked' frontal planes which increase in density by the entrance balcony and interior stairway.

Hanselmann House, mural representing layered space and diagonals, green earth and blue sky.

MICHAEL GRAVES, *Gunwyn Office Conversion*, Princeton, New Jersey, 1973. Curved tubes, portals, frames, steel trusses, lighting fixtures, glass block and various colours all focus into a Gris still life and then go out of focus. The experience of space is rich and ambiguous again being a movement against a series of real and implied planes.

pulling away the entrance and making it ceremonial, he creates a big outdoor room, a public space which is in fact a cube of empty space identical to the positive volume of the private space. Thus a certain drama and significance of entry is created, so potent that the house could be more appropriately used as a shrine.

After you reach the ceremonial bridge, you head straight at the centre of the cube noticing such distinctive features as a diagonal to the left (indicating the stairs down to the children's level) and a balcony overhead (articulating the second entry). Certain Corbusian elements are exaggerated. Steel tubing and white picture windows framing the sky, a slight curve recalling the ever obsessive guitar shape of Cubist paintings. Even the underlying Corbusian order of columns detached from white planes is emphasized.

You open the front door, arrive at the public level, and are confronted by stairways at right angles to each other and an idealized, Cubist mural of the house – a kind of totemistic representation of the whole thing. The mural is then a transformation in two dimensions of your experience in three – rather like an Eisenman drawing. Except elements are even further fragmented and made more complex than the architecture. Another notation is set up in terms of colour – blue for sky, green for nature – thus, if you are aware of it, underscoring views out of the house. (Graves has written on the 'celestial soffit' and he often curves this element making a visual pun on clouds in the sky.) In all of his buildings, there is a heightening of the vertical dimension: the sky is always brought in by frames, by columns and beams reaching out into space.

In fact there is always an ambiguity of space, perhaps best seen in his Gunwyn office conversion where elements are so tightly packed that you have trouble distinguishing foreground from background. Essentially space is collapsed in two dimensions to appear as a Juan Gris still life (the Cubist Graves most admires). The movement through portal frames is so rich that it foreshortens the experience into a single flat plane. Everywhere you look mechanical, structural and wall elements compose into a two-dimensional collage. The trick, like all good architecture, calls attention to itself and takes time to experience.

Obvious doubts arise. Why should Graves confine himself to a 1920s semantics? Clearly his emphasis on the significant points of architecture – doors, windows, walls – is valid and exemplary at this time, but he refuses to perform an essentially traditional role with a traditional syntax. No mouldings, capitals and pediments, no popular signs which would have a wider resonance of meaning. Furthermore the symbolic cues necessary for an understanding are essentially esoteric. For instance in his Benacerraf House, you need a Reader's Guide to understand that a blue balustrade is really a 'column lying on its side'. There is an infinitude of such hermeneutic meanings in the Five's work.

Influence of the Rats

The work of the Five and the Italian Rationalists has had an enormous influence on architects who aren't directly in the tradition. Arata Isozaki has, since 1970, been producing variations on cubes and grids and Palladian plans. His Gunma Museum is a sequence through an implied deep structure of large cubes, which is everywhere articulated by a surface structure of small grids. Isozaki even elaborates the Rationalist style – the non-joint joint, the window or door opening as 'absence of wall', the smash together of grids without any mouldings or visual junctions.

Cesar Pelli and the 'Silvers of Los Angeles' have been developing their own version of spatial ambiguity based on refinements of the curtain wall which bring transparency, reflectivity, translucency in a sequence of views.[14] The Silvers also reify the grid.

In England, Alan Colquhoun and John Miller use a restrained form of Rationalist style reminiscent of the work of Max Bill, while James Gowan produces a kind of Neo-Neo-Palladianism and James Stirling, slightly influenced by his former draughtsman Leon Krier, practises a type of Modern Neo-Classicism.

Stirling's shift in this direction, noticeable since the Derby scheme of 1970, is interesting because it indicates a general move of many architects towards urban and historicist meanings. A building as a part of the historical fabric, rather than as a discontinuous monument, becomes a prime focus. His museum scheme for Düsseldorf shows much of the Rationalist historicism I have already mentioned.

On the level of details, he uses the German flattened-arch common to public buildings in this area, as well as masonry and the classical grammar of Schinkel. The base of Schinkel's Altes Museum in Berlin becomes the elevation for a good part of Stirling's scheme, which also has a facsimile facade on one side (to carry on the nineteenth-century street facade) and even a real pediment on top of two columns.

ARATA ISOZAKI, *Gunma Museum*, 1974. Here the Rationalist grids actually appear represented on the outside and throughout all the surfaces, being suitably rendered in a religious, polished aluminium. This main exhibition hall is turned at an angle to the rest of the grid, thus gaining importance as the 'head'. The space beneath is a mirror image of the volume – cube and anti-cube.

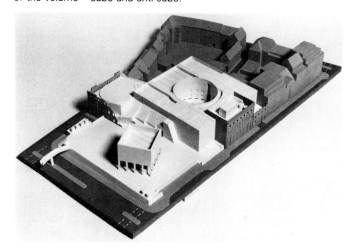

JAMES STIRLING, *Düsseldorf Museum project*, 1975. The open circle becomes the covered square. Like Kahn and Rossi, the architect is fascinated by these basic primitive forms conveyed with a stripped Classicism. The building fits, on one side, very neatly into the city fabric, taking up the street facades and cornice line. Then the square element, raised on a podium is turned to the side picking up major site lines and acting as a symbolic entrance.

In volume, Stirling's museum scheme fits into the city fabric and gives a very enjoyable twist to the existing pedestrian street: it becomes first an open outdoor room to the sky, a circle, and then a glass roofed portico, a square. Positive square, negative circle, conceptually one tries to square the circle. The same opposition can be found in Aldo Rossi's urban projects, although made with less tension and irony. In fact the ironies of this Düsseldorf scheme become a bit black when one reflects on certain references. The windows of the open circle recall the Nazi work of Albert Speer and they seem to sink into the ground. They are placed way below the roof line and emerge half above the ground implying that Nazism is still present, but that it is sinking (or is it rising?). The only remains of the old Stirling, the Futurist, are in the ramps and curved, patent glazing. All in all it shows how strong the Rationalist influence has become (although as mentioned Stirling himself created an aspect of this in the sixties).

King Rats or Rat Killers? – Surrationalism

We have seen that Rationalism taken to an extreme becomes absurd and that practised as a half measure it's simply irrational. Of course its twin, functionalism, was never functional and there are few movements that live up, or down, to their slogans. This is not altogether a bad thing since any doctrine is bound to be simplistic and its followers will therefore spend much of their time trying to balance if not altogether refute it. Thus it is appropriate that from within the movement come two supreme ironists whose Rationalism is so explicitly extreme and thorough-going as to make all the pitfalls and beauty of the approach abundantly and deliciously clear. They push Rationalism so far it becomes surreal or Surrationalism; they are the King Rats or Rat Killers, depending on where their extremity leaves the movement. Either way it can't go on any more pretending to be straightforward and sensible. Either it evolves towards an empirical base and becomes *Critical* Rationalism, or it evolves in more absolutist directions towards the Surrationalism of these two Kings.[15] Both have been influenced greatly by Surrealism and both, not surprisingly, haven't built anything – but their projects are no less persuasive for that.

Big John Hejduk, who must be over six foot six and who speaks like a John Wayne from the Bronx, likes to build little, tiny, miniscule models of his unbuilt houses (some are 1½ inches small). I'm not sure why he likes this massive disjunction in scale (he does of course carry the models in his pockets) but it is entirely fitting to the rest of his message which thrives on absurdity and paradox. Magritte is one of his exemplars.

Hejduk will take an essentially prosaic and normal idea and then belabour it so long that it becomes extraordinary and abnormal. First, in 1954, he worked over Palladio, planning houses based on nine squares until he had exhausted much of the magical potential for filling these squares with columns and chimneys. This research on pure geometric relations and a trabeated, caged system of space lasted until 1962 when – miraculously like Theo Van Doesburg – he rotated his geometry by 45 degrees. The result? 'Diamond Houses'. For the next four years diamonds were to be explored. All sorts of diagonal properties were discovered which Mondrian and Van Doesburg only just touched on: the meshing of two grids produced no end of nice collisions. Space seemed to whirl about like a centrifuge, stairways and chimneys went into 'three-dimensional torque', the edges or corners became 'charged and filled with maximum tension'.[16] The effect was so mesmerizing that Ken Frampton used this formal twist as the second theme of his justification of the Five, an article he called 'Frontality and Rotation'.[17] This was rotation all right, every corner of the room reminded you of the fact. For initiates into the hermeneutic code of the Five, there were also other cues. Whenever one saw a round column one was meant to think 'rotation'. When one saw a square column one thought 'frontality'. As Hejduk said of Le Corbusier's Carpenter Centre – 'the shape of the structural columns is round, indicating a centrifugal force and multi-directional whirl'.

Or as Frampton said of Eisenman's 'House 1':

> . . .The unresolved tension between frontalization and rotation [is created by] the presence and/or absence of stainless steel cylindrical columns.[18]

Oh those absent square columns are just so . . . frontalized! This is all very interesting and it reminds one of the traditional Japanese, indeed Shinto, distinction

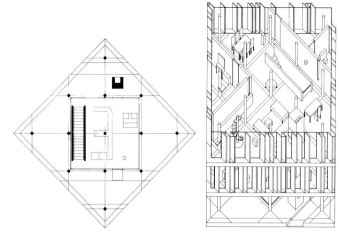

JOHN HEJDUK, *House 8, Diamond Series*, 1962–66. Two squares rotated at 45 degrees create the major opposition between frontal layered space and whirling, centrifugal space. Everywhere you feel the opposition between the two systems because every element of structure and furniture takes up one or another of the themes.

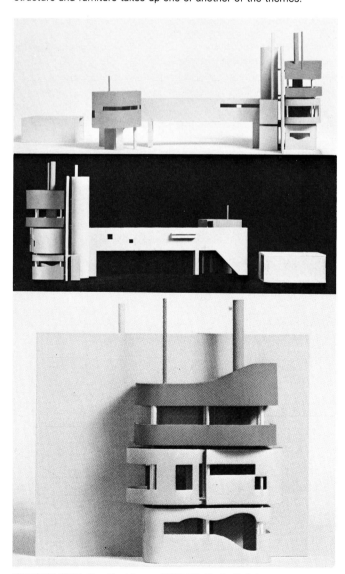

JOHN HEJDUK, *Bye Residence*, 1972–74. Basically living space on one side of the wall and functional space on the hall side of the wall, periscopes over the top. The guitar and stomach-shaped rooms are painted in muted primary colours. At one point Hejduk was considering that these rooms should be rendered like an architectural drawing with scratchy shadows. 'Everybuddy asks me how we gonna doh dat, but a house can be rendered. Ed Bye, like me is a cunsuvative and said what I want ta hear – I like it?' It took Hejduk two years to make working drawings for this house which may be built.

between round, untreated cypress columns symbolizing tree (nature) and squared-up wooden beams symbolizing man-made (culture). But of course this Japanese code was neither so esoteric, nor based on *missing* cues for its interpretation.

Anyway, Hejduk moved on from his diamond fixation to concentrate on what he really came to love – walls. He designed one project, somewhat racist in overtones, which consisted of two houses, one black, the other white, which were separated by a high wall. Then he provided holes and periscopes so these opposite neighbours could surreptitiously monitor each other – the wall uniting them in a mutual obsession. Hejduk then looked at Philip Johnson's wall houses and the canonical Rationalist building Hadrian's Villa, with all its types of wall, and of course Hadrian's Wall itself.[19]

By 1964 he was really into the wall in a big way and he started designing houses whose drama consisted in constantly penetrating through an outside wall to find yourself – outside. ('You goh truh da waal ta make yah way back to da house'.)

For instance, on one side of the Bye Residence there are three superimposed rooms of living, sleeping and dining which are separated by a flat (frontalized) wall plane from bathroom, stairs, study and long linear hall. A periscope is thoughtfully provided 'so Ed can come intuh

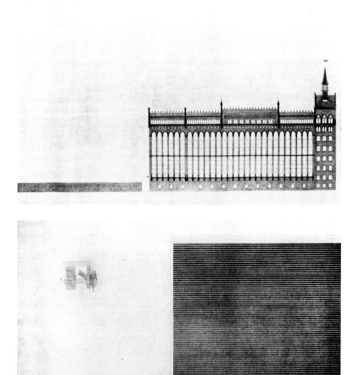

JOHN HEJDUK, *'Cemetery for the Ashes of Thought'*, Venice Biennale project, 1976. An old factory is kept empty and many walls, 600 feet long 4 feet apart with black and white sides, are placed at right angles (see plan). Various transparent cubes and plaques commemorate dead authors such as Marcel Proust. 'Most Rationalists I hold in high regard, but they are dealing in an architecture of death. This is a commentary and answer to them.' Visiting dignitaries would inhabit the memorial for a limited time.

his house and luk ovah his waal'. Putting a large, structured wall, a shield between these two types of room (rendered in Cubist shapes and pale primaries) gives them a felicitous kind of schizophrenia, as if they belonged to two different families (one horizontal, one vertical). It also increases the drama of transition and, a functional point Hejduk might not like to make, is very sensible if there is a lot of traffic and noise on the garage side.

The fascination for walls ('Wallism' – a well-known disease of bad neighbours)[20] reached a pinnacle (if that is the right architectural word) with his project for the Venice Biennale in 1974. This was called a 'Cemetery for the Ashes of Thought', a kind of museum or mausoleum for thoughts that weren't quite dead, or at least ones that Hejduk wished to commemorate. Hejduk made it an explicit commentary on Rationalism, since it was a project for Italy, a 'commentary on and answer to the architecture of death', those schemes of Aldo Rossi which appear so quiescent and necrophiliac. His answer was a lot of wall. Many (it's hard to count because of optical vibration) walls to be twelve feet high, to be placed four feet apart and run straight for six hundred feet. 600 feet of wall, one side black, the other white, holes every 2 or 3 feet! You'd feel like a termite lost in a straightened Bridget Riley.

What was the point? Hejduk said that various plaques and cubic gravestones would be placed throughout giving the titles of old thoughts (e.g., *Remembrance of Things Past*, *The Counterfeiters*, various titles of books he admires). The main house, an abandoned factory, would be painted deep black, would have more plaques now with the authors' names, and it would be inhabited from time to time by a visiting dignitary (who presumably would spend his time recalling those previous moments of time past, *Death in Venice*, etc.).

Hejduk spent a whole month colouring in the spaces between the walls. Such projects starting from a Rationalist concern with first principles, and architecture about itself, render the principles authoritarian. They grow to consume everything else. Like a traditional Surrealist, Hejduk focuses on everyday aspects of reality, but then gives them an independent life of their own, cut off from their original function. Doors, walls, triangles, chimneys, linear halls dominate everything, like Magritte's apple that expanded so much that the inhabitants were forced to flee their room. This impossible likelihood, like magic, forces us to reconsider the prosaic, and the assumption of what really is rational.

That other Rat Killer, or King Rat, Rem Koolhaas and his team of metropolitan enthusiasts, is also very influenced by Surrealism – particularly the 'paranoid-critical method' of creativity practised by Salvador Dali.[21] Central to this method is the projection of dreams, phobias, ideologies and obsessions onto the real world, until they become true by sheer force of repetition and willpower. The history of civilization, and particularly that of New York City, looks from this angle like a sequence of such projections. Koolhaas says of Manhattan (and he quickly turns this *aperçus* into a philosophy, Manhattanism), that it was 'a compression of all the best of Europe'. It was a successful paranoid projection of the Dutch phobia – 'New Amsterdam'; its history has suffered successive projections, those of endless ethnic groups and paranoid Rationalists such as Le Corbusier, until each part of it represents the distillation of some ideal dream. To take this tendency even further and bring it to self consciousness, Koolhaas has designed 'The City of the Captive Globe'.

This project gives to each city block a self-consistent and self-referring style and ideology – or 'mania'. Thus Le Corbusier's serrated towers stand next to Expressionist pointed arches, Malevitch near Superstudio, the ever present globe and needle (1939 World's Fair) is next to what looks to be the Plaza Hotel and Mass Housing. Other Rationalist icons are strewn about – the World Trade Center looks down on 'the captive globe' at the centre.

The point of these blocks, like the paranoid-critical method, is to banish any reality which does not serve the original mania – what could be a better critique (and celebration) of Rationalism. In Koolhaas' words (and he is the son of a Dutch poet):

> Each science or mania has its own plot. On each plot stands an identical base, built from heavy polished stone. These bases, ideological laboratories, are equipped to suspend unwelcome laws, undeniable truths [sic], to create non-existent physical conditions to facilitate and provoke speculative activity . . .
> The changes of this ideological skyline will be rapid and continuous, a rich spectacle of ethical joy, moral fever or intellectual masturbation.[22]

In a sense this is just real New York intensified.

Koolhaas and OMA developed their theories in 1972 with a study of the Berlin Wall (walls again), and their scheme for London called 'Exodus, or the Voluntary Prisoners of Architecture'. When I pointed out to Hejduk the remarkable similarity in wall obsession he drew back in disdain, muttering something indecipherable about plagiarism, reacting with near paranoia. Obviously there is no place for two King Rats occupying the same territory, but the similar obsessions turn out, in this case, to be fortuitous (although perhaps psychologically connected).

Is it true that people, not only designers, love to be 'voluntary prisoners of architecture'? Can the history of architecture really be seen as the self-imposed incarceration into walls, skyscrapers, globes and needles? In a dream-sense, yes, and it's this unwritten dream which Koolhaas wishes to record, and reinforce.

'Every skyscraper in New York wanted to be a sphere and every sphere secretly wanted to be a needle. . .' The drama of 'delirious New York' unfolds like an illuminated nightmare, with the two protagonists, the Chrysler Building and the Empire State in bed with each other. There they lie, the feminine Chrysler curving over to meet the larger Empire State, while the Statue of Liberty holds a flaming lamp above them. Their tryst is over, symbolized by the spent rubber balloon of the Goodyear Tyre Blimp. But then suddenly the jealous RCA building intrudes, and casts its search-light on them. The best of New York skyscraperdom looks on aghast (or is it with an interest in morals?).

What is the message of this *in flagrante delecto?* Out from underneath the bed is born the magical New York Grid, Central Park and the spaghetti of roads, tubes and services (the underground, deep collective unconscious). Manhattan is being killed (by recent architects) and in the next set of drawings we see that the only hope is for more spaghetti, more fanatical obsessions which produced these two former 'largest needles in the world'.

In many such drawings and water colours Koolhaas and Vriesendorp portray what they call 'the secret life of buildings'.

To introduce explicit figurative, symbolic elements in the urban realm, OMA is developing a quasi-Freudian language to identify and analyse the psychological characteristics and properties which could be ascribed to architecture.[23]

With a kind of remorseless, surrealist wit Koolhaas shows what psychological characteristics have existed; the evolving globe and needle become more and more sick and finally degenerate into the awful slab blocks. Wallace Harrison, who has been instrumental in this evolution with his RCA and United Nation slabs, still feels a throb of the Manhattan blood in his clotted arteries, so he is capable of utterly inexplicable gestures – such as the slight curve. Koolhaas finds these curves becoming more and more obsessive after the RCA building (he studied Harrison's curves for three years) until they reach a spasmic crescendo in the UN building. The weak curve

REM KOOLHAAS and ZOE ZENGHELIS, 'The City of the Captive Globe', 1975. What New York City is trying to be, a distillation of ideologies which have been 'inflicted' on the world. Each block is a complete and pure expression of 'a certain form of madness' – notice the Rationalist block of ice-cool cubes, lower right. The captivity of the globe in the centre is the final subjugation of the reality principle by the 'paranoid-critical method'. All blocks are isolated on rectangular podia which carefully exclude unwelcome truth – the censorship practised in every nation. Incidentally, of all nations, South Africa has the highest level of paranoia; West Germany is second.

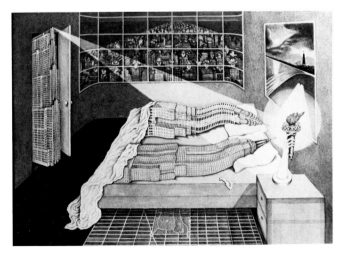

MADELON VRIESENDORP, In Flagrante Delecto, 1975. The Chrysler Building, female and the tallest until 1931, curls up to the Empire State, while other skyscrapers sprout heads and watch. The print-out under the bed is the offspring of this illicit encounter – the neutral grid of New York which absorbs all paranoid projections equally. This gouache is part of a series 'The Secret Life of Buildings' and the drama continues.

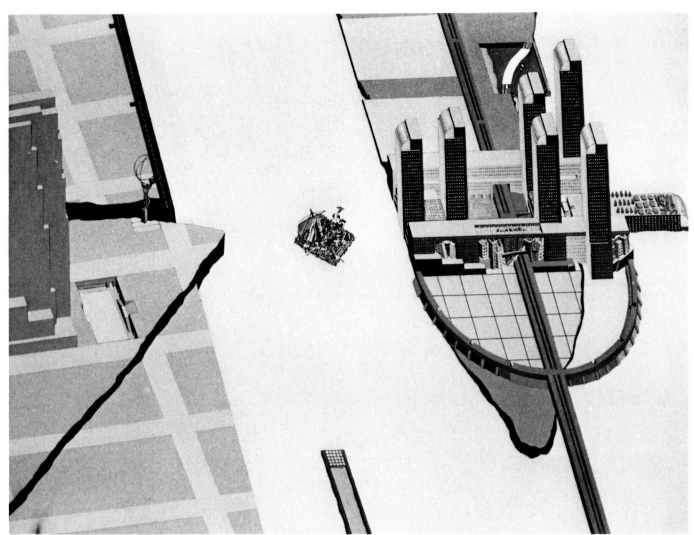

REM KOOLHAAS, *Welfare Palace Hotel*, 1975. This hotel of towers
faces Harrison's RCA building and New York with its glass walls and
seven heads. A fault runs through the hotel and one tower has fallen
over on its back. The site is a graveyard for discarded schemes, an
architectural parking lot full of Rat beauty and monotony.

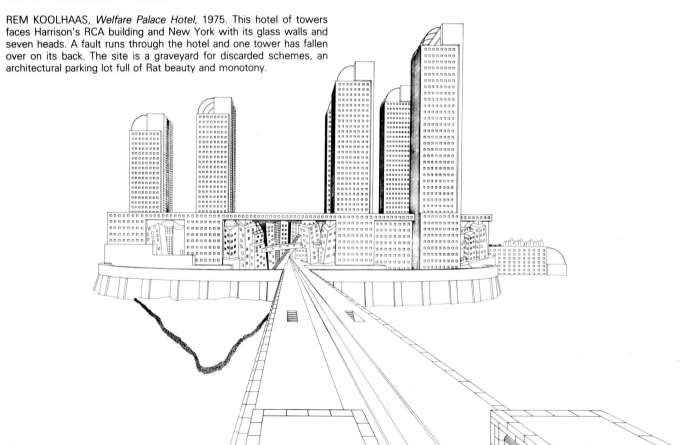

of Harrison recurs here fifty times! Whatever can it mean? Koolhaas decodes it; 'That means there's something the matter with it. It's the *limp curve of humanism* which betrays the perpetual representation of guilt feelings.' The same limp curve of humanism disciplines Harrison's Opera House at Lincoln Center which is a 'marble cyclotron that twists and turns people until they lose reality'.

This psychoanalysis of architecture is then turned into

a utopian paranoid conjecture, a scheme for Welfare Island. The grid of Manhattan and Harrison's limp curve are there as well as other recognizable manias: in fact Koolhaas calls his scheme 'an architectural parking lot, a graveyard for discarded schemes', tinged with the 'humiliating setbacks' he prefigures in his future. The skyscrapers are there with their 'heads' looking at Manhattan and the RCA, while one of them has collapsed on its side as a 'groundscraper'. The Rat emphasis on repetition is there, brought to a new pitch of boredom. So is the Rat jumble of buildings, a collision to rival New York which is also a 'shipwreck of architecture'? To 'take the temperature of this shipwreck', Koolhaas has devised his 'architectural dipstick' in the form of Gericault's *Raft of Medusa*. This he inserts at various points to see how healthy is the paranoia. The raft is in a sense the perfect image of Manhattanism, a group of survivors from a shipwreck, who cannibalize each other in order to survive.

> According to the Classic Chronicle, their parachute dropped the castaways of the Medusa and their raft on the rescue-ship 'The City'. It appeared like a serene monument bursting with the ornamental frenzy that its inner life provoked. It was an unknown, a new form of life, inside a timeless architecture: an innumerable mixture of activities generated by the ship's hedonistic daily program. It was a spontaneous Planning Centre governed by the continuous satisfaction and shameless application of human passions. Amongst the protagonists of the inspired state of anarchy, Jesus Christ and the Marquis de Sade were engaged in a mutant form of behaviour which was echoed by the splendid order of the architecture. . .[24]

And so Rationalism born in the paranoid conjectures of an eighteenth-century monk dreaming about the lesson of the Primitive Hut ends two hundred years later on a wooden raft of Surrationalism, the Rats unable to leave their sinking ship and eating each other to save their lives.

REM KOOLHAAS, *The Raft of Medusa*, 1975. If New York is an architectural shipwreck which is sinking, then the buildings, like the survivors on Medusa's Raft, will have to eat each other. Welfare Island proceeds to eat New York City. All of a sudden everything is saved – 'They had recaptured a lost paradise: the ability to love. not so much each other, but themselves'.

3. SERIOUS JOKES

3.1 PHILIP JOHNSON – THE CANDID KING MIDAS OF NEW YORK CAMP

Since this piece was published, AAQ Winter 1973, Philip Johnson has gone through another creative period, perhaps the most original of his career. As the buildings illustrated show, he is at once a protagonist of Late and Post-Modernism, and in a loose sense, by consulting history for its examples, he has always been a Post-Modernist. Unmentioned in this essay, written in the Neo-Hysterical Style, is Johnson's personal kindness and generosity. He has been a patron of Modern artists and architects for two generations, and remains something of a power-broker in American architectural politics even today. He supports unknown, but good, emergent architects. 'Doctor Johnson', as Peter Eisenman calls him, was even generous to me after I wrote this piece, which is not a balanced assessment of his work. This will have to wait for the future. The work has, I believe, an easy and icy beauty.

Nikolaus Pevsner has denied the innuendo on page 157 (see AAQ vol. 6 no. 2 1974, p. 58). The quotes from Johnson come from two tape-recorded interviews I had with him and the numerous other published statements he has made.

The professional rogue

There he sits on Christmas Eve, Philip Cortelyou Johnson, in his weekend See-Through House turning up and down the outside flood lights while all around him gentle snow flakes fall, fall, fall – poof, poof, poof – each one picked out and highlit by the floods . . . 'With the lights out inside and the snow coming down, it makes you seem to go up – like a great celestial elevator!'

Philip Cortelyou Johnson ascending into a weekend heaven in his quarter-of-a-million dollar Glass Box, his cosmic fish bowl, all tucked in by central heating, shrubbery and plenty of stone walls . . . thinking out the next way he can send up the Modern Movement, outrage the socially responsible, deny the underpinnings of Le Corbusier, Gropius, Fuller, 'Epater le Mouvement Moderne?'. After a hundred years of smashing the nerve

Glass House, New Canaan, Connecticut, 1949. When first built in the heart of New York's commuter-belt, this see-through house caused a lot of local consternation. Johnson had to build a six foot high stone wall to protect himself from the gaze of the curious, Sunday strollers. But also, to whet their appetite, he would conduct an occasional tour of the open-planned house. Pointing towards an empty space: 'This is the library, Madam, you see it's an *American* library – no books.' When she objected that this open planning was unsuitable for family life – 'It's a nice place but I could never *live* here', Johnson replied, 'Madam, *I* haven't asked you to'.

The function of the glass wall was to minimize the imposition on the beautiful landscape and allow for changing views of the four seasons to become the subject of architecture – 'the most beautiful wallpaper in the world'. Actually, Johnson's love for landscaping and exotic plants equals his love for architecture (see the garden for the Museum of Modern Art).

As in so many of his Neo-Classical buildings, the structure is raised on a plinth, has a cross-axial plan with doors on all four axes and is extremely precise and closed in outline – caused by painting the steel picture-frame a sharp black.

endings of the bourgeoisie, Modern architects have found that the old neurons won't fire any more, the synapses are worn out, there is nobody left to shock except a fast-diminishing group of themselves, the last people on earth who still can be surprised, outraged, ethically repulsed.

When Philip Johnson built his See-Through-It-Isn't-There-Glass House in 1949, he provided a set of programme notes (like a nineteenth-century, Romantic composer), published them in *The Architectural Review* for all the professionals to follow his sources, his eclectic stealing, his architectural cleptomania – seventeen (17!) different sources ticked off. The See-Through House was entirely made up of sources pillaged from the Greats of the Past – nothing original, but all acknowledged right there for everyone to see: 1) site plan and spiderweb walkways taken from Le Corbusier, 2) sliding arrangement of volumes stolen from Mies, 3) asymmetrical composition lifted from Theo Van Doesburg, 4) Acropolis planning from Choisy, 5) straight-on symmetry from Schinkel . . . 8) the Glass House from Mies . . . 13) glass walls by Mies . . . 17) open plan from Mies . . . after this building Philip Cortelyou was called Mies van der Johnson because he robbed I-beams, corner details, open planning, tinted glass, chairs, tables . . . English, moralist critics love it! The English critic and Defender of the Modern Movement, Sir Nikolaus Pevsner, loves to catch Philip out playing at his eclectic game: '. . . that brilliant rogue Philip Johnson . . . is a virtuoso at playing with stylistic materials old and new . . .' and Sir Nikolaus is a brilliant rogue-finder with his searching out of every possible stylistic source – 'sourcery'! The English critics love to catch Philip playing at sourcery. They come in droves on their pilgrimage to the US to visit Johnson at his New Canaan House, to tour the grounds, to look at his Pop Art collection, to be deliciously outraged at his Camp sensibility.

James Stirling, the English architect committed to a functionalist base, drives up to Johnson's New Canaan Compound. 'Look at this', Philip says, pulling out a devastating assault on his work and character from *Architectural Design*, 'you Englishmen always attack my work with such style. It's absolutely fabulous, only an Englishman could have written this':

> One step further along the road to complete architectural decadence has now been taken by Philip Johnson, with yet another addition to his idyllic estate in New Canaan. Although it is passed off by the architect as a 'folly' by virtue of its entirely false scale it is, nonetheless, in its trivial historicism, quite typical of Johnson's recent work . . .

'Complete architectural decadence'! And Johnson likes this attack because of its style? Indeed – his Glass House is a temple decorated to the celebration of style. Besides the sourcery already mentioned there is a painting by the seventeenth-century classicist Nicolas Poussin – the *Funeral of Phocion* – a life-sized Nadelman portrait of *Two Women* (these two women are chatting and embracing and they are monobosomed and made out of white *papier-mâché*.) There is a small Giacometti *Thin Man* inching his way across the floor, a Claes Oldenburg – *Bursting Banana Split* (of course) – and as for the accompanying elements – low cabinet units which look as if they were made out of Chinese teak; shaggy potted plants; a soft, white, wool rug which creates a conversation island on the polished redbrick-herringbone-floor; a seating pool made up of Miesian leather chairs reclining

couches . . . LEATHER. Johnson loves leather. The only enclosed room in the house, the bathroom '*la salle de bain*', is covered in oily, pigskin panels and the tiles on the floor are all leather.

In his Guest House which is located diagonally to his Glass House, Johnson inverts the open, flowing style and encloses two bedrooms in a brick cube which only has small, Peeping-Tom portholes for windows. The effect is inward-looking, protective, womb-like, a 'feeling of cuddle' (Johnson calls it) caused by the warm curves of the hung-plaster domes and the honey-dew arrases of gold and silver which tinkle and caress the indirect light that gently spills and cavorts down them. The wandering-wire sculpture especially designed for the space over the bed is lit like the nimbus of some Byzantine saint but it dims and brightens when Johnson turns up and down the rheostats. With this building and more particularly with its paired column domes, Johnson finally broke with the Modernist commitment to structural honesty and straightforward expression. 'This is my High-Queen Period' Johnson says with a wicked smile directed at the ascetic priesthood of the Modern Movement.

But the building which really brought out their collective wrath was his 'pleasure pavilion', his 'follee', his underscaled forest of pre-cast white concrete columns placed in his *artificial* moon viewing lake in the west part of the Johnson Compound. Here it is, the final insult to functional purpose and everything the Pioneers of the Modern Movement had fought for – relevance, social

Guest House with its golden arras and aedicule. (Photo Ezra Stoller Associates).

utopianism, a non-historicist style. To them it would be a practically useless piece of under-scaled wedding-cake whose purpose was, as Johnson put it, 'to make giants of the visitor (an idea borrowed from the dwarf's chambers at Mantua)'. The classical colonnade, which appears to be twelve feet in height (but is actually half that), appears suddenly even smaller when the hundred foot high *jet d'eau* explodes into action at the press of a button.

In the 'follee' are gigantic Erie Canals, of gushing water ten inches wide that pour over herculean precipices, of two inches, and thunder to the bottom of the lake with a resounding tinkle. This tinkle is then taken up again in a visual form as it reverberates off the interior of the gold-leaf domes (which are only three feet wide).

The British magazines sprang into action. *Architectural Design* shot out its 'complete architectural decadence', its 'trivial historicism', its condemnation of these 'feeble forms'; *The Architect's Journal* drove in the message: '. . . we all have this ugly romantic urge in us . . .for too many people, this sort of disincarnate architecture is the real thing, and the attempt to ally form with social purpose an irrelevant bore'. The British critic Reyner Banham answered this mounting attack on what he termed 'one of the most sincerely hated buildings in the world'. But the defence was hardly needed. Johnson himself turned the joke back on his critics in an interview presented right in the heart of the debate – on the BBC with Susan Sontag:

P. Johnson: . . . I got the idea that it was good to imitate the British, you know our betters, as we always say in this country, and, er, so I decided that we would have a follee . . . we hear the splash of water, we see the floating, dying leaves and it gives us a sort of Keatsian sense of fairy casements forlorn – I'm copying this wrong – I'm quoting this wrong, but you know what I mean . . .

Susan Sontag: Very eighteenth-century –

P. Johnson: . . . an out of scale island away from the world and you get that feeling that a boy gets in a tree house or a girl gets with her doll house, the idea of a miniature . . .

Just previously in the interview, Johnson had gone to the root of his conception of morality – a conception very like that of Oscar Wilde who never stopped attacking those whose good intentions led to the ultimate sin of boredom, of obviousness.

P. Johnson: . . . and incidentally the English that are so good about morals and city planning and have all those London County Councils and things they are so proud of, have ruined their city in the name of morality – even worse than New York in this hopeless chaos.

Chiding those with a bloodless common sense or a pretension to social purpose has always been a constant goal of Johnson, who has the unsuppressible desire to deflate pomposity especially when it happens to be the not inconsiderable magniloquence of himself. This kind of candid self-deprecation, a particularly New York and Jewish virtue, comes out in almost all of Johnson's pronouncements on himself:

Do we lack convictions? Do we just flit around in all directions like butterflies as we are accused of doing

Opposite above
PHILIP JOHNSON & JOHN BURGEE *Boston Public Library Extension*, 1973. Heavy, indeed gargantuan, use of a stylized classical language which is meant, somehow, to harmonize with the adjacent nineteenth-century library. Such pompous formalism was characteristic of American civic centres of the sixties and criticized for falling, heavily, between classicism and Modernism.

Opposite below
PHILIP JOHNSON & JOHN BURGEE, *Boston Public Library Extension*, interior, 1973. Diagrammatic, flat, pristine and still classical with a typical Late-Modern doorway: i.e. absence of wall, no mouldings or transition. The black cantilevered stairway divides the unitary material into two different elements.

'Follee', 1962. Cocktails are served in this six foot high Acropolis while two, white, aristocratic ducks paddle from shore to shore. The sylvan silence is broken by a hundred foot *jet d'eau* and a two inch waterfall. (Photo Ezra Stoller Associates).

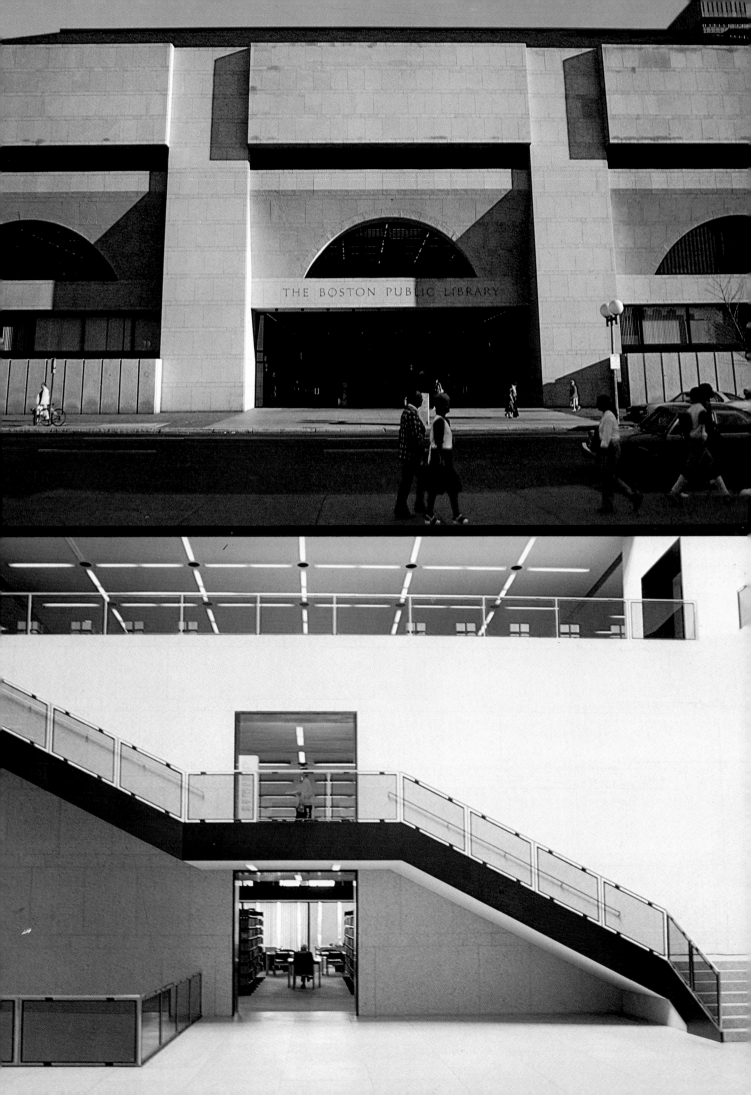

New York State Theater, Lincoln Center, New York City, 1964. Computerized fountain in front of the grand foyer with gold-leaf ceiling and Nadelman sculptures. Red plush and the glitter of crystal head-lights.

Termed Neo-Fascist by its many critics, at least this theatre has a certain ruthless conviction and Camp playfulness. The entrance is through a set of paired columns and up a flight to the grand foyer which rises through four levels of balcony to a gold-leaf ceiling. At either end of this space, which looks like a Mississippi steamboat turned inside-out, are two, gigantic, white, nude Nadelman statues that survey the theatre-goers like a race of icy-frozen Titans. Throughout the theatre, crystal headlights glitter like diamonds on a tiara.

The traditional, continental seating provides the traditional virtues of·maximum viewing with minimum disturbance. ('How can you improve on the shape of a Georgian spoon?')

Susan Sontag: 'The peculiar relation between Camp taste and homosexuality has to be explained . . . Homosexuals have pinned their integration into society on promoting the aesthetic sense. Camp is a solvent of morality. It neutralizes moral indignation, sponsors playful-ness.'

Opposite, left
PHILIP JOHNSON & JOHN BURGEE, *Thanksgiving Square Chapel*, Dallas, 1977. A spiral ziggurat based on many historical prototypes including a ninth-century tower in Samarra. The historicism may be considered Post-Modern but its unlikely presence, as an oversimplified corkscrew in Dallas, makes it typical of Late-Modernist unintended humour. Basically a diagrammatic spiral, where the stained glass follows the twists, it is conceived as precisionist sculpture not meaningful or carefully detailed form.

Opposite, right
PHILIP JOHNSON, *Kline Science Center*, New Haven, 1965. What Yale students called 'the tootsie rolls' and German critics faulted for having several 'false columns', this building nonetheless established a strong urban context and focal point at the end of an avenue.

by the people who are still with the International Style? The English, being articulate critics, say that we are all crazy here and that the functionalist tradition of the Bauhaus, as continued by the likes of Stirling, is the only answer. Well it may be, but it certainly isn't evident in the way things are getting built . . . I copy an eighteenth-century theater for Lincoln Center. My point is that everybody does; I am the only one who admits it?

Candid? The only one in a group of clowns, a group of court jesters, who will admit that he's joking?

Sleeping in Chartres

Philip Johnson was born in Cleveland, Ohio in 1906, the only son – he has two sisters – of a very successful corporation lawyer and a mother who taught the history of art in school. His first two architectural experiences, not untypical for the wealthy, young American boy on the Grand Tour of the Continent, were at the Parthenon (age 22) and Chartres (age 13). 'Catholicism was a great mystery to a young Puritan from the Midwest. There was a funeral going on. I was so moved I don't know why *I* wasn't dead.' In 1923 Johnson went to Harvard University where he became interested in piano playing, the Greek Classics and finally Greek philosophy. However, uncertain in his direction, he had several breakdowns and did not graduate for seven years. But then in 1928, half-way through an article on Modern architecture, the vision struck. 'The Conversion from Saul to Paul took place'. Johnson had found his Christ and seen the light. It was an article by the young Wesleyan instructor and emergent historian of the Modern Movement, Henry Russell Hitchcock. On the spot he realized what to do. He dashed out to the nearest bookstore and treated himself to a handsome German portfolio *Architecture in the Newest Age*. The following two summers he teamed up with

Asia House, New York City, 1960. By the late fifties, the sleek, supercool, glass facade had become standard New York architectural practice. This design by Johnson has all the usual qualities – a high reflective surface, transparency, smoothness and very shallow relief – with the additional property of being highly articulated. The dark tinted panels on the bottom vary in size and proportion while the top four floors are treated with a consistent transparency. All the high single panes and all the small, horizontal spandrels are picked out by silver coloured frames.

Actually, this building was the third and best of three alternative proposals, shown here, that Johnson had prepared for his client. Returning to his Harvard practice of designing for different tastes, Johnson was also returning to the pluralism of Sir John Soane and his 'Alternative proposals for Commissioner's Churches'. Many deplored this seeming lack of conviction – as if any one problem had one and only one solution – but the plurality of proposals seems to be much more realistic to actual conditions which are under-determined. Also it allowed Johnson to avoid compromising his conviction on any single project.

Harvard classmates and Hitchcock and went on a pilgrimage to the Holy Land of Modern architecture – Germany. Mies Van der Rohe said later: 'This [1930] was the year of the American Invasion.' The Americans, Hitchcock, Johnson and Barr came to Europe, discovered the International Style, took it back home and sold it in an exhibition at the Museum of Modern Art (which had just been founded by the Rockefellers, the Blisses, the Goodyears and other such families, some of whom were to become Johnson clients). In 1932, along with the exhibition, a book appeared called *The International Style: Architecture Since 1922*. It explained to Americans what the Modern Movement was all about: volume, asymmetry, flat roofs, white planes and – in spite of misguided attempts of certain pure functionalists who were then the strongest voices – aesthetics. There was a modern *style* suitable to, indeed a direct result of, the Machine Age. In 1934, Johnson produced another exhibition and book at the Museum of Modern Art – he was now Director of the Department of Architecture there – this time called *Machine Art*. Here were all the clean, clear, well-polished forms of industrial civilization: an all-chrome cash register, an all-chrome flush valve etc. The kind of industrial products which were carefully selected for their consistent purity seemed to support Bauhaus arguments, Herbert Read arguments, Le Corbusier arguments, that the machine led directly to Plato – pure, polished, Phileban forms.

And yet Johnson had doubts and a return bout of uncertainty. Perhaps his vision was a mirage. He became involved in all the fringe groups of the thirties. 'I think the only one I didn't get mixed up with was Communism – Communists weren't very amusing even then.' His first involvement took him down south to fight the Depression at the side of Mr. Huey Long, the populist demagogue and the man who did more for the under-privileged than most of the New Deal Democrats. Unfortunately Huey Long didn't quite understand the contribution of Harvard intellectuals in saving the South (Johnson was with a classmate) and they only saw him four times – so they left, depressed.

First project.

Second project.

Built project.

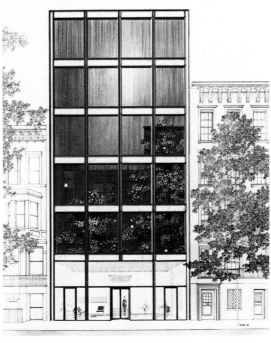

After returning home to his father's farm in Cleveland and having another unsuccessful try at populist politics, Johnson then got 'mixed up with all the right-wing fringes'. He wrote an article for the Harvard-based magazine *Hound and Horn* on Nazi architecture. It was an impassioned plea for the Nazis not to 'set the clock back' in a reactionary and racist return to the past. Johnson

Kneses Tifereth Israel Synagogue, Port Chester, New York, 1956. That Johnson should here be influenced by the eighteenth-century 'Revolutionary' architect Claude Nicolas Ledoux is very revealing – they both share a mixture of monumental formalism combined with a sometimes reactionary politics. Here two, white, pure forms, the rectangle and oval, are separated with an uncompromising boldness. The black picture-frame of steel further emphasizes the volume. On the interior, the bay rhythm is accentuated by suspended plaster canopies which recall visits to the Sir John Soane Museum in London while the domed vault of the vestibule reminds one of architectural pilgrimages to Baroque Rome.

This historicism and Neo-Classicism had a wide impact on the Modern Movement in the middle fifties, when they were both vehemently praised and condemned. (Photos Ezra Stoller Associates).

distinguished between three types of Nazi architecture and then pleaded for the Nazis to pick the third type – Mies Van der Rohe's purist monumentality evident in his design for Hitler's Reichsbank. After the Nazis became more clearly historicist, rejected the Modern style and the implications of their politics became known, Johnson lost his latest found faith, had yet another conversion and change of direction.

In 1940, at the age of thirty-four, he enrolled at Harvard's School of Architecture which was now under the directorship of the German refugee and leader of the Modern Movement – Walter Gropius. Being much older than the other students and having a penchant for luxurious expression which went way beyond the restraint of Gropius, Johnson found himself in natural conflict with the school. 'By the second year I was doing two designs for every problem – one for myself and one for the school. I still recommend that procedure today to all students.' Perhaps Johnson's conflict with Harvard was as much due to his style of life as to his design method since he started off living in Cambridge in a luxurious hotel suite until he subsequently moved into his own private 'Court House' – which he had in fact designed and submitted as his graduating thesis in 1943. After serving his time in the academy, Johnson then served a few years in the army as a latrine orderly, Private First Class Number 31–303–426. Johnson kept out of trouble and was, uncharacteristically, part of the background.

When the war finished, Johnson returned into the limelight in his old position as Director of the Department of Architecture and Design at the Museum of Modern Art – and embarked on two projects which had a wide influence both in Europe and America. These were his book on Mies Van der Rohe and his Glass House in New

Amon Carter Museum of Western Art, Fort Worth, Texas, 1961. This little Greek Temple of five archways was built to house the collection of the Fort Worth millionaire Amon Carter. The art consists mostly of bucking bronchos and whooping cowpunchers solidified in bronze – the 'Museum of Yippee-Yi-Yo' as *Time* magazine called it. In his quest for immortality, Johnson has claimed that his ultimate ambition is to be *L'Architect du Roi*, even if the King turns out to be a latter-day version of Horatio Alger, the self-made oil magnate.

The exterior peristyle of the museum is made of hand-carved, Texas shellstone columns which taper downwards and contrast with the black-tinted plate glass behind. The whole facade with its tapered columns and flat segmental arches is like an attenuated version of Le Corbusier's High Court at Chandigarh. On the interior, the lighting by Richard Kelly is recessed while the *cella* is covered in teak and pandanus.

Boissonnas House, New Canaan, 1956. A further development of the interplay between open and closed – Johnson's Glass House and his Guest House. Certainly the plan is his most masterful to date – a rich interlocking of spaces which both separates functions and unites areas where this is possible. Again the formal units are a glass and brick wall, but here a brick pier is also added on a square grid system to give a kind of intellectual ordering to the sprawling layout. By opening or closing this square bay, by using it in double height and by letting it enclose outdoor space, Johnson achieves a kind of spatial sequencing which is quite rare. (Photo Ezra Stoller Associates).

Canaan. Perhaps of equal influence, according to the historian Vincent Scully, were his talks at Yale University where he contrasted the functionalism of Harvard with his more formalist approach: 'I would rather sleep in the nave of Chartres Cathedral with the nearest john two blocks down the street than I would in a Harvard House [of Gropius] with back to back bathrooms.' Scully describes the effect of these 'pronouncements of the Devil' on him and other students in terms of their religious conversion from Saul to Paul, from building to architecture as an art. Indeed for the next twenty years Yale, with its lavishly tasteful magazine *Perspecta* and its articles on Johnson, was to lead the movement of American formalism. More particularly, Johnson's lapidary epigrams and historicist buildings were to justify it: 'Where form comes from I don't know, but it has nothing at all to do with the sociological aspects of architecture.' This summing up of his approach which occurred in *Perspecta* 1954 could be made by any number of American formalists five years later – the Harvard formalists Paul Rudolph, Ulrich Franzen, I. M. Pei, Victor Lundy or even Walter Gropius (by 1960) and the big name practitioners Eero Saarinen, Minoru Yamasaki, Ed Stone, Wallace Harrison etc. Indeed the formalist movement was international, sparking off such returns to the past as Neo-Liberty in Italy, Neo-Katsura in Japan and Neo-Ziggurat in Israel. However only Johnson among these historicists would admit what he was really up to and bring out the evasion of others with his laconically Camp pronouncements:

> Mies is such a genius! But I grow old! And bored! My direction is clear; eclectic tradition. This is not academic revivalism. There are no Classic orders or Gothic finials. I try to pick up what I like throughout history. We cannot not know history.

This history which Johnson could not not know amounted first of all to Mies in his Hodgson and

Museum of Modern Art Annex, New York City, 1964. The black steel and glass addition to the old, white Museum of Modern Art is an emphatic *hommage* to past technologies. Here the Miesian detailing reaches the level of jewellery. The polished, black-tinted glass and rounded corners recall the Art Nouveau of Victor Horta while the overall effect is mordant, even quite terrifying.

The outdoor garden shows Johnson's great interest in landscaping and the dendrological promenade. One strolls around sculpture, walks along canals, climbs over bridges, steps carefully between creeping myrtle and wandering roses, ducks under weeping beeches, slides through Japanese styrax, gaggles over Japanese cryptomerias, gurgles through a tangle of greenbriar and honeysuckle, gazes along the ligneous legumes of an ailanthus, ten European hornbeams and finally rests the eyeball on an evergreen groundcover of verdant pachysandra.

Boissonnas houses, to Sir John Soane and Claude Nicolas Ledoux in his Port Chester Synagogue and to the German architect K. F. Schinkel in his museum buildings. Architectural historians have already identified historical allusions at length, but basically they break down into two types: Miesian influences up to about 1960 and Neo-Classical influences from about 1954. But this breakaway from Mies, which was extremely criticized at the time as the beginning of American formalism, is more apparent than real. In fact if one studies the purely architectural evidence, what is striking is the consistent classical style of the whole. All the work could be described in this terminology. Thus even the Miesian architecture has a plinth or stylobate, entablature and some kind of trabeated structure. The external columns are usually too widely spaced to speak about a true intercolumniation, but still their relation to the infill walls is conceptually like a Renaissance *palazzo*. Furthermore either the overall form is symmetrical or a carefully balanced asymmetry which gives the classical feeling of harmony and resolution. This is further reinforced by the inclusion of cross axes and the heavy visual stops at all corners. At times Johnson produces an even more closed architecture than the classical. For instance he contrasts black and white at points of articulation to achieve the extreme visual closure that is comparable to a picture frame. His various attempts to produce an open architecture of interlocking spaces, such as the Boissonnas House, have not been followed up. Rather he has turned to the heavy arcuated rectangles of his museums or the gigantic columnar temples of his laboratories. In both cases he has chosen the emphatic visual *Gestalt* of classicism in preference to the light, open-ended aesthetic of recent engineering.

Partially this preference must be traced to his method of design which consists in working on detailed models – working like a sculptor on a homogeneous block of material, rather than either drawing or relying on picturesque accretions due to new technologies. A television aerial or mechanical duct would be as disturbing to his unified simplicity as it is to Mies' buildings. While Johnson is admired for his professionalism, it consists in the visual perfecting of well-known motifs rather than the creating of new ones. Indeed his originality is in the refinement and obsessive elegance of the building as a whole. Few other Modern architects, except some Italians, can compete with the finesse of this sensibility. At times, such as the New York State Theater, it falls into historicist allusion and strained pomposity without the saving grace of wit or polished overstatement. Architectural historians sometimes follow Johnson into this trap, identifying influences rather than concentrating on the more relevant question of his sensibility and place in American society.

Children like a bridge to cross
When visiting New York I went over to photograph the Seagram Building (designed by Mies) and pay a call on Vincent Scully's Devil himself (who has an office on the top floor). I brought along my pocket-sized Kodak Instamatic, this superior piece of goon technology, to photograph Seagram from directly below. I wanted the vertigo shot, the dizzying, New York shot of Seagram receding into heaven like some celestial railroad track – zzzsswooooosh – parallel bronze bullets shooting up thirty-nine floors to the knife edge roof which – boooiinnggs – out like some kind of bronze Arabian scimitar. The roof line is *actually* flat, but it appears as a curve because it isn't corrected for optical distortion like a Greek Temple. Anyway, I wandered around zig-zag, drunk, with head cocked back like some baby dicky-bird in feeding, picking out the historical overtones – Phidias, Michelozzo, Schinkel, Doric columns, intercolumniation and – well, never

MIES VAN DER ROHE and PHILIP JOHNSON, *Seagram Building* from below entrance; unlike a Greek Temple the architecture has not been corrected for optical distortions.

Four Seasons Restaurant, Seagram Building, New York City, 1959. This four and one-half million dollar restaurant is located on the first floor of the Seagram Building. It represents Johnson's first Camp departure for affluent New Yorkers determined to enjoy themselves on a gustatory binge (*Time* magazine: 'as hedonistic as a Caesar's court'). However, *Time* moguless Clare Booth Luce 'can't stand the place . . . because the curtain ripples make her nervous'. These are made out of thin chains of anodized aluminium which are looped across the windows and chatter and clatter when the air-conditioner is turned on. The cluster of brass rods, designed by the sculptor Richard Lippold, the thin rods of the stairway and the bubbling pool all add to the effervescent tinkle of money changing hands and food being served.

mind. I snapped back my head into forward drive and coasted into the open and bare lobby (travertine, bronze, stainless steel etc.) and thence into an express elevator to the top floors. Once on the thirty-ninth floor, the walls slid silently apart and we were debouched onto deep black marble with white veining. As I turned left, suddenly I felt this gentle hand on my shoulder – 'You must be going to my office' (I was wearing my English three-piece-Glen-Plaid-identibadge). 'You must be Philip Johnson', I said, quickly stuffing away my Kodak Instamatic. He looked across at me with that benevolent, relaxed smile, that 'we know how to handle things here' look that makes you feel warm molasses inside. He ushered me past a glass entrance, a Picasso tapestry, a few Pop paintings, Robert Indiana's *A DIVORCED MAN HAS NEVER BEEN THE PRESIDENT* and then into his private office overlooking the East River. A large expanse of tinted Thermo-plate, a few bronze I-beam mullions, one or two potted palms, an Indian Rubber plant, a few chairs and a polished walnut table upon which was that fantastic piece of architectural literature, the colour-illustrated *Philip Johnson* (which was subsidized by Philip

Johnson, composed by Philip Johnson and even, modestly, reviewed by Philip Johnson).

After explaining the purpose of my visit – to obtain permission to quote from various articles and interviews – Johnson launched into one of his favourite subjects: the lack of a civic-minded tradition for which large, monumental public spaces could be constructed.

> Why is it the nineteenth century and even the Robber Barons had so such more public spirit than we do today? They knew how to enjoy themselves, they had the buccaneering spirit, they drained the West of its wealth – but for a purpose. To build grand spaces like Pennsylvania Station, which we just tear down, or Grand Central Station, the greatest space in New York City, which we go and ruin with all those Kodak advertisements.

I pushed my Instamatic deeper into my pocket and asked Johnson the rather delicate question of whether I could quote from his article on the Nazis – delicate because no other publication on Johnson had gone into his connections of the thirties. 'Sure, what did I say?' Johnson was ready to come out with the truth even before he remembered what it was. Just as I finished reminding him of his triple-decker distinction between three types of Nazi, we were interrupted by some invisible sign on his command module that indicated clients had arrived and it was time for me to be extricated.

As I reached the door, shook hands and started to leave, in walked three Fat City New York Clients all lit out in their blue Alumicron suits, Countess Mara ties (Countess Mara, the hundred dollar tie) brilliantined hair swept back over their sun-tanned creases like Hollywood moguls circa 1947. The place was literally exploding with signals, status badges, pecking-orders, classifiers. Johnson was sporting his it-had-to-be a Tripler Broadcloth shirt, shooting his cuffs through reticent grey pin-stripe, out-signalling everybody in sight – exuding so much easy-going self-confidence that you'd hand over your nest-egg in a shot. Safe keeping? The super-rich find it all but irresistible. Culture centres, museums, the 4½ million dollar Four Seasons Restaurant, private houses for the Rockefellers and the Henry Fords, the Dallas monument to JFK, the New York Pavilion for the World's Fair, all his commissions are prestige jobs in a monumental style. Johnson had written of the new Nazi Regime in 1933 an analysis which was coming true for both America and himself:

> . . . architecture will be monumental. That is instead of bath-houses, Siedlungen, employment offices and the like, there will be official railroad stations, memorial museums, monuments. The present regime is more intent on leaving a visible mark of its greatness than in providing sanitary equipment for workers.

Critics compare Lincoln Center and Johnson's New York State Theater to Mussolini's Third Rome – Noam Chomsky says that what is needed in American society at large 'is a kind of denazification'. The accusations of 'Fascism' are ricocheting around the country from New Left to New Right and nearly everyone is agreed that labels from the thirties apply. But where is the Fascist Regime, the philosophy of power, the takeover group? It doesn't exist except as some kind of covert, deep instinctual drive which even the political demagogues prefer to keep in hiding today – as opposed to the thirties when they were openly proclaiming Fascism. At that time, even the poets and architects of Futurism were openly proclaiming their aggressive commitments to war and the beauty of destruction. Fillipo Tomaso Marinetti, the founder of Futurism, could find the greatest possible aesthetic delight in the Italian Colonial War against Ethiopia:

> For twenty-seven years we Futurists have rebelled against the branding of war as anti-aesthetic . . . Accordingly we state . . . war is beautiful because it establishes man's dominion over the subjugated machinery by means of gas masks, terrifying megaphones, flame throwers and small tanks. War is beautiful because it initiates the dreamt-of metalization of the human body. War is beautiful because it enriches a flowering meadow with the fiery orchids of machine guns. War is beautiful because it combines the gunfire, the cannonades, the cease fire, the scents and the stench of putrefaction into a symphony. War is beautiful because it creates new architecture, like that of the big tanks, the geometrical formation flights, the smoke spirals from burning villages, and many others . . . Poets and artists of Futurism! . . . Remember these principles of an aesthetics of war so that your struggle for a new literature and a new graphic art . . . may be illumined by them.

This is probably about as far as an aesthetics of war and enjoyment of destruction can go and when I questioned Johnson about his commitment in the thirties he was much more circumspect.

CJ: Well, what was your attitude towards the Nazis there. You were connected somehow –

PJ: On no – totally outside. I did . . . um . . . go to Berlin after the War started. Which was very, very challenging . . . in 1939 . . . for just the sheer excitement. I mean nobody got nowhere . . . I knew some American correspondents who hated my guts and thought I was a spy. I don't know really how they figured that one out???

Actually it was William Shirer whom Johnson met in Danzig then – who describes this meeting and the suspicions it aroused:

> Dr. Boehmer, press chief of the Propaganda Ministry in charge of this trip, insisted that I share a double room in the hotel here with Philip Johnson, an American fascist who says he represents Father Coughlin's *Social Justice*. None of us can stand the fellow and suspect he is spying on us for the Nazis. For the last hour in our room here he has been posing as anti-Nazi and trying to pump me for my attitude. I have given him no more than a few bored grunts.

PJ: Shirer's a very irresponsible journalist . . . very third rate writer . . .

CJ: You were in Danzig then . . .

PJ: Yes, I went on one of those expeditions you'll find . . . Yes it was that night in Danzig that Shirer writes about. But uh . . . I really, I'd suppose that anyone who wasn't actively crusading was suspicious and I probably did lean over backwards . . . No I was wrong . . . I hoped something good would come out of it. No this was *before* concentration camps were started of course. But still no excuse. Speer has it right, I know. But of course I weren't no spy . . .

We had previously touched on the Modern Movement's ubiquitous compromises with all the Fascist regimes of the time and Johnson had underlined the apolitical position of Mies – which seemed somehow particularly relevant to his own pragmatic position.

PJ: . . . If the Devil himself offered Mies a job he would take it.

CJ: Yeah, quite . . . Well that's true of all the major architects . . . the Pioneers of the period. I mean Le Corbusier going to Vichy.

PJ: Corbusier going to Vichy, Neutra wishing that Hitler would give him a job.

CJ: Gropius.

PJ: I mean – semi-joking – but-uh-of course! But then – uh – a lot of people – Sibyl Moholy-Nagy can't forgive Mies. But it was going on . . .

CJ: But you even find Gropius writing a letter to Goebbels in 1934 – have you seen those?

PJ: – Don't tell me!

CJ: Oh yes, saying you must not get rid of the new Modern architecture – it's 'Germanic', it's Schinkelesque, it harkens back to the Gothic period . . .

PJ: Pevsner –

CJ: What?

PJ: Sainted Sir Nikolaus . . . wanted to become an honorary Aryan and stay on . . . I forget where this is . . . but uh – Gropius????

CJ: Yes there is a book written by Barbara Miller Lane called *Architecture and Politics in Germany 1918–1945* . . . page 181 . . .

PJ: Thanks, well I probably won't read the book.

CJ: But it's surprising – all those architects were trying to make overtures. The problem I think was, among other things, that Hitler and Goebbels both came out for a 'crystal-clear functionalism' in 1932 . . .

PJ: Of course –

CJ: And you could read it either way.

PJ: You could read it *both* ways. Oh, reading Speer is one of the really exciting things. Have you read the

Sheldon Memorial Art Gallery, Lincoln, Nebraska, 1963. One of Johnson's masterpieces of Middle Camp of 'failed seriousness' at its best. The gigantic columnar order on the exterior contradicts the two-storey reality within. 'The essence of the exterior design, of course, is the splayed column. I don't know where I got it. But the idea of these curving columns, curving up from their bases and then into the arch itself; that is the fascination of them.' The fascination of travertine columns turning into a wall, arch, entablature and ceiling exists also on the inside which is like a homogeneous piece of marble carved away by a diamond cutter. The eye easily spills over these gently modulated surfaces until it comes to rest finally on the other objects, the stairway-bridge, the gold-leaf lighting discs and an occasional *objet d'art*.

Susan Sontag: 'Camp is the consistently aesthetic experience of the world. It incarnates a victory of "style" over "content", "aesthetics" over "morality", of irony over tragedy'. (Photos Ezra Stoller Associates).

architectural section? Oh, but read the architectural part. Because Speer was an extremely sensitive man and really a businessman architect – he'd be good in America, a really great skyscraper architect, an organizer. But with this *mad* architect – uh – Hitler, who didn't have any intention to run the country at all – during the war. Spent the time designing – and made the drawings *himself* sometimes. Oh, you must take a glance at the book.

What the . . . HITLER! An architect? *Mad* architect? Somehow it made a lot of fortuitous sense as if Johnson had suddenly illuminated a whole area of the architect's dreams, the secret desires and warped fantasies which usually cannot stand the light of day and remain hidden – even to the architect himself. But Hitler! A Thousand Year Reich . . .

The Sheldon Memorial Art Gallery, Lincoln Nebraska. The Sheldon Museum, a clear reference back to Fascist designs of the thirties: massive, blank arcades from Mussolini's Third Rome which appear as fashion backdrops in *Vogue* magazine; Hitler and Troost's House of German Art in Munich with its classical colonnade and classical composition – stripped of any historicist ornament to combine Modern purity with Greek propriety – these are the roots of the Sheldon Museum. The exterior temple front, raised on a travertine stylobate, filled in by a travertine blank arcade is all surrounded by hand-carved splayed pilasters that curve up from their bases in concave swoops to merge with the entablature in an eye-ease symphony of unified, moulded travertine. It's as if a sculptor, a jeweller, took some gigantic block of homogeneous marble and went at it with a scalpel and polishing gun. All the surfaces melt into each other including the concave, four-sided, hand-carved columns – which were chosen specifically for the purpose. 'The problem, as usual, was the corner column. A concave

curve at the cornice was unthinkable, so it is convex, warping toward the typical concave base.' Not only were these columns hand-carved, but they were first erected in Italy to '*test the play of shadows*'. The columns for a museum way out in the boondocks of Lincoln Nebraska were first erected in Italy – to test the play of shadows where even *the light is different*!

The interior. Well the interior is made up of this thirty foot high Great Hall, glazed both sides so that you can see clear through from one side to the other as you pass under a central bridge – a free-standing, gold-hued, scissor staircase which cuts up the space and leads almost *nowhere* like some Baroque stairway of Balthasar Neumann in the *corps de logis* and like that – a pure architectural *promenade* meant to display people in their latest finery and to make everybody into children. 'The point of this is it is so much fun to be on a bridge. It is like a little child. He longs for a brook with a little bridge to cross. And then he runs back and forth across the bridge. I think we are all children at heart. It is always nice to cross the bridge.'

The whole space glows with a lemon-yellow hue of

gilded sunlight – honey curtains, gold carpets, golden staircase, gold-leaf lighting discs whirling above like flying saucers made out of 14 carat bullion – Johnson has this kind of failed Midas touch – everything he touches turns to gold . . . leaf.

Keepers of the architectural conscience shuddered. *Architectural Design* said: 'What commenced as a continuation of classical tradition, now ends up as the most gargantuan piece of mannerism.' Bruno Zevi condemned the Neo-Classicism *in toto*: '. . . the dullest and most reactionary monumentalism, the most arbitrary and insignificant caprices'. Johnson had achieved another *succès de scandale*, another one of 'the most sincerely hated buildings in the world'. And yet, characteristically Johnson himself, with his unsuppressible perception and candour, was out in the field gently mocking his own uncertainty, his own insecurity, which would lead him to design Camp symbols to a non-existent public realm while asserting at the same time that this lack of belief was itself a possible cause of destructive potential.

The only principle that I can conceive of believing in is the Principle of Uncertainty. It is a brave architect that

can possess convictions and beliefs, and keep his tongue out of his cheek . . . I really don't know why I designed these [buildings] the way I did. Others will tell me.

In a sense, Johnson's buildings represent this loss of belief as does so much other formalist architecture. Yet the desire to believe and produce credible monuments is still there, even if it has no acceptable outlet, even if there is no credible public realm or religion.

What we have lost is a public passion for greatness. No cathedrals? Not even great public nuclear plants? What is our generation going vicariously to enjoy as in old days, the palace, the church, or the Acropolis?

It almost sounds right – but 'vicariously enjoy'? This is the Camp reading of High Culture. All Johnson's best works have this 'failed seriousness', this heroic gesture which backfires, which explodes into the grin of a sardonic clown. At best – in his self-mocking comments or his Sheldon Museum – he attains a level of candid introspection and exaggeration usually reserved as moments of truth for the court jester.

3.2 BRUCE GOFF
– THE MICHELANGELO OF KITSCH

This article, written in 1978, hardly does justice to the complete architecture of Bruce Goff, which is often serious, beautiful and complex. Rather it illuminates one angle which has been overlooked. For a balanced view see the issue of Architectural Design *on Goff, No. 10, 1978, (and the books mentioned therein), where this article first appeared.*

Recall your worst architectural experience; think back to the moment when you entered that sleazy bedsitter all decked out with its bathetic knick-knacks and *el cheapo* furniture. Remember your first encounter with the sad, pretentious world of Babbit, of lower-middle class taste run amok with chintz on the kitchen cabinet, of Ideal Home decor, of plastic strip-on chrome, in short of Yuk-Taste. Remember the revulsion, the horror followed by simple distaste? The basic discovery that schlock is unredeemable, beyond the pale, even too much for Robert Venturi and friends to rescue? Well you were wrong, there is a poet of the unredeemable and his name was Bruce Alonzo Goff (*was* because the Alonzo was dropped after an early attempt to mimic the three-worded Frank Lloyd Wright, his constant friend and paragon). Goff is a better architect than Wright, 'Wrightier' one is tempted to say, at least when it comes to the obsession with geometric themes and ornamentalized geometry. His spatial flow is flowier, his houses are much funnier and lighter and cosier. His yellow-pea-green thick-pile carpets climbing off the wall and into the conversation pit are thicker than Wright's. So, asks the Department of Architectural Justice, why isn't Goff on a two cent U.S. stamp like his *liebermeister*? That is a question which all Americans, concerned with popular taste, should ask themselves.

Undeniably Goff's houses are popular with those who live in them. They are also popular as a form of entertainment, one might even say 'performance', having been featured in *Life* magazine, *Popular Science* and a Chevrolet trade magazine called *Friends* (a fact which leads to more commissions). Build one 'Umbrella House' and the Mid-Western Harder family who see it while getting a grease job on their Chevy will have you build them a Japanese 'Turkey House'. Why a house that looks like a lot of clucking turkeys – and with orange carpet on the roof? Why? Because the owners are turkey farmers, and conscientious objectors, and Goff has just returned from Japan where he has seen endless upturned roofs and orange is the colour of turkey combs, and besides outdoor carpet is probably a good roofing material.[1] And why not? After all this is the MID-West where there are no Vitruvian rules, and free-association architecture has always had a hold. It's the architecture of allusion, of throwing together parts *ad hoc* – for the specific purpose of making something new and saving cash. Orange outdoor carpet on the roof! (Liberace at least put it on the ground, and it was green). According to a time-honoured formula one never does this sort of thing on the *outside* of a house, where it can cause traffic accidents. It could never happen in Boston ('I don't mind what you do, as long as you don't do it on the street where it will frighten the horses.'). It would never happen in London as Inigo Jones insisted ('Outwardly every wyse man carrieth a

Glen and Luetta Harder House, Mountain Lake, Minnesota, 1970–2. Orange carpets and orange rainplates dance across the prairie plains around the rugged fieldstones over the waving corn and near the clucking turkeys. Architecture that is responsive to local metaphor, to the animals of the farmyard, architecture suggestive of previous work – Richardson citadels and Japanese eaves. In plan the buildings have a symmetry and centrality not so apparent on the exterior: giant chimneys, made from rounded fieldstones with hidden mortar, are at opposite ends of a living space which focuses on a larger fireplace, the 'heart' of the home. Conventional ornament is transformed not disregarded: a continuous line of light bulbs follows the exposed ridge beams; glazed mosaic tile contrasts with the fireplace boulders; strip lighting is between bolted two-by-twelves with exposed bolts and triangular mirror mosaic. The ultimate *ad hoc* ornamentation? Buttons, sequins and artificial insemination tubes, for turkeys, were used as see-through decoration.

graviti in Publicke Places, yet inwardly hath his imaginancy set on fire, and sumtimes licenciously flying out, as nature hirself doeth often times stravagantly.').

However in Mountain Lake Minnesota it's the *outside* that sumtimes licenciously flies out with its orange, pulsating thick-pile, and its swooping corner chimneys, its random turd-like rocks held together with 'outta-sight' Japanese mortar, its floating swallow-tail rain plates which hover over the flues like so many Calder mobiles – orange carpet!!! It will frighten the turkeys . . .

When Bruce Goff finished the Ledbetter House in Norman Oklahoma in 1947 with its interior lily pool garden-cum-waterfall ramp and Woolworth Ashtray Decoration (forget your old Egg and Dart) 14,500 people from Norman trudged through the house in a two day charity event – and Norman only had 22,000 people. It was the 'largest non-athletic event in Norman's history', and as one appreciative Normatron said 'It's the biggest thrill since my first ride on an elevator'.[2] Goff has turned architecture into a performance, a popular art form that *happens* and doesn't just sit there dumbfounded holding onto its reinforcing bars. When the Bavinger family built their own Goffouse in Norman (Goff gets his clients so involved they have to give up their normal work) their spiral, helicord house, their SNAIL HOUSE, 50,000 people came out to watch over the years, and the Bavingers, knowing a performance art when they see one, charged the people an entrance fee – 1 dollar per view, – $50,000 just to see this crazy snail get built out of stone.[3] It helped pay for the house. But the Bavingers and Goff didn't stop exploiting life there. Two-thirds of the

house is thrown together out of used parts, cast-offs, rocks which had been cluttering up neighbouring farmland, uprooted walnut trees nobody wanted (the stair-treads are solid walnut), and sixty shiny, stainless steel cables which cost them five cents each (and that wasn't much in 1952).

These steel cables are in fact biplane braces, lifted from their airborne context and hung on a central mast – which itself is robbed from the oil-drilling industry. Adhocism, *bricolage*, coping with what's at hand, do-it-yourself, what Reyner Banham called *à propos* Goffism 'the Army and Navy Surplus Aesthetic' (he left out the Airforce).[4] Goff's greatest *ad hoc* victory on this site was not the carpet on the ceiling, not the fish net balconies swooping over twenty open feet of indoor conservatory living ('You don't use a vacuum cleaner here you clean with a hose.') . . . but the lighting fixture in the conversation pit, a glass bowl under the parent's sleeping pod, which is kind of a conversation piece, which is in fact . . . an old gunner's bubble robbed from a B.52 bomber! ADHOCISM! Fantastic! But . . . why bother? Especially when they make similar kinds of glass bowls anyway, *real* lighting fixtures. Because behind Goff and these Mid-Western Yankees is a kind of pride in doing it the hard way, and not paying for it, a pride in using coal waste as rustication (black anthracite as basement), discarded glass cullet as a decorative crystal . . . which even tells the time (the shifting sun changes prismatic hue, 'can you give me the colour, please?'), a pride in using old cellophane strips below a skylight ('PLASTIC RAIN'), a pride in using creosote rope as a decorative moulding, cake tins as light reflectors, translucent coasters, more plastic rain, over the High Altar of a church of oil drillers, and goose feathers cuddling a skydome . . . YUK-TASTE . . . yuk, yuk, yuuuckk.

Metaphors and taste cultures

When Goff designs a house (and 98% of his commissions are private houses for the just-arrived Mid-Westerner) he designs it like an Abstract Expressionist – from rhythmical themes, rather than from explicit visual images. He composes a two-dimensional abstraction, building up by stages according to a method comparable to the early abstractionist Kandinsky – 'from point, to line, to form'. The end forms can be either hard and geometric, like the hexagonal shingle of the Nicol House, or soft and flowing like the glutinous curves of the Gryder House, or a combination of both, as in the Harder House already mentioned. In any case they are inspired by geometry, the paintings of Klimt or the music of Debussy – kind of unleashed on the world after an initial inspirational uncorking by one of these sources. The rhythms take over, a design idea emerges, some damn hexagonal pattern becomes so obsessive that it marches right through the bedrooms and bathrooms (hexagonal toilets?) and erupts way outside on a cantilevered pole, as Holy Christmas, a green, translucent outdoor, Woolworth night-light. What the hell are these green, bug-eyed, sparkling Woolworth ashtrays doing in our Kansas

Bavinger House, Norman, Oklahoma, 1951–5. A continuous open space spirals up in which various saucers of living space are suspended: no doors or partitions in the conventional sense, but instead a division by plants, carpets on the ceiling and fish net. The house was built by the owner, an artist, and his wife, from various sources including a 55 foot mast made from two deep-well drilling pipes, rubble masonry, sewing machine frames (used as scaffolding), biplane braces, and 'bomber-blisters' used for light fixtures and lavatory wash bowls.

City suburb anyway??? Everywhere else are colonial clapboards and Half-Witted Tudor with their sprawling lawns and gentle refeenment and then comes these glowing, schlocky Five-and-Dime cigarette coffins that march all over the house, and even right up the front door. What does Dr. Hyde think he is doing!!! It'll run down the neighbourhood, all that plastic rain on the inside, and soon we'll have neon, and billboards, and yes, the arrival of the Great Unwashed. (Goff's first teacher Endacott, of Rush, Endacott and Rush, where he apprenticed at the age of twelve (12!) confided to the young designer that the Tulsians *are* the great unwashed, when seen from the well-groomed shores of the East Coast.)[5]

Actually, Goff's clients are, for the most part, sensible professionals like Dr. Hyde – bankers, artists, farmers, collectors of Americana, Mid-Western self-made individualists – who have seen or read about a Goff house and like the aesthetic of low-cost *ad hoc* building. As Jeffrey Cook says 'Goff has orchestrated the great dreams of small people and not the reverse', not the Palladian or Miesian fantasies of the Fords and Rockefellers.

The surprising thing is that with a method of abstract design, which could be almost Modern and Miesian in its abstraction, very representational buildings result, quite by chance. And it is these implicit metaphors which have proved so popular with a certain taste culture. The Ledbetter House, 1947, was seen as a 'solar house', and the first to be featured in a *Life* article as some kind of freaky Martian deposit. The Ford House, Aurora Illinois 1948, was inevitably called the 'Umbrella House' because of its explosion of quonset ribs around the central mast. But, as the usual mixed Goffian metaphor, it was also called the pumpkin, the tomato, the spider trap, hangar, Hollywood Spaceship, and the fat sprout flanked by cotyledons. In short the metaphors fixed to these strange new shapes were mostly organic as they were with Antonio Gaudí's similar work in Barcelona fifty years earlier.

Ford House, Aurora, Illinois, 1948. Quonset ribs radiate from a central core which marks the heart of the house. The immediate associations are with natural forms – an explosive fountain, a sunburst or flower blooming out. Salvaged, creosoted rope is used decoratively for important areas around the front door and coal waste and glass cullet are used to cast a coloured light which, if the sun is shining and the owner thinking, can indicate the time. The 'Umbrella House' raised some eyebrows in suburban Illinois and the Fords put up a temporary sign 'We don't like your house, either'.

Hyde House, Kansas City, Kansas, 1965. This house constructed for Dr. Hyde and his family features the green Woolworth ashtray – here skewered way out, nine of them placed on the diagonal, to enclose a night light. Such long cantilevers jut out all over the roof giving it the vague appearance of a multiple-bug-eyed Martian insect with, of course, Indian decoration. The roof of the house is thankfully flat, something that saved it from the tornado that went directly overhead. Other 'Prairie Style' details include clerestory lighting and low overhanging eaves.

Conneil Gryder House, Ocean Spring, Mississippi, 1960, was built for the owner of a family chain of shoe stores who was also an elder in the Presbyterian church. The parents' and children's wings are at either end of this preying mantis – that is they open out onto the conical balconies, the ears, which balance precariously in a water garden. The entrance is over a bridge, through some circular hoola-hoops in steel and an insect's mouth which is set off from the violet stucco and gold trim.

Indeed if Goff has an obvious precursor it is not so much Frank Lloyd Wright, whom he does claim as the influence, but the much more fantastic Catalan who also took nature and rhythmical construction as his departure points. Both Goff and Gaudí are led to excess as nature is, whereas Wright, except for his later work, remains more balanced and moderate. One can imagine Goff producing the equivalent of a century plant, a venus fly-trap, a passion flower – in fact he has produced a 'liveable orchid' at the Gryder home, whereas Wright more often than not stayed away from such conceits as his 'Holly-hock House'.[6] For Goff as for Gaudí 'originality is going back to origins', that is to nature; deriving ornament from crystalline structures, plant-forms, insect forms. Occa-sionally they both derive ornament from mechanical left-overs such as used sewing-machines.[7] The major differ-ence between these two adhocists is that Gaudí was motivated by social, religious, indeed, public symbolism, whereas Goff's representation is essentially private.

But this private language is not uncommunicative because it is rooted in accessible metaphor and local reference. In addition to the popular epithets mentioned above, his houses have been called 'airplanes' because of their struts and cables, and 'insects' because of their spikey feelers which shoot out from the 'head' or 'tail' of the roof. In several buildings such as the Gryder House an insect face is visible, but it is definitely an Oriental insect with turned up eyes slit at the corners. Often the 'body' of the house is symmetrical like an animal body, placed on legs and centred on the 'heart', the hearth, the fireplace or conversation pit – so a subconscious identity is felt between our body and the building.

One projects a bodily metaphor, a clear set of human dimensions – beginning, middle and end, up/down, left/right – that help fix orientation in a possibly chaotic field (and Goff's work *is* possibly chaotic).[8] But beyond this basic human coordinate system and image are the sensual human parts, the erogenous zones of architec-ture that Goff especially dresses up. Doors, windows and other orifices are outlined with ornamental bands or decked out with a plumage of coloured glass and beads. Fireplace and chimney, the definite focii of the house, both heart and face, are surrounded by mosaics and plastic strips, which scatter light in all directions. Roofs flare out at the corners, protective wings in one instance, and funny heads in another. While these erotic images are similar to the Art Nouveau buildings of Nancy, with

163

their tits and bums and other less mentionable delights (barely concealed in the fireplace), the anthropomorphism is not total and certainly not preconceived by Goff, but rather allowed as a possible consequence of organic design. Whenever a non-historic language of architecture is used people will compare the unusual shapes to familiar objects, they will find metaphorical images, and in Goff's unique shapes these images are closer to the body than they are to the machine, to weird insects than to the Parthenon.

Hence another reason for the popularity, for the many features in *Life* and *Popular Science*, for the crowds which mill around the latest Goffery. The images and themes appeal not to the whole populace, not to the elite and high culture of the profession, but to the lower-middle taste culture – the readers of *Life*: thus the accent on the hearth, symbol of familial security, the omnipresence of water and indoor growth, common themes of relaxation and escape. The easy beauty of shimmering crystal, the comforting softness of thick-pile carpet and goose feathers embracing an orifice. This is not the last word in Brutalism, this is not the five shades of white of the New York Five – this is the architecture of the solar plexus meant for another audience, sensual in orientation and non-intellectual by inclination.

Herbert Gans, the sociologist who developed the notion of differing taste cultures, marks out five basic (but not rigid) American types, varying from High Culture (that of the creators) to Upper-Middle (basically *Time* and *Newsweek* readers and Leonard Bernstein) to Lower-Middle (Harold Robbins, *Readers Digest* and 90% of what you last saw on T.V.) to Low Culture (the followers of Spiro Agnew and John Wayne) to Quasi-Folk Low Culture (rural and ethnic groups that sometimes express themselves 'with elaborately painted and colourful graffiti'). A sixth taste culture is added to these called 'Youth, Black and Ethnic' which covers such things as Hippies, Yippies, Drop Outs, Jesus Freaks, Pill Poppers, Blacks, the readers of the *Village Voice*, that is to say basically all those left out in the first five categories.

Most of us, it would appear, just consume what we like and call that culture, or its equivalent, and reserve less savoury terms for everything else which is beyond the pale (like Goffisms). But a dispassionate analysis like that of Gans, or perhaps any market researcher, reveals the actual variety of values and the conflicts, not to say disjunctions, inversions and hiccups that exist between them. These disjunctions lead to strange feelings of unreality when one is confronted by strong values from another taste culture. As T. S. Eliot put it in *Sweeney Agonistes*:

> If he was alive then the milkman wasn't and the rent-collector wasn't
> And if they were alive then he was dead.

An extreme example of taste-culture-shock, which an upper-middle suburbanite might feel when driving past a lower-middle Goff for the first time. Herbert Gans:

> Numerically [the Lower-Middle Taste Culture] is America's dominant taste culture and public today. It attracts middle- and lower-middle-class people in the lower-status professions, such as accountancy and public school teaching, and all but the lowest-level white-collar jobs . . . The aesthetics of lower-middle culture emphasize substance; form must serve to make substance more intelligible or gratifying. Dramatic materials express and reinforce the culture's own ideas and feelings . . . Its heroes are

Joe Price House, Bartlesville, Oklahoma, 1956. Price describes his ultimate 'bachelor's' pad as 'an escape from business . . . Away from the stifling blanket of false morality . . . I wanted everyone to sit on the floor . . . so soften it with four inches of carpet and foam pad. Without support the back gets tired, therefore the walls are sloped, running the soft carpet up them and even continuing it onto the ceiling . . . Sink a hexagonal pit in the centre of the room for conversations . . . since music must be a basic principle in this house, give the main room a triangular shape so that . . .' 'Plastic rain' hangs from the ceiling, a sculpture is made from green string, and white goose feathers stuck into latex cement help modulate the light and sound.

ordinary people or extraordinary ones who turn out to be ordinary in that they accept the validity of traditional virtues, such as 'wholesomeness', and traditional institutions, such as religion . . . The lower-middle public provides the major audience for today's mass media; it is the group for which these media program most of their content . . . this public probably uses much less nonfiction than the upper-middle public (except for self-help and 'how-to' content that aids people in solving personal problems and taking care of home, car, and other consumer goods) . . . Lower-middle culture does not often treat subjects in a manner that would disturb or upset its public, but then neither does any other culture, including high culture.

Lower-middle art continues to be mainly romantic and representational, shunning harsh naturalism as well as abstraction. Still, . . . [they] are also ready to accept popular adaptations of nonrepresentational high and upper-middle culture art: imitations of cubists like Feininger in which the cubist method is altered in a more representational direction, and op art which is softened and romanticized by the use of pastel colours. Reproductions of the work of high culture artists can also be found in lower-middle outlets; for example, the landscapes of Cézanne and Van Gogh, the dancers of Degas, and the cityscapes of Buffet.[9]

Goff's work is accessible to this public because it is always designed around clear-cut themes – prisms, trapezoids, spirals, crystals, lozenges, amoebae – which are repeated insistently. The lower-middle taste culture wants high definition of these themes – and they get it in America with Morris Lapidus, John Portman, Minoru

Yamasaki . . . and Bruce Alonzo Goff. But he alone is the real master of these themes, the Prometheus of the Woolworth Ashtray Style, the Pied-Piper of the Woodbutcher's Art, the Big Daddy of the Lone American Architect. So many American architectural students are now given advanced training on Levittown and Las Vegas by Robert Venturi, PhDs in mobile homes by Vincent Scully, Disney seminars by Charles Moore – 110 credit hours of Camp, Kitsch and Schlock at Yale University – these *experts* of the *démodé*, these professionals of bad taste can't begin to reach the nightmarish beauty of Goff's work because their heart and taste culture aren't in it. Goff has a heart of pure tinsel, pure cellophane rainstrip, pure gold-anodized metallic roof-strip, pure yyuk!

Surrealism and Beauty

Goff has remembered among his storehouse of quotes, the vast collection of varied reading that the self-taught feed on like yeast, one that justifies both the acceptance *and* rejection of his work: 'someone once said that the perception of beauty itself is always accompanied by feelings of strangeness . . . it's part of the process of the recognition of beauty.'[10] Strange, queer, outlandish, awful, new, avant-garde, marvellous, terrible, outta-sight, shocking – the Marquis de Sade put his finger on the theory of the avant-garde when he said 'man likes nothing so much as a shock to the nervous system' (or something like that). Right, 110 volts, jack up the power, beat the avant-garde, fire those old tired neurons that have been dulled by 100 years of The Tradition of the New. Make it so outrageously new that even Wright looks positively Renaissance, make the Expressionists look like nineteenth-century Goths, make every Modern architect from Mies to Corb look like some Beaux-Arts classicist on a gridiron – yes, Goff is so extreme that he makes the rest of the avant-garde look like a bunch of prep-school conformists wearing the same school tie.

In the twenties a group of underground German architects started producing an equivalent of Dada nonsense, to wit a preposterous sexual architecture that was so *outré* that it has remained censured to this day. Certainly no European architect could build these ejaculatory exercises because the society wouldn't have them staying around on the streets frightening the tourists. If one wanted a 'convulsive beauty' then a Surrealist painting or collage, or at best a staged happening was possible. Beauty as 'the fortuitous encounter of a sewing machine and an umbrella on a dissecting table', the nineteenth-century epigram of Lautréamont, might be perfectly acceptable hanging on the wall at a Surrealist exhibition and contained by an art gallery context, but a whole city made up of such encounters would be so beautiful and stimulating, that it would drive the popula-tion to ever-increasing levels of ecstatic madness, higher blood pressure, hypertension, hyperthyroid – hyperrealism, just plain HYPE over the top. Drugs and suburban madness.

You're driving down one of the main rolling roads on the outskirts of Kansas City, past the University of Missouri, past collegiate Gothic fantasies all covered in their well-kept ivy and discreet vegetable salad, past your Scarlett O'Hara Southern Mansion, row upon row of Stockbroker's Tudor, Ad Man's Castellated and Doctor's Palladian, when you see appearing out of the manicured verdure these funny coloured spikes with little round balls on the end, kind of Martian tentacles waving out there (maybe they have five television sets?) above this shaggy-shingle, zig-zag TEEPEE! What the . . . ???? . . . is this zwoopy, shingle wigwam doing to our Palladian neighbourhood? The Indians returning to reclaim their plains, some kind of ethnic pavilion put up by the U of M? And what are those glowing, lozenge-shaped, green . . . *Woolworth* ashtrays doing crawling up the front door? Holy Toledo, what do they think this is, Coons Bluff Iowa or Paris Georgia?

Opposite, above
Joe Price House, new additions, Bartlesville, Oklahoma, 1974-8. Triangular geometries control the plan and ornament which consists of a Goffian mixture of sequins, glass cullet, coal, thick-pile carpet, prismatic mirrors on the ceiling, tea coasters and gilded insect-like feelers. The glass wall decor is reminiscent of Klimt's paintings.

Opposite, below
Hyde House, Kansas City, Kansas, 1965. Green Woolworth ashtrays frame the sacred hearth of family life and the plastic rain which sprinkles down from the light filled dome.

Nicol House. The oculus is an abstraction of lozenge-shaped shingle, repeated from the outside. The use of a conventional religious form – the eye of God, the dome of heaven – is modified by the tinkle of domestic equipment, the plastic tea-coasters and balloon(?) decoration.

It's the James Nicol House, commissioned in 1965 for a local banker, his wife and three children. You walk in through the front door, past all these hexagonal shingles and sharp, pointed triangles, past your glowing Woolworths and you hit the thick-pile, *really* thick, and warm and soft and kind of yellow-pea-green soup colour that you know couldn't just happen by chance, but had to be picked by somebody who really wanted it. Off with the shoes, as in all Goff's Japaneserie, and onto the thick-pile – everywhere: down it goes into the conversation pit, climbing over the octagonal pit around the ambulatory right into the bedrooms . . . endless, wall to wall, deep, thick-pile pea-soup! It's fantastic, it soaks up the sound, you can hear your heart beat it's so silent, this is the ultimate tactile architecture that Moore and Bloomer write about, the most touchable, all senses going, enveloping body-bath that an architect ever fashioned, more incapsulating than Rococo, more epidermic and cuddly than Art Nouveau – you can actually fall down and crawl through the building like a mouse on a featherbed touching every last part of it – HAPTIC ARCHITECTURE!

You snuggle down into the furry conversing pit, preparing for some really good repartee, and see across the octagon, behind your concertina shutters these bedrooms changing colours like a Munsell Colour chart – from indescribable deep-purple red to orange and yellow – all the way around the octagon the colour chart rings

Opposite

Nicol House, Kansas City, Missouri, 1964. Octagonal plan, lozenge-shaped shingle and teepee imagery while on the interior the sacred hearth again but here uniting earth, air, water, fire and green carpet. Note the furniture, and colour clashes.

Nicol House, dining-room. Carpet climbs up the wall in triangles to kiss the triangular windows coming down to meet them while the Mod furniture explodes out in glass bubbles and the Top Hat, right, cools the champagne.

the changes, while every now and then there are these punctuations in see-through acrylic, these perspex womb-chairs and plastic tables that you might have last seen in a fifties Sci-Fi flick, or maybe a sale of down-market, replica Saarinen. The great thing about these plastic accoutrements is that they seem totally without pedigree, without provenance, they cry out 'anonymous craft-kitsch'. They are emanations from the hidden psyche of the Great Unwashed.

Overhead is the central skylight and its decorative insect giving an undeniable focus to the heart of the house. Light comes through this central octagon and focuses like the oculus of the Pantheon (yes it does) on the surrounding octagonal dome and its coffers of tiny hexagonal shingle. And from the top of the Pantheon, this religious space given over to sacred conversation, comes down a most miraculous thing. As if from heaven, picked out by the central eye of the Supreme Being, and down, down, down the thin copper wires come . . . DROPS OF WATER, sliding one by one down the oiled wire, slinking with all their little capillary actions working to cool the air. Yes, it's a Goffairconditioner. Beads of water on copper wire cooling the Kansas City 110° in the shade . . . and why not, we perspire little beads of sweat for the same reason. And where do these little beads of coolth arrive? Why – at the central, circular, conversation *pool*, where else, where there is a halo of copper wire, surrounding a lake of water that in turn surrounds a ring of gas jets! The FIREPLACE, the hearth, the archetypal heart – of course, how could we have missed it? *Earth, air, water* and *fire* and thick-pile carpet, the five elements of the Goffiverse, meet at the centre of family life. How indescribably yuk-beautiful, how incredibly outrageous – give up all you Surrealists, throw it in you Schlock PhDs, back to the Beaux-Arts Venturi, out of the woods you self-build neophytes, you failed Hippies and would-be Slummers – this is the poetry of the unredeemable, the rescue of ersatz, the Michelangelo of Kitsch.

4. HISTORY AND THEORY

4.1 THE TORY INTERPRETATION OF HISTORY

On David Watkin's book Morality and Architecture, *Oxford University Press, London and New York, 1977. This review-article, commissioned with others on Watkin's book by* The Architectural Review *(February 1978) shows once more the 'mythic' element behind history writing and how we have not gotten very far in dealing with this necessary but contentious aspect. I have discussed this aspect in 'History as Myth' I and II (1966, 1977) and the question of 'morality', that Watkin raises, in the next chapter.*

David Watkin charges out onto the field with his sword flashing and his visor drawn firmly over his eyes. He wheels about, spies an enemy and with perfect aim delivers a mortal blow. But lo, the enemy is already dead! For the last fifteen years or so other knights, indeed veritable battalions, have been killing off the *Zeitgeist*, the idea underlying Modern architecture that there is an all-encompassing spirit of the age. Watkin, like some of these other warriors, considers himself unique, a most curious affair. Like the very Modern architect he hates he is not entirely aware of his own tradition, by now the orthodox tradition of anti-Modernism and Popperian argument (see appendix). Having myself tilted at the same windmills, with virtually the same weapons and words, I am, of course, put out that my victories aren't honoured (or even footnoted), but more I'm annoyed with the tone underlying the attack. It merges on contempt and over-statement, perhaps because Watkin is insulated from, not the odious *Zeitgeist*, but its reputable cousin 'the climate of opinion'. Because he thinks he's alone, he fights like a cornered man with all the weapons of bombast. He reacts to the tight alternatives of his Cambridge university with a rage reminiscent of Mumford. Consider his attack on the leader of the Modernists there:

> [Sir Leslie Martin's] 'Centre for Land Use and Built Form' [is] a title which indicated clearly enough a belief that architecture as an art involving taste, imagination, and scholarship should finally be abolished and replaced by a scientifically plotted utopia in which tamed collectivist man with all his wants defined by technology and gratified by computerized planning would contentedly take his apportioned place as in some gigantic rationalistically constructed beehive. (p. 12)

Of course the 'Centre for Land Use and Built Form' is a pretentious title for a pretentious study, but does it really prove that unfortunate Sir Leslie is intent on all the other crimes? Watkin cites no evidence but merely footnotes another piece of savoury, Cantibridgean polemic by R. Scruton called 'The Architecture of Stalinism'. Here we find the unlikely idea that Sir Leslie is not only an advance guard of Stalinist worker bees, but that Constructivist architecture is Stalinist too. Pausing for a moment of silence in memory of those Constructivists who were sent prematurely to their graves by Stalin (and who are now rolling over there because of Scruton's blasphemy) we are reminded of yet another piece of Cambridge

character assassination: the historian Hugh Brogan's attack on James Stirling and others as 'anti-democratic: structural fascists', with again the comparison to Stalin and Hitler. These last characters and their unfriendly use of the *Zeitgeist* appear several times in Watkin's book with the latent and sometimes explicit connection to Modern architects and historians. With judicious cross-quoting Lewis Mumford's arguments are equated with Hitler's (p. 47) and most of the be-knighted collectivists – Sir James Richards, Sir Nikolaus Pevsner, Sir Anthony Blunt, Sir Leslie Martin, Sir Herbert Read – appear as opportunistic fellow travellers intent on collectivizing architects and artists into our communal, Siberian beehive.

Now whatever the merits of this argument are, it has one enormous fault. It treats the 'enemy' with contempt. A suspicion emerges which grows with each overstatement that Watkin is being as intolerant and uncharitable as, should I say, a Stalinist or a Modernist? So passionate is the condemnation, so single-minded is the inquisatorial zeal, that the *tu quoque* argument is continuously called to mind. The problem is that all institutions tend towards the closed shop, all friends towards a coterie, all 'fellow travellers' towards a collective movement, and all universities into traditional places of privilege. This is no more than a tendency, but it is not one either recognized or guarded against by Watkin's argument.

A critique

The theoretical side of Watkin's position suffers somewhat from agnosticism or underdevelopment. He quite rightly attacks the naïve moralism of Pugin, Richards and Pevsner but then never suggests an alternative moral base, or explanation for architectural form. He overlooks the moral arguments in the classical tradition he knows best – the injunctions of Vitruvius, Alberti and the Palladians. We can agree that moral probity does not inevitably follow any 'spirit of the age', but disagree with the statement that architecture doesn't 'express social, moral and philosophical conditions' (p. 4). Of course architecture *expresses* these values by convention and usage as any good history shows, and so we don't have to accept just the aestheticism and personal taste which Watkin advocates as the alternative. He says, quite often, that taste is a matter of individual choice (and so it partly is), but is unaware of its social and institutional nature – how it is also shared. Thus:

> The architect can certainly decide that he wants his building to look like a building that contains advanced technology, but that is an aesthetic decision which we should be free to accept or reject as we wish. (p. 11)

Of course it's also a *social* decision and we can give moral and social reasons for accepting or rejecting the image. Certainly it's more than a purely aesthetic decision, or one as Watkin would have it, that should be confined to the internal world of 'artistic tradition with its own canon of judgement' (p. 25). If proof were needed of this fact we wouldn't have to look any further than

Watkin's book itself and the Cambridge or Peterhouse tradition from which it stems – hardly unmoral or a purely aesthetic tradition, or an argument to be accepted or rejected 'as we wish' like a flavour of ice cream.

The basic aestheticism of Watkin's *conscious* position is similar to Geoffrey Scott's and it has all the same problems: in trying so hard to purge architecture of one fallacy after another (The Romantic Fallacy, The Ethical Fallacy, The Mechanical Fallacy, and The Biological Fallacy were the villains of 1914) Scott fell into the grand Reductive Fallacy. He rescued architecture from being turned into Something Else at the price of making it concerned Mostly With Empathy. Indeed such is Watkin's hatred of Modern architecture and its symbols of collectivism that he, like Scott, wants to throw overboard symbolism itself, or an architecture which refers to 'religion, politics, sociology, philosophy, rationalism, technology, German theories of space or the "spirit of the age"'(p. 1).

Well, the throwing away of symbolism isn't quite as radical as this long list implies, because Watkin doesn't have a theory of symbolism to jettison. He's unaware of architectural semiotics and its development over the last fifteen years, or perhaps he regards it as one more collectivist conspiracy to be avoided. In any case the agnosticism on this point once again makes his position out of touch. He refers to 'the public' and its rejection of planners (p. 12) as if there were a monolithic body of public opinion, and not the actual plurality of groups with their differing values and architectural codes. He fails to understand how architecture can be experienced through a moral code, and chastises James Stirling and Marcel Breuer as well as Pugin and Pevsner, implying that all moral experience is conditioned by the ideology of the *Zeitgeist*.

But clearly when Stirling refers to the 'moral rightness of the new architecture' we are dealing with cultural values which express an individual choice that can be explained and understood (p. 13): in this case Stirling's rejection, when he was a student at Liverpool, of a weak Neo-Georgian for a more creative International Style. Given the alternatives at the time it was a perfectly moral and comprehensible decision. His recent return to 'historicist' forms when designing for historical centres is equally understandable. The same is true of Pevsner's equation of 'sham materials and sham techniques' with immorality; although it is not an equation we have to accept (and I certainly wouldn't in many contexts) we know what it means whenever Vitruvius, Bellori, Winckelman or Pevsner uses it. I give these classical 'moralist' examples because Watkin's sympathies lie with classicism. Indeed he admires E. H. Gombrich and it is precisely Gombrich who has shown to our generation the connection between 'Norm and Form' (in an essay and book of that title). Gombrich shows not only that there are links between artistic and cultural norms and the forms of art, but that any attempt to deny them will end in the absurdity that art cannot be explained. Furthermore Watkin focuses on *part* of Gombrich's theories and, like so much else, exaggerates the rest. For instance he says 'We *know*, too, that our inclination to enjoy a thing precedes any attempt to rationalize or defend that enjoyment' (p. 5, my italics). This is questionable, and his footnote on Gombrich meant to support the supposed knowledge shows it is really something else. Gombrich says 'Apologists for certain kinds of art often plead that if we would only understand it, we would also like it. *By*

and large, I think, the sequence is inverted.' (my italics). From the careful qualifications of Gombrich we leap to the dogmatic certainties of Watkin. Many counter instances could be cited where *understanding* precedes enjoyment, even if in the majority of cases it is the reverse. Hence we don't *know* any iron law that Watkin forces on the evidence, because there is no such law.

Perhaps the strongest charge that could be brought against this book is that it pushes the argument too far. It strains the evidence, it exaggerates the points so strongly that they either become unfair or false. Basically it is lacking in balance and proportion – that is in architectural virtues. This is not the place to try to refute Watkin's over-statements, but let me show how uncharitable and contentious he is:

1. Pugin is attacked for writing about architecture as if it were religion and then Gropius and F. R. Leavis are accused of doing similar things for their respective arts. But clearly the latter aren't treating their 'subjects as though they were religion' (p. 18). The charge is absurd since both Gropius and Leavis are making quite explicit *moral* not religious arguments. Watkin easily fudges the difference because he lumps together all arguments that aren't aesthetic. It's typical of what he censures as 'slipshod scholarship' (p. 63).

2. The gratuitous attack on Stirling's History Faculty Building is made because Watkin doesn't like it, not, as he implies, because Stirling has justified his building as a 'technological necessity' (p. 28).

3. Although Watkin is probably right to attack Le Corbusier's mechanolotry it is not a 'functionalist argument' (p. 40) as Le Corbusier himself stressed so many times; and while Bruno Taut may have seen architecture as 'a socially manipulative force', so did Alberti. Nothing is gained by dismissing these so called 'pathetic fallacies' so quickly. Once again sympathetic criticism is needed to distinguish plausible from implausible morality.

4. Again, while Siegfried Giedion is somewhat guilty of many misdemeanours pinned on him, it's an overstatement to have him giving 'an all-embracing totalitarian argument' (p. 54). Nor is he only interested in architects 'in so far as they conform to the unarticulated spirit of the age'. Giedion's history as well as Pevsner's and the rest are full of contradictions which incorporate Expressionists and others which don't fit into their scheme.

5. Frank Lloyd Wright's 1903 *Manifesto on the Machine Age* is dismissed as 'just uncouth and arrogant philistinism' and full of 'blatant crudities'. Whatever its undeniable faults it still has some merits and the contemptuous dismissal sounds as if Watkin is trying to outdo Wright's inimitable style.

6. So zealous is Watkin in hunting out his conspiracy that he even finds the historicist argument in Hugh Honour and Henry-Russell Hitchcock. He calls the following statement by the latter 'palpably empty': 'Lutyens, one feels, in a different time and place – a generation earlier in England, say, or a generation later – might have been a greater architect' (p. 114). The assumption of Watkin is that generations, or periods of cultural history, have no influence whatsoever on the individual. Clearly it's a matter for reasoned argument about how much Lutyens was limited by his time, as well as helped. To say this doesn't make one a believer in any 'spirit of the age' – merely traditions, a climate of opinion and social realities.

JAMES STIRLING *Cambridge History Faculty Building,* 1964–7. Stirling did not justify this use of glass as a 'technical necessity'. In fact he appealed to historical precedent (The British Museum etc.), as well as 'convenience, construction, or propriety' – although of a different sort than Watkin's. The fact that such values are experienced *in a code* eludes Watkin and thus the fact that Cantabridgeans experience the building in quite opposite ways becomes incomprehensible to him. As I have found through interviews roughly half of the students respond positively to the Constructivist aesthetic – the exhilirating cascade of glass, the three extract units splayed overhead like bugs, the gantry crane – while others, particularly women, feel exposed in these spaces. Some Cambridge historians have damned the building, and Stirling, using a language even more abusive than Watkin's, while others respond positively to the visual clarity and hard-edge geometry. The section of the building is projected on the end elevations and here one can literally see that 'iceberg principle' of organization where most activity occurs at the bottom. The extreme emphasis on logic, circulation, and mechanical equipment make this another key building of Late-Modernism. Views show large reading room between glazed corridors and classrooms; reading stacks on the ground floor; and twin elevator shafts mark the entrance.

The positive side

Having said all this I must admit to enjoying Watkin's polemic and the cool relish with which he hits so many nails on the head and right through the body of their victims. We can obviously learn something from a biased view of Modernism that we cannot from a critique that comes from within the tradition. Listening to Watkin, or Conrad Jameson or Gavin Stamp attack Modern architecture is chastening and illuminating because they have, by and large, avoided being infected by its assumptions (unlike the rest of us). This gives them the privileged position which a Martian might enjoy, or someone recently arrived from the eighteenth century. They apply standards which we have lost, with a certain disinterest, and since Modernism has broken up as a living ideology it's even more necessary that its successor build from fragments taken from the past (among other sources). While Watkin doesn't supply these fragments he does insist on the importance of artistic traditions and individual excellence within them, obviously one alternative to the *Zeitgeist*. His major contribution is to kill this beast once again – perhaps necessary every three or four years because it has an awful habit of surviving lethal attacks.

The execution is remorseless and starts with one of the sillier clichés of our time, expressed by Sir Herbert Read, that 'a belief in Marx should be accompanied by a belief in, say, Cézanne'. The quote from Read is perfect, not only because it is one of the funnier ideas around, but because it illustrates so many current fallacies at once – the *Zeitgeist*, the notion of a unitary 'health or sickness of society' and the idea that taste is homogeneous.

> . . . the cause of the arts is the cause of revolution. Every reason – historical, economic, and psychological – points to the fact that art is only healthy in a communal type of society, where within one organic consciousness all modes of life, all senses and all faculties, function freely and harmoniously. We in England have suffered the severest form of capitalist exploitation. (p. 6)

The metaphor connecting the social body with the individual life, which makes the arts a thermometer which registers its sickness or health, goes back to Vasari and beyond. While there is something to recommend the metaphor it usually ends up by dominating the historian. We only have to think of the Borgias along with Leonardo to dispose of the notion of a sick or healthy Renaissance, or think how, say, both Watkin and Stirling love Thomas Hope, to dispose of the idea of unitary taste. Stirling has one of the largest collections of Hope furniture and Watkin has written a book on this designer. Taste varies in its development across classes and within individuals and, I would guess, most people have 'reactionary' and 'revolutionary' tastes across a spectrum of the arts (as did Marx and Lenin).

Watkin, time after time, attacks the notion of 'holism' which makes taste homogeneous and it's only a pity he doesn't have some concept such as 'the semiotic group' or 'taste culture' to put in its place. Clearly if architects are finally to get rid of the *Zeitgeist* they'll need some such substitute, a theoretical basis on which to design for a pluralist society.

Watkin's main attack is on the concept underlying Modern architecture that it should always represent and further the cause of 'levelling social differences' (in Pevsner's words). He traces this idea from Viollet-le-Duc to Mies Van der Rohe ('The individual is losing significance') which culminates in England with the group

around *Circle* magazine and the writings of J. M. Richards. Richards, in 1940, uses the medical metaphor once again and pronounces the nineteenth century suffering from its 'malady' of individualism and eclecticism. The confusions that holism leads to are then exposed by Watkin. Richards supports the idea of a common vernacular, but has to reject the vulgar one of the speculative builder because 'His products *form no part of the socio-cultural whole*' (p. 50). In other words Richards is trying to impose Modernist notions of the vernacular on 'the people' in the name of 'the people' while it is clear 'the people' want to speak some other language. The language Richards favours is a simple, collectivist one that suppresses individual differences, supposedly like the Georgian '. . . it is people as Society that architecture has to cater for . . . It has been said before that great architecture is more a product of the times than of personalities' (p. 52).

While Watkin shows a lot of evidence that Richards *et al* were advocating a form of collectivism and socialism, he doesn't analyse the particular type but rather connects it by implication with Stalinism (following Scruton's mistake). This lacuna is a pity. One wants to know, for instance, what form of socialism these historians and critics supported since, among other things, so many of them have accepted knighthoods and a place in the non-revolutionary Establishment.

Of course since Modern architecture has ended as a live tradition one expects confusion as to what it meant previously. The more old-time Modernists I ask, the more definitions I come up with, but I think this pluralism also reflects, partly, an actual variation of approaches at the time. For instance F. L. Wright's organic architecture was conservative in many senses and opposed to Mies Van der Rohe's collectivism which was equally conservative. Both were different from Bruno Taut's populist romanticism which in turn differed from Le Corbusier's syndicalism of the thirties and Hannes Meyer's Marxism. The fascism of Terragni and Nervi and the Communism of the Constructivists start to fill out the positions (which are of course only labelled here). Philip Johnson and others were involved with right-wing politics. Given this heterogeneity of social and political attitudes and the fact that they changed from the twenties to the sixties as Modern architecture became the Establishment Style (to replace varieties of Classicism), it becomes particularly difficult to generalize about ideology. From Watkin's book one would get the false impression that a vague kind of collectivism characterized all those who shared the *Zeitgeist* theory.

In any case, Furneaux-Jordan's 'populistic chauvinism' (p. 64) stands out in this context with Pevsner's well-scrubbed 'Protestantism'. Apparently the latter's healthy spirit of the age was being 'impeded even in Germany, by imperfectly cleaned teeth' (p. 100). We can thank Watkin greatly for ferreting out such delirious arguments, but they are made more often by Pevsner than other historians and are not so general as they appear from the book. Two other aspects make Pevsner a special case: he has not had much influence on practising architects outside of England (Watkin often argues as if England were the world) and ever since the early sixties he has cut himself off from developments by, on the one hand adopting a hardened Modernist stance and, on the other hand, implicitly promoting Victorianesque (which he is explicitly against). Watkin gets him on the latter contradiction, but doesn't press an analysis of the former position.

It creates some curious problems. One, which Watkin mentions, is that such modest managers as Frank Pick, Vice-Chairman of the London Passenger Transport Board in 1933, is termed a 'modern counterpart of Lorenzo the Magnificent'! (p. 102). This second delirious comparison makes Pevsner less a Protestant than a Surrealist, a point which almost could be sustained given the evidence which Watkin cites. Pevsner won't back down on his 1936 view of a collectivized, International-Styled world and the more the real world challenges his view the less he seems willing to change it. He sticks to his old principles at the cost of making them unlikely. Consider writing the following sentence:

> No doubt many of the abstract painters of today consider self-expression their principal mission; but history will decide against this.(p. 94)

Clearly this sentence shows more than a belief in the *Zeitgeist* or even a desire to censure self-expression. It shows a kind of Expressionist outburst, a wild Nietzschean rage that parallels the proclamations of those that Pevsner attacks, an attempt to force 'history' into a mould by assertion. Indeed his ending to *Pioneers of Modern Design* also does this (as Reyner Banham pointed out).

> It is the creative energy of this world in which we live and work which we want to master, a world of science and technology, of speed and danger, of hard struggles and no personal security, that is glorified in Gropius' architecture . . . (p. 95)

Such apostrophes, which recur with regularity and increasing vehemence in later years, are closest to the writings of the Futurists, and underneath Watkin's dour Protestant is a kind of scholarly Marinetti trying to get out. In fact this gives Pevsner's writing a lot of its power – no matter how much we may disagree with the message.

So Pevsner the Surrealist and Futurist is one helpful implication which emerges from this study. Another is that the social collectivists of the thirties have become the knighted conservatives of the sixties, replacing Classicism with Modernism as an Establishment Style. A third implication is that another kind of history could be written of Modern architecture, from a right-wing position. Watkin, however, is no more explicit in his political sympathies than are so many of the historians he discusses. Nonetheless his book raises this question and the overwhelming support it has received from, among others, John Betjeman, and *Apollo* magazine suggests that there is a political tinge to it. At the outset of his book Watkin quotes the mentor of the Peterhouse tradition at Cambridge, Sir Herbert Butterfield, on *The Whig Interpretation of History*, 1931.

> . . . the Whig historian sometimes seems to believe that there is an unfolding logic in history, a logic which is on the side of the Whigs and which makes them appear as co-operators with progress itself (vii).

No doubt Watkin is right to connect this with the historicism of the Modern Movement, but it does suggest, given his latent conservatism, a corresponding characterization of an opposite approach. The Tory Interpretation of History, to give it a title, sometimes seems to believe that the present order of society is all right, that innovators tend to be philistines just as reformers are apt to be Stalinists and that traditions and institutions should always be given the benefit of the

doubt over doubters. This characterization may be overdone, but it's not wildly off the mark. It suggests a history to be written which, although dubitable politically as all histories are, is still welcome as another approach, and as a corrective to a previous orthodoxy.

Appendix

As Watkin mentions there are two opposite uses of the word 'historicism'. The one which Karl Popper attacks, as opposed to the one Pevsner attacks (which is Revivalism), 'is out to find The Path on which mankind is destined to walk; it is out to discover The Clue to History' (p.6). This Popperian tradition has been quite strong in theory and historiography although Watkin is unaware of the fact and writes as if he were unique (p. 113). The tradition starts sometime in the early sixties (1962) with the writing and seminars at the AA in London and MIT in Cambridge, USA. Roy Landau and Stanford Anderson first introduced Popperian arguments into architecture (as far as I'm aware) and I can remember a few seminars, lectures and articles on the subject by E.H. Gombrich, Thomas Stevens, Colin Rowe, Marcus Whiffen (1964), and W.W. Bartley III. In 1966 George Baird and myself were writing on the subject along with Alan Colquhoun and Norris Kelly Smith — some of this material was published in book form in *Meaning in Architecture*, 1969, particularly my own attacks on the *Zeitgeist* and Pevsner's and Giedion's use of it (p. 245, pp. 251–2). Also in *Modern Movements in Architecture*, 1973, I pointed out Pevsner's use of 'totalitarian' arguments and the use of the *Zeitgeist* by Mies and other Modernists (pp. 11–14, 50–51, 105–107, 113–114, 120); the first chapter is concerned with the varying political views of the Modernists. The other tradition which Watkin overlooks, which is of course much larger, is that of anti-Modernism, and no more than a summary of recent polemic can suffice here. Starting with the attacks of the twenties, and continuing through the thirties, with Goodhardt-Rendel, one has by the early sixties a kind of systematic critique summarized in the work of Jane Jacobs (1961) and Lewis Mumford 'The Case Against Modern Architecture' (1962). There is then the planning attacks of Robert Goodman, Oscar Newman and Conrad Jameson, and in architecture a sequence of polemic — Malcolm MacEwan's *Crisis in Architecture* (1974), Brent Brolin's *The Failure of Modern Architecture* (1976), Peter Blake's *Form Follows Fiasco* (1977) etc. My own *The Language of Post-Modern Architecture* (new edition 1980) discusses the seven departures from Modernism since, roughly, 1952 (Historicism, Straight Revivalism, Neo-Vernacular, Adhocism and Contextualism, Metaphorical buildings, Post-Modern ambiguous space and Radical Eclecticism). All these departures, except the second, are transformations, not rejections, of Modernism, much the way Mannerist architecture was a transformation of the Renaissance approach. Strong attacks by Robert Venturi, Vincent Scully and others date from about 1966. The popular press, architectural press and TV start taking up the arguments about 1973 in America and Britain, and somewhat earlier in Italy. It is obviously time that someone collected these anti-Modernist attacks and explicated this tradition. Apparently G. Blomeyer is doing this in Germany.

4.2 ARCHITECTURE AND MORALITY

A section of this essay, that on 'multivalence', was written in 1968 as part of my doctoral thesis which later became Modern Movements in Architecture (1973). *The concept of multivalence underlies all of my writing as the basic theory, which I have not been able to develop further than here. Obviously this could and should be done but the reader may feel that the theoretical apparatus has already reached sledgehammer proportions – and that the 'nut' of architectural morality is much easier to crack. I don't think so.*

It might seem curious that we experience architecture morally. Many people claim to look at buildings from a purely aesthetic point of view and try to exclude ethical considerations. But even in this seemingly pure case, a moral component is bound to enter. For when we judge a building as aesthetically beautiful or unified or picturesque there is a hidden ethical value smuggled into this judgement. We say such a work has 'integrity' and, as the overtones of this word suggest, there is a tinge of ethics involved. Even if we say a building is just pretty or amusing there is an aspect of moral judgement in these remarks. We mean it is pretty or amusing to *us* and therefore it promotes our pleasure and well-being, rather than frustrates or depresses us – a moral pronouncement even if a limited one.

The converse of this is also true. 'Ugly' buildings seem to weigh us down with their heaviness, triviality, or brutality and these reactions are soon generalized beyond their aesthetic source. One may object that such reactions are misunderstandings, examples of the pathetic fallacy, of responding empathetically to inanimate objects; but if that's true then it's equally true that we all commit the fallacy. Reactions to much Modern architecture bear out this truism as indeed did those of Pugin and Ruskin to Renaissance architecture. What we don't like for aesthetic reasons, we tend to find oppressive and then, possibly, immoral. And yet while this moral reaction is a psychological constant in our experience of architecture, it raises curious ethical problems that have hardly been faced.

These have been touched on in David Watkin's *Morality and Architecture* (see section 4.1), but have not been adequately treated by our generation. Confusions and problems remain. How, for instance, are we to condemn whole periods of architecture, as Pugin and Ruskin did, when we know that every period produces some architects of unimpeachable integrity. The moral experience of architecture, necessary and irreducible, has led these moralists to the paradox of 'immoral' generalization and intolerance.

We may pride our age as being more open-minded than the self-righteous nineteenth century; but is it? Does it tolerate as many approaches and styles? Have we not condemned whole periods of history in the name of the 'spirit of the age', the modern *Zeitgeist*? It would be unthinkable today, or unlikely, for an architect to design in the Classical or Gothic style because we have somehow moved beyond these prior periods in terms of technology, belief and social make-up. Our modern building, so the argument runs, is based on the recent technics of glass, steel and concrete fabrication, and on agnosticism and egalitarianism. Yet today it is precisely such assumptions which are being questioned. We now

begin to feel that older, vernacular technologies are just as valid as recent ones and to suspect that previous beliefs – national, ideological and religious – are not to be outmoded like a used car. So we are in a complex and perplexing historical situation caught between a too-simple Modernism which has rejected past languages of architecture and a reaction against this which seeks to return to a previous tradition. As an example of the latter there is the return to the Classical language advocated by Quinlan Terry, Allen Greenberg and others, or similar movements in Europe.[1] This alternative to Modernism thus appears as another equally coherent and limited language of architecture.

This debate, however valid, will not be engaged here, since I have already said too much in a book on Post-Modernism.[2] Rather some of the general ethical questions involved in experiencing building will be raised. We need, it seems, to distinguish more clearly and delicately between two types of judgement: that which values a building because of its ideas (or the contribution it makes to society and history), and that which supports an architecture because it is well done. There are two types of judgement involved here which inevitably get confused, the extrinsic and intrinsic, the relation of a building to other buildings, and the relationships between parts within a building. At stake is the distinction, which is now widely debated, between architecture as a social art and architecture as an autonomous discipline.

Ideology and integrity

As a first step in this polarized debate we might seek a proverbial balance, or at least the Rabbi's proverbial advice to his son: 'Whenever faced with two extremes, always pick a third.' The third, in this case, would naturally be a synthesis of the first two. Architecture has a moral component both because it relates to and changes other architecture, that is the course of history, and because it is a small world of internally related meanings.

An extreme example of the latter position are today's 'Rationalist' architects.[3] These Italian, Spanish, French and Japanese architects, loosely grouped around the figure of Aldo Rossi, have emphasized the autonomy of architecture – its independence from society, history and politics. And no one has been more wrapped up in his own autonomous creations than Peter Eisenman, an architect who has said he doesn't care much about the function of a building, its context, environment, and sometimes, even, the owner. For him, as indeed for Massimo Scolari or Superstudio, architecture is beholden only to itself, its own laws, beauties and possibilities.

Surprisingly, this is a major tradition of Western architecture. Theorists since Vitruvius have always concentrated on rules and proportions intrinsic to the language of architecture, and the history of architecture can almost be adequately taught as the succession of changes in rules. Like it or not, architectural history is mostly about monuments and nothing, as Rossi has pointed out, is more autonomous than this building type. The Villa Rotunda, the Palladian villa, is often uninhabitable but such is the virtuosity of its formal coherence that we don't seem to notice. The case for architectural morality here rests on the integrity with which internal meanings are related and new meanings are suggested.

PETER EISENMAN, *House 6 for the Frank Family*, Washington, Conn., 1975. View from the entrance side shows the frontal layering of planes and 'pilasters'. The living room is partly visible below and stairhall above. The building is unrelated to both the site and the nearby vernacular style of building.

House 6, interior of the master bedroom showing the 'virtual' door, a pier in different shades of white and grey which pivots on hinges thus leaving the door open when closed.

Thus we might look at Eisenman's House 6 like we look at one of Karpov's winning chess games, to see what new moves are being played. The autonomy of architecture is like the autonomy of chess except one is allowed, indeed asked, to change the rules from time to time.

As I have argued elsewhere House 6, in its supreme autonomy, does not relate to its woodland setting, the Frank family that inhabit it, the tradition of clapboard building in the area or any contextual fact.[4] It may look, to the uninitiated, as much like a dentist office as a house and it doesn't matter too much which way you turn it, even if altogether upside-down. It stands, like a Palladian villa, apart from nature and relates to, if anything external at all, the De Stijl buildings of the early twenties. In relation to these it is less colourful and readable in its functions and more enclosed at the edges. In a word it is a Classicist version of De Stijl.

The meaning it creates, the rules of Eisenman chess which become apparent as you walk through the house, are concerned mostly with the relations between wall, window, 'column' and 'pilaster'. A basic antinomy is set up between solid, blank wall and long thin rectangles – either slits of space or concrete members painted white or grey. It is a sensual and amusing experience to discover the tricks played with these elements. The way the 'column' is either present or absent from its proper place. For instance an 'absent column' (a rectangular void) even cuts through the bedroom separating the marital bed, while a 'present column' descends elegantly through one side of the dining table dividing up the family meal. We are prepared for these architectural jokes by the exterior 'pilaster' cantilevered from a useless wall that hangs six inches above the ground (as indeed does much of the 'base' of the house). These contradictions (a pilaster which hangs, a base which doesn't support) are akin to Mannerist contradictions and like them they heighten the perception of normal elements. It is as if Eisenman, using the conventional language of prosaic Modern architecture, were intent on disproving every one of its functional rules. The ultimate functional absur-

dity, and sensual delight, is a hinged 'column' in the bedroom placed where the door should be. Here the 'present/absent column' has its final revenge on utility as you turn it, because it merely turns beautiful shades of grey and white leaving the door quite open – a void of three feet – through which the (split) marital bed is quite revealed. For a small private house it questions the rule that we need closed doors.

All of these jokes, and there are more, establish the building as an architectural example of black (or at least grey) humour. But to see the integrity with which these meanings are carried through and reinforced we have to subject the building to fairly detailed formal analysis. If we compare the south facade to Gerrit Rietveld's Schroeder House the Mannerist and Classical aspects of Eisenman's work become apparent.[5] Whereas Rietveld's house has a spinning, dynamic quality caused by volumes sliding past each other and a strong contrast between solids and voids, Eisenman's house is relatively static and sombre. This is caused by the edge stops which I find Classical. By contrast, Rietveld explodes the corner and several edges thus setting up a pinwheel motion around the central reference plane.

Like a Classical building, Eisenman's is more symmetrical as well. There is a near symmetry of the left glazed area set against the dark grey plane on the right. If we adopt this reading then we actually get a Mannerist emphasis on the sides, that is, roughly, an A B[1] B[2] A[1] rhythm. Secondly, there is another Mannerist aspect, which historians have called 'the principle of frustration'.[6] According to this formal principle, visual movement is cancelled or frozen. In Eisenman's building there is no visual pull towards the centre as in Baroque; an emphasis of neither top nor bottom. There is neither beginning nor end, and no movement towards a crescendo. The eye jumps around, in its restless search for a theme, a theme which it finds everywhere neutralized.

Closely related to this, and also very Mannerist, is what Wittkower calls the 'principle of ambiguity', the fact that one element has many different equal roles so that its exact meaning is unclear. This is also a frustrating principle. Here for instance vertical 'pilasters' relate to two or more contiguous systems and also, at the extreme right, one becomes the wall itself. These 'pilasters' are further ambiguous because they have no base and capital, no direction, and are perhaps not pilasters at all (yet they *represent* interior structure and space as pilasters do, and are non-utilitarian like pilasters). Another ambiguity is the implied equality of the top 'parapet' and bottom 'base', as if they were the same thing, or as if the building could be extended. This reading of indeterminancy applies to other elements which are, ambiguously, equated: beams, floor lines, wall ends, partitions and pilasters all have nearly the same shape.

Finally to confirm our reading that Eisenman has produced a very Mannerist (and mannered) joke on Modern architecture we should mention two further sixteenth-century aspects. Like a Michelangelo interior this building has a supreme intellectual sophistication and coldness; it has like all Eisenman's work an almost cruel obsession with showing formal logic, showing the steps by which it has been designed, 'marking' these steps. The Mannerists were of course equally fascinated by showing their skill at creating and then overcoming 'difficulties' (*difficultà*).[7] And in both cases it is a skill exhibited as an end in itself, not for any supra-architectural purpose. Finally there is the Mannerist 'principle of variety' exhibited here by the abundance of window sizes, the tense, nervous movement of the profile, and the different treatment and colouring of rectilinear elements even when they fulfil the same role.

Our formal analysis could go on, but I think it has established the point the House 6 is a Mannerist version of Late-Modern architecture and that it conveys, if we can attach any meaning to it, a fundamental nihilism.[8] It is of course a sensual and dignified cancellation of all positive belief, a counterpart to Michelangelo's *terribilità*, but a nihilism nonetheless. Each autonomous, unrelated element proclaims it, the shades of grey reinforce it. Even Eisenman's commitment to communicate the process of design, the transformations, is cancelled by the seemingly random painting of exterior members. It is true one can understand binary distinctions (the painting of pilasters light grey indicates they are non-structural) but there is no overall consistency, or sense to the colouring. This building of 1975 then, foreshadows Eisenman's explicit nihilism of 1977 and his House 10.[9]

To see how these meanings relate to the agnosticism of Modern architecture, the neutrality of the curtain wall and 'Chicago frame,' and the blank incomprehensibility of Modernism in general would take us beyond the scope of this essay. Suffice it to say that Eisenman's nihilism is held with great conviction, even religiously, and that if we are concerned here with morality as shown by the integrity of meaning, then House 6 obviously has it.

But we are also concerned with another kind of morality, the ideas behind architecture, its ideology, and here of course his position may be questioned. In effect we are applying two standards of morality, intrinsic and extrinsic, and thus it is not surprising if our judgement is mixed. This split valuation is, furthermore, bound to be usual in a pluralist society, for a variety of belief is not only the norm today but institutionalized as such. It leads to some curious paradoxes. At the very least it leads to contention, the low-keyed battles between movements one sees in the avant-garde today. In America there were the 'Whites' led by Eisenman versus the 'Greys' led by

GERRIT RIETVELD, *Schroeder House*, Utrecht, 1924. Volumes and elements slide past each other and around a centre; edges are open, when compared to House 6, and the profile more dynamic.

House 6, west elevation. More sombre and Classical than the Shroeder house because of the dark and neutral tones rather than the colours. The full edge stops and near-symmetry increase the static quality.

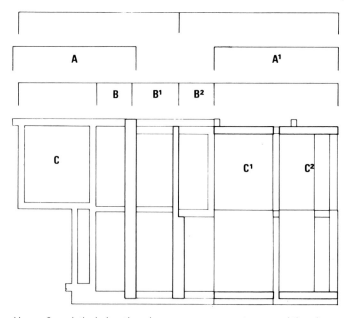

House 6, analytical elevation shows a near symmetry around the glass-gridded service areas. Reading from left to right a rhythm of A,B[1],B[2],A[1] can be discerned, with an internal repeat C,C[1],C[2] of the dark wall bay.

House 6, transformational steps which are sometimes 'marked' on the exterior: e.g. the column line continues across the ceiling and slices up volumes on the outside. One can also see the two stairs, one real the other 'virtual', and the large reference planes which accentuate the frontality.

Robert Stern, Robert Venturi and Vincent Scully. In England and Europe there has been a similar conflict between the Rationalists led by Aldo Rossi and the other positions, not so explicitly formulated. Meanwhile Modern architects and the general public have their own ideologies and their own languages of architecture, which are different from all of this.

Probably a degree of pluralism and strife has been common in all ages, yet ours has these qualities to a greater extent than either the Renaissance or eighteenth century. Then there were only two or possibly three competing modes of design (the Gothic, Classical and vernacular) and one of these usually had the upper hand. This established a general consensus of informed opinion and so architects and their patrons could assume a commonalty of architectural language and ideology. Today no such consensus exists and the general result has been to turn the critic, as indeed user of architecture, into an ideologue. That is, he supports and promotes the style he knows best and ignores or condemns the rest. The result of this is a provinciality of opinion and a lowering of architectural standards, things which are evident throughout the world. If the standards are always shifting, if the rules and goals are always in dispute, then architecture will not generally reach a very high level as an art form. Hence my plea that the critic suspend his disbelief for a time and judge architecture quite clearly as a small, coherent world, before he goes on to make extrinsic comment. What type of comment or judgement is this?

A representative example can be taken from Sir Nikolaus Pevsner's *An Outline of European Architecture* (1970 edition). It concerns his partial attack on Le Corbusier's Ronchamp, and the movement of Neo-Expressionism. I quote selectively to give the main outlines of the argument:

> Brazil is the country in which the fascination and the dangers of the mid-century irresponsibility appear most concentratedly [i.e. 'structural acrobatics' and 'bizarre forms'] . . . the pilgrimage chapel of Ronchamp [1950–5] not far from Besançon is the most discussed monument of a new irrationalism . . . In the same way the sham streamlining of the motor-cars of yesteryear cannot be acceptable to reason. It can in addition hardly amuse, because on an auto-bahn or in the thick of traffic of a city one does not want to be amused by the machine one is operating . . . And architecture can rarely afford to be silly; it is as a rule too permanent and too big merely to amuse. . . . What [architecture] cannot be is irresponsible, and most of today's structural acrobatics, let alone purely formal acrobatics imitating structural acrobatics, are irresponsible. That is one argument against them. The other is that they are not in conformity with the basic social conditions of architecture . . . The architect still has to build predominantly for anonymous clients and large numbers of clients – see the factories, office buildings . . . and he has still to build with industrially produced materials. The latter combination excludes decoration, since machine-made decoration, i.e. decoration not made by the individual, lacks sense; the former also excludes it, since decoration acceptable by all, i.e. decoration not made for the individual, also lacks sense.[10]

Leaving aside the content of this history, a content with which I disagree, there are three notable aspects to it. First it is more clearly ideological than most criticism and for this we may be grateful since polemical issues are clearly expressed and coherently thought out. Secondly, when extrinsic beliefs take over, then the analysis of actual buildings stops, as it tends to do and therefore their artistic integrity, or that type of morality, is over-looked. Thirdly, the kind of things usually said have to do with the understanding of where history is going – here, according to Pevsner, towards an irrationalism, and Neo-Expressionism. Now this understanding may well be wrong in even the most well-informed experts. In fact, the Modern Movement did not take the direction Pevsner feared when he wrote these lines in the middle sixties; it continued to fragment in several directions at once.[11] But, and this is the point of citing such ideological criticism, it assumes a direction to history and then tries to influence it.

If we look at any current history writing or criticism we'll find similar ideological direction, or else presumed direction, and this entails that the critic act, from a moral point of view, rather like a conscientious traffic cop. He holds up the flow in one direction, and waves the other along; he favours one lane of movement rather than another; he tries to steer the flow *towards* something. He may have no clear idea of what this something is, indeed the majority of writers and the public couldn't say what end state they want, but he usually has a very good notion of the direction to take. For Pevsner it is away from decoration and individuality and towards anonymity and machine production. We see behind these ideological statements there is a metaphor of directionality and position. 'Go towards this, away from that.' There is also the metaphor of balance and equilibrium: 'We've too much of this, let's have more of that, until that is overbalanced.'

This kind of morality may lead the critic, as it has certainly led me, to praising buildings which are not intrinsically very good, and to condemning those which have a great internal integrity, because they 'point' in the wrong direction. To cite personal examples, I have criticized Mies Van der Rohe's buildings because they do not portray and communicate their functions, and this shortcoming I felt was typical of Modernism.[12] Overlooking, for the most part, their internal brilliance, an integrity I thought was overpraised by Giedion and Pevsner, I sought to reset the balance, and the direction of this tradition.[13] Yet how was I to know where architecture was moving? If perchance Mies' buildings were unique, or placed in a Renaissance environment, then I might have praised them. If the Miesian aesthetic were not the reigning approach of large offices would it then be all right? And maybe, despite all appearances, the Miesian aesthetic is not triumphant. It may be confined to the major American and European city centres, and thus in terms of volume the leading style of our time might actually be ersatz Modern or ersatz traditional. In that case, and I think we have to consider it seriously, then both Pevsner and myself, not to mention other critics, have got our perspectives wrong. For the elite movements in our century have merely thrown up the new stylistic options. They have never led society at large, nor captured its imagination. And it's probably in the nature of a mass consumer society that traditional elites no longer have the power to lead, at least in cultural fields.

If this is true then it would cast the continuing controversies and conflicts in a new light, because none of them has made much of a difference to the overall form of the environment. It would also suggest a greater tolerance and unity among the elite. In any case it should suggest a greater descriptive accuracy as to where architecture is and is going. Let us hazard a guess: perhaps fifty per cent of architecture in England is commercialized Trad/Modern, a hybrid style: another thirty per cent is mainstream Modern, perhaps ten per cent is influenced by the avant-garde in one of its five or

RALPH ERSKINE, *Byker Community*, Newcastle, 1974. The architecture of participation, or at least consultation with the inhabitants. Aesthetically the results are unrelated, perhaps making up in vitality for what is lost in control, but in any case less than an integrated work of architecture.

six styles, and ten per cent is unclassifiable. Such a description, even if it is inaccurate by ten per cent, at least shows the pluralism of the situation and how it can accommodate Modernism, Post-Modernism and many shades of 'ism' to either side. Everyone in a consumer society has a small interest in continuing this pluralism, for it allows their own elite approach to continue. While the cost may be high in social terms, the alternative, a single ruling elite, is far worse. For these reasons the critics' moral role should be directional among elites, and for these reasons I have supported the participatory architecture of those such as Ralph Erskine and Lucien Kroll. But, let me reiterate, not because it is great architecture, but rather because it points the direction towards which architecture should go: from *my* perspective. The fact that we may have different perspectives makes, of course, morality possible, because it allows choice, judgement, mistakes.

Megaperiods and key figures

Given the fallibility of an individual's ideology, or even that of the group, it may seem impossible that a fair perspective of architectural worth ever emerges. And yet over time historians and critics begin to construct one. A collective picture is built up, never complete, or filled out and always in need of repainting, to use the visual analogy. But the picture does become clearer, the

The Baroque Megaperiod. Part of an evolutionary tree showing the richness of approaches which are usually subsumed under the heading Baroque. With the continuation of Gothic, Classical, Mannerist, and highly decorated Classical, the period was, as usual, richer than the historians' simplifications.

perspective more balanced, as successive historians inquire into periods and more details. This collective picture, or consensus among experts, no doubt makes such things 'universal' or world history possible, not to mention the art market.[14] It is true the perspective can change suddenly, the price of Victorian painters can rise or fall; or as T. S. Eliot said of the literary tradition, every new master makes us read previous authors in a new way. A new architectural movement also changes the way we look at the past; for instance Modernism and Expressionism made us revalue Mannerism and the Baroque period during the twenties.

And yet as our view of these periods becomes clearer they become more stabilized in valuation. A 'somewhat

universal' history emerges independent of both fashion and current endeavour. We now know a lot about the Baroque megaperiod, from 1620 to 1700, know who were its major architects and what were the reigning ideas and social forces. There are not going to be any major surprises concerning this period – as there were when Borromini and Guarini were re-evaluated at the turn of the century. Nor are we going to write the Baroque off at a stroke as Pugin and Ruskin did.

But there may still be funny distortions in our view of the period caused by our use of the classifying term. During the Baroque megaperiod there were many minor periods such as Northern Mannerism, Realism, Gothic Revival not to mention full blown Classicism. And these minor movements tend to be overlooked or distorted by the historian always searching for the Baroque. This perspective distortion is why I have constructed 'evolutionary trees' of different periods, diagrams which attempt to clarify the variety of approaches and terms. Whether we use such a diagram or not, some such constellation of relative worth and influence is built up in every historian's mind, and by the writing of history itself. The key figures of a period become clearer as does their contribution.

This on face value must be surprising. For if historians have such varying ideologies how do they agree that certain architects are worth discussing and not others? There seems to be an unconscious agreement on the value of particular architecture, and I have suggested that it is due to the integrity of meanings within the work. In short, the *way* forms, ideas and techniques are treated, quite apart from ideological meanings, provides the basic substructure of consensus. It is this quality which I want to focus on as a key to morality in architecture, because it keeps a building alive and reinterpreted with each generation.

Multivalence

Considered in the most abstract way, we could say that every object, poem, tool, etc. is a sign that continually sends out signals to those who are willing and prepared to receive them. Why certain of these objects have continued to remain alive when even their original meanings have become obscure continues to be a mystery; but it is an undeniable fact and one that asks for explanation. Obviously it must have something to do with the object itself, for otherwise the revival and enjoyment of all past artefacts would approach an equal average. Instead of this, we find that certain works remain in obscurity, while others oscillate in and out of favour, while still others remain in fairly steady favour – as 'classics'. It is this continual popularity of classics which has caused the most speculation in the past and made the critic search for some abstract, general quality of 'beauty' or 'significant form' or 'expressionist essence' which they all must share in common. The problem is that if *Hamlet*, the Pantheon, Chartres or *The Night Watch* continue to have an unremitting effect on people, in spite of cultural vicissitudes, then this must be because of some general quality *within* them. Perhaps one imagines that the accounting has been too short and that in geological time, in a few million years or so, they will all merge indistinctly into their background. Still, even given this ultimate perishability in terms of cosmic time, the local significance of these privileged works has to be explained and, it seems to me, that its explanation in terms of 'beauty' or '*Gestalt* form' or 'shared ideology' is too narrow. Instead of these works being constantly alive for only these reasons, they remain potent because they are open to reinterpretation. And this is because they have within their structure enough different meanings in a highly interrelated state to invite or allow new interpretation. They are simply multivalued in a *particularly* organized way, a condition which I will call multivalence, but it has been termed other things by different critics.[15] Because of such multivalence, or density of meaning, *Hamlet*, among plays, finds a new audience and interpretation with every generation.

For example, the Romantics interpreted the play as the story of a melancholic Dane who was given over to fits of brooding, neurotic madness and one who was forced to delay committed action because he was excessively intellectual or 'thought-sick', as Coleridge said. However, in a contrary interpretation, recent critics have argued that Hamlet is really the ideal, Elizabethan hero who is in fact avenging a horrible crime, withstanding political subterfuge, acting with the utmost moral scruples and realizing his fate in a tragic triumph of will. Or, again conversely, some have seen him as the archetypal male, suffering from an Oedipus complex, who delays in his actions because of the 'unconcious repugnance' of wanting to sleep with his mother and kill the substitute for his father.[16] Now the curious fact about all these and many other interpretations is that they are plausible, and realized in time. That is they refer to real qualities within the work which have remained hidden and only *possible*. The tantalizing fact is that what exists in a multivalent work, as a latent possibility for all time, can only be discovered and brought to consciousness within time. Even though there exists a single correct or most plausible interpretation of *Hamlet,* one can still insist that it continues to be relevant because the multivalent meanings are extracted or discovered by each new generation.

If this is true for a single object, it is even more true for a whole period. In a remarkable book on the various ways the Gothic has been interpreted for eight centuries, Paul Frankl has demonstrated the paradox of this situation.[17] First of all the term and concept 'Gothic' were created for reasons which now appear to rest on a grand historical mistake: to denote a form of building supposedly conceived by barbaric hordes of Goths who had invaded Rome in the fourth century and destroyed classical civilization. That these same Goths had created an 'irrational, barbaric' architecture which was 'not strong enough to bear the slightest weight' and was so full of 'many projections, gaps, brackets and curlicues' that it was 'out of proportion' was all apparent to Vasari and the Renaissance who condemned it. Equally apparent to succeeding generations, who however praised the Gothic, was that it was the work of Bavarian woodsmen who tied the tops of large pine trees together to achieve the elaborate ribbed vaults; or it was the pious work of dedicated, anonymous craftsmen who were sacrificing their labour to the single glory of God. Now none of these interesting interpretations was in fact historically correct – if by correct we mean the way the actual architects conceived and built their work. And yet they are no more implausible than the interpretation that Hamlet, or even Shakespeare, was suffering from an Oedipus complex. That is to say, they point to implicit structures within the works, a condition which Erwin Panofsky has termed 'iconology'.[18] These speculative hypotheses are illuminating and plausible interpretations which keep the objects

concerned of interest. To generalize from these examples, we can say that there are many wrong interpretations which simply do not work and, in the case of multivalent works, a smaller but open set of plausible ones which can only be actualized in time. Nothing would be more destructive of our intercourse with objects than to insist that there is only one right interpretation of them, even if it is claimed to be that of the creator's original intention. This interpretation may be a privileged and primary one, but its exclusive acceptance can only be reductive and lead to the sterility which stops growth of the mind and our interest in the object itself.

That this is so has been long realized, especially in the nineteenth century when the succession of historical styles and new interpretations of them took place at an accelerating rate. In order to explain this increasing rate of change, the architect and professor Adolf Göller sharpened the concept of aesthetic fatigue – or the way forms are used up and exhausted through familiarity.[19] 'Familiarity breeds contempt', '*déjà vu*', 'monotonous knowledge'. Göller's explanation was that when forms and ideas become so completely stamped in the memory that we can reconstitute all their dimensions with ease, then there is no pleasure left in them because there is no mystery or possibility of discovery. One has the feeling of claustrophobia induced by being restricted to well-worn paths, the paths of habit and mechanical certainty. Given the familiar object X, out pops the usual interpretation Y, as mechanical and certain as the message from one of those audio guides now found in Gothic cathedrals. This mechanical nature of the memory thus points to the other side of the equation concerning value – that is ourselves.

It is apparent that since meaning depends on human perception, any holistic theory of value must be irreducibly dualistic in nature: both concerned with relations *intrinsic* in the object, and the *extrinsic* knowledge and beliefs within the observer. Thus we may accept the importance of ideology and fashion in determining the value of a work even if it is less important than ideologists would wish. In our time historians and architects have appropriated ideology under the umbrella of 'the spirit of the age', and we are still a long way from being able to discuss ideology openly, without being unduly pushed to accept one position rather than another.

Imagination and multivalence
By now it is probably obvious that the theory of value or multivalence is in one sense hardly new. The idea is similar to that of the 'organic whole' which as a critical term goes back to Plato. And it is one which has been revived by almost every Neo-Platonist from Aristotle to Plotinus, and in architecture, from Vitruvius to Alberti, to Frank Lloyd Wright and Le Corbusier.[20] For instance, the Neo-Platonic architects of the Renaissance insisted, following Alberti, that in a perfect work 'nothing might be added, taken away or altered, but for the worse'. Why? Because the meanings, and proportions, were so carefully worked out that they were all interrelated. Baroque architects refined this idea of the integrated whole by showing that it partly depended on the presence of an overriding idea or *concetto*.[21] A single idea, or set of related concepts, unified disparate parts, just as recurring motifs at different scales pulled together a variety of images.

If so much could be taken for granted in Neo-Platonic aesthetics, then the next step, which insisted on a *discordia concors*, 'a combination of dissimilar images', was less obvious. Samuel Johnson in the eighteenth century was one of the first to explain what the Metaphysical poets had shown: that when 'the most heterogeneous ideas are yoked by violence together', then, assuming some sort of sufficient yoking, a positive conjunction, the result was more provoking and interesting than simple integration. Such antithesis as 'complex simplicity' came to be preferred to 'easy simplicity'. Works that showed 'controlled passion' were to be preferred to works that were simple, passionate, cloying or gratifying alone. The 'higher' art forms were held superior to farce and doggerel because they showed a greater maturity, complexity and balance in their structure, as well as in the audience's response to that structure.[22]

In the twentieth century, with the work of the New Critics, T. S. Eliot, I. A. Richards and others, this notion of the complex unity, or 'tension', in Metaphysical poetry for instance, was further sharpened. Eliot argued that the Metaphysical poet could 'devour any kind of experience' and form new unities out of the most diverse sort of material, while Richards developed a theory of imagination, which showed why this complexity was itself psychically nourishing. To see how much more refined the theory had become since its Platonic origins, one only has to think of how it could be used to justify such apparently unorganic, non-wholes as T. S. Eliot's *The Wasteland* or Duchamp's *Ready-Mades* which were composed by taking away and adding on different parts – in direct contradiction to Alberti's injunction. The idea of an 'organic whole' had become generalized to mean a work which had so many internal linkages, and such strong ones, that even unintegrated matter could be accepted into its pattern for the tension it caused in a reading. Thus the 'simple whole' was resisted by contradictions in Robert Venturi's notion of 'the difficult whole'. In such notions we are taken back to an idea which Samuel Taylor Coleridge had developed in the nineteenth century.

What Coleridge did was to place the emphasis on the 'synergetic' power of the imagination: show how it fused opposites into a new unity by mediating between thinking and feeling, conscious and unconscious aspects of the mind. He formulated the theory of how the poet's imagination fused disparate material, a theory which applies as well to the artist and architect.

> The poet, described in ideal perfection, brings the whole soul of man into activity, with the subordination of its faculties to each other, according to their relative worth and dignity. He diffuses a tone and spirit of unity, that blends, and (as it were) fuses, each into each, by that synthetic and magical power, to which we have exclusively appropriated the name of imagination. This power, first put in action by the will and understanding, and retained under their irremissive, though gentle and unnoticed control (*laxis effertur habenis*) reveals itself in the balance or reconciliation of opposite or discordant qualities: of sameness with difference; the individual, with the representative; the sense of novelty and freshness with old and familiar objects; a more than usual state of emotion, with more than usual order; judgement ever awake and steady self-possession . . .

There are many interrelated ideas on creation here, but in this particular context, the following points should be underlined: the imagination is an active *power* which *fuses opposites* into a new whole where they are no

longer just opposites, but have something new in common, (*a new creation of links and tone*). This synthetic power mediates between the conscious will (or choice) and the unconscious (or emotions and memory); it diffuses a tone or spirit of unity (the tone is something the poet actively creates, the unity is something he finds through new linkage). All these points had been made before by theorists, but Coleridge was the first one to shape them into a coherent critical tool and counterpose them in a most important distinction: that between the *modifying* power of the imagination and the *aggregating* labour of the fancy:

> [The imagination] dissolves, diffuses and dissipates, in order to recreate; or where this process is rendered impossible, yet still at all events it struggles to idealize and to unify. It is essentially *vital*, even as all objects (as objects) are essentially fixed and dead.
>
> FANCY, on the contrary, has no other counters to play with, but fixities and definites. The Fancy is indeed no other than a mode of Memory emancipated from the order of space and time; while it is blended with, and modified by that empirical phenomenon of the will, which we express by the word choice. But equally with the ordinary memory the Fancy must receive all its materials ready made from the law of association.[23]

This distinction between imagination and fancy is of course a logical construct as there is no physical locale where each is placed within the brain. In fact, the distinction points to a very real difference in the workings of the mind, or rather the whole personality. It is precisely Coleridge's point that the imagination, as distinct from the fancy, co-ordinates more faculties than just reason. For instance, it mediates between the kinaesthetic centres which are responsible for rhythm, sound and movement and the higher centres which are responsible for thought. Thus it produces multivalent works where 'the sound is an echo', or perhaps a contrast, to the sense, whereas the fancy would produce a univalent work where the relation between sound and sense is neither positive nor negative but merely fortuitous.

In short, we see that what is at stake in the distinction is the number and density of the relations or links and not, as Neo-Platonic theory averred, whether all the elements are unified in terms of style and content, and point in a common direction. As mentioned above there is evidence to show that strong movement towards a goal which is resisted by counter-movement, or tension, is of higher value than unrestrained movement, because it brings into play opposite faculties of the psyche – thinking and feeling – which make contrary demands. On an analogous level tragedy is considered as of greater importance than propaganda because it engages more aspects of our personality and also because it is more fitted to the complexities of life.

The last distinction of Coleridge's which should be brought out is that the imagination is essentially creative and 'vital' because it 'dissolves, diffuses and dissipates in order to recreate'; whereas the fancy is essentially passive and uncreative, because it works under the control of the will with 'fixities and definites'. In short, the fancy does not change or modify the elements with new linkage. Thus the products of the fancy are cool and relatively dissociated like discursive prose, whereas those of the imagination are intense and compacted like a resonant symbol.

There have been several developments of this theory

in the twentieth century which have extended and sharpened the ideas of Coleridge. One of them, by I. A. Richards, is a direct application of Coleridge's theory to poetry.[24] This clarifies the fact that it is the number and interrelation of links that distinguishes imagination from fancy. We see in this formulation the similarity between imaginative works and those which Christopher Alexander has characterized as rich in linkage. He shows that 'organic cities' and objects are richly linked as 'semi-lattices' rather than 'tree' diagrams.[25] Using Alexander's terminology, we could say that the greater the set of elements (M) and the greater the linkage between them (L) then the greater is the imaginative fusion. But there is a problem with this model which brings out a crucial aspect of the imagination: Alexander's method is too rational and thus it doesn't allow that breadth of approach which brings into play sensual and emotional aspects of design.

Another sharpening of Coleridge's theory, albeit in entirely different terms and with different purposes in mind, is Arthur Koestler's *The Act of Creation*, 1964. Koestler, like Coleridge, shows that creation is essentially the finding of a new link in previously dissociated material – a 'bisociation of matrices' he calls it, underlining the idea that two or more developed skills, or objects, are fused into a new whole. Again the point is made that

CHRISTOPHER ALEXANDER, *Semi-lattice diagram compared with a tree*, is much richer in linkage. If we substitute for his nodes the meanings (M) of a work, and the linkage between them (L), we see how his 'organic' semi-lattice is multivalent by comparison to the univalent 'tree'. The number of connections are roughly comparable to the chains of associations between meanings. The 'organicity' of a work thus relates directly to the number of meanings (M) and the number of links (L). This model does not, however, make clear several crucial aspects of multivalence: the inventiveness of the links, their newness, nor existence on non-intellectual levels of perception.

when successful creation occurs, as opposed to a mere aggregation, then the parts of the new whole have had their internal structure changed. This is true whether the creation is a scientific concept such as space-time (which modified the ideas of both halves) or a banal joke such as – 'The definition of a sadist is a person who is kind to a masochist'. Koestler comments:

> The link-concept is 'kindness', bisociated with two diametrically opposed meanings; moreover the whole definition is open to two different interpretations:
> a. the sadist does a kindness to the masochist by torturing him;
> b. the sadist is torturing the masochist by being kind to him.
> . . . we can get around [the paradox here] by deciding that in either interpretation 'kind' should be understood both literally and metaphorically at the same time; in other words by playing simultaneously two games governed by opposite rules.[26]

If, as Koestler shows, creation in all fields follows this same principle of bisociation of previously separate matrices, it is also contingent upon unconscious and semi-conscious action in order to make the new linkage. In many examples of scientific creation from Kekule's dream of an organic compound as a snake eating its own tail to Einstein's image of himself riding a light ray, Koestler shows how semi-conscious processes can discover the new linkage where conscious thought, because of its tendency to remain within habitual patterns, cannot. Thus we are led again to a critique of Alexander's method for attaining multivalence as the limited and unlikely case.

Before we apply the theory of value to a work of architecture the abstract criteria of multivalence should

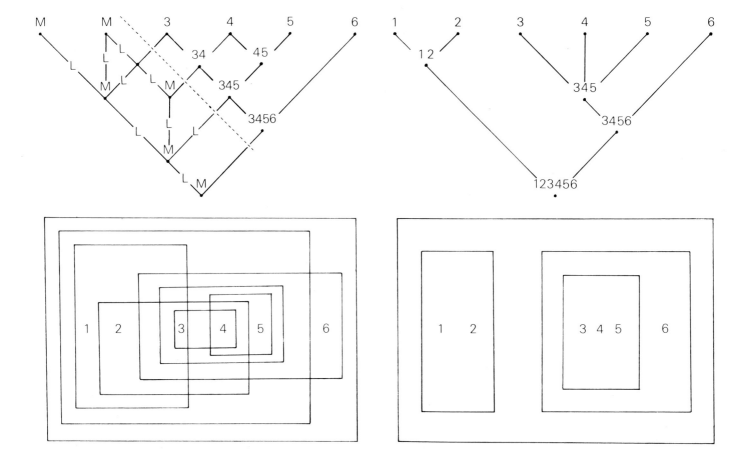

be summarized. It has three general properties: 1. it refers to the imaginative bisociation, really multisociation, of *new creations*; 2. it refers to the *amount* of material, or the set of elements (M) in a matrix, and 3. it emphasizes the *linkage* (L) between the elements, which causes them to modify each other.

Francesco Borromini's 'dome' of S. Ivo della Sapienza

It makes sense to examine an acknowledged master work of architecture which is rich in creative meanings, rather than an ordinary work, if we are to appreciate the qualities of multivalence. Borromini's church of S. Ivo in Rome, 1642-50, is such a work and it's so rich in multiply-linked meanings that we will confine our analysis to just one exterior aspect, the 'dome'. Inverted commas are necessary here, as in much original work, because it is not so much a dome as a bisociation of that form with others – a spire, ziggurat, temple etc. and, for us, multi-stage rocket. This last image may seem far-fetched at

FRANCESCO BORROMINI, *S. Ivo della Sapienza*, Rome, 1642–50. This university church, planned on a six-pointed star the symbol of wisdom, carries the themes of intellectual light (carried by Divine Wisdom) into its structure and elevation. On the interior dome various papal symbols converge on the armorial sun, another symbol of the Barberini family, wisdom and papal supremacy. On the exterior, the seven distinct layers combine and contrast themes of the papacy and S. Ivo as the *Domus Sapientiae*, the house of wisdom. The spiral may symbolize the Tower of Babel 'redeemed' by superior Christian symbols; it may also refer to an Early Christian symbol of the Church as a spiral winding around a pillar. The semantic meanings of this form extend to signs of growth, change and ascension, while the overall syntactic meaning – the spiral as a synthesis of the horizontal steps and vertical pilasters is a bisociation of forms.

first, and we know Borromini couldn't have intended it. But it does relate to similar astral images of the form – comets, stars, and quick, explosive movement in general – and a primary quality of multivalent works is to suggest future meanings. Here this unlikely image is made more plausible by the various vertical attachments – booster rockets – balls, flaming obelisks and a flaming crown, all of which seem to burst upwards.

What Borromini *did* intend was a combination of the 'dome' with other forms in such a way that it was both present and absent. The swelling, curving domes of Rome – St. Peters and others – are only just barely visible, pushing through the six concave curves of the drum and the swell of the 'steps'. On the inside it actually exists as a six-sided ribbed dome, but on the outside this is mostly concealed by the straight vertical drum (as in North Italian examples of the time).[27] So it is an enigmatic form, bulging onto the surface in the forms of convex or stepped shapes, a dome trying to 'break out', and at the same time a 'non-dome', a pyramidal spire. This ambiguity was at once a cause for consternation and excitement. Immediately the scaffolding was off the architects and citizens of Rome reacted, either with praise at the invention, or censure at the distortion. But, inevitably, it

S. Ivo della Sapienza. Besides the symbolism already mentioned there is a numerological basis to the dome: the 12 steps ascend and are confirmed by the 12 lantern columns (Durandus: 'twelve [stands for] the glorious company, the Apostles and, tropologically, the whole Church'). The 8 church doctors and 4 Evangelists (four turns of the spiral) are also symbolised. The figure of Divine Wisdom carrying a lamp, which illuminates the intellect, is perhaps latent in the flaming torches on the last spiral.

wasn't just the 'dome' which could be read in various new ways, but also the forms to which it was being visually linked, or equated. The church spire and bell tower, one French the other Italian but both well known, were also being distorted by this new linkage. These distortions of popular codes were enough to cause Borromini trouble for the rest of his life, while at the same time assuring him the devoted support of his admirers. It is difficult today to see how creative his solution was because so many Baroque domes and towers were based on his inventions.

Here something like seven distinct elements are combined in this multi-staged rocket, so the linkage is much more complex than a simple bisociation. At the base, the six-sided drum swells out a thinner convex shape to counterpoint the larger concave base, the *cortile* designed by Giacomo della Porta previously. So well integrated is this opposition of curves, and continuation of centralized movement, that many people have believed one architect designed the whole complex. The formal integration, the similarity of colour, material and window shape, is itself a kind of linkage, of equal importance to the linkage of ideas.

To either side of the 'dome' are further similarities of form, small versions of the overall shape, the superimposed mountains and stars which are papal symbols, and signs of the powerful Chigi family. These are imaginative transformations of this conventional sign *and* sculptural accents of the main shape, so that like every other form they have more than one meaning. Their pyramidal outline matches up with the 'dome', the mountains reappear again further up as hovering globes, and the starburst is recalled at the top in the crown and cross (the Chigi sign was often a globe with a cross). Thus, as with bisociated ideas, we get two different readings brought together by a 'link concept', the similar pyramidal form. According to one reading the sign is an exaggerated 'pop' advertisement for the power and glory of the Chigi family (Borromini intended at one point to use the motif as a giant entrance door).[28] A certain irony may be intended through the gigantic size. According to the other meaning, however, the forms are a natural and conventional sign of sanctity. Profane or sacred, or both, these are the meanings which cohere to these forms as they do to the whole church. And the meanings modify each other so that we read each one as 'more than' itself (e.g. a symbol of heavenward aspiration plus a propagandist argument for the supremacy of one family, one faith and one city).

Perhaps the multiplicity of forms, and their eclecticism, should be seen as providing an overall argument for a syncretic world view (a Catholicism meaning 'universal to opposite cultures'). Borromini may be trying to reconcile pagan and foreign meanings with Christian ones; summarize in brief the history of Rome and relate it to Islam and the supremacy of the Catholic faith.

Above the drum is a 'stepped pyramid' which is not only Eygptian in overtone, but also Christian – 'stairs to heaven'. These steps are divided by swooping buttresses which also have double meanings – they recall the Gothic buttress that Borromini knew well, and the Classical pilaster and impost. They also function visually in two quite different ways: to continue the vertical thrust of the lower pilasters and to form a ring, which will be echoed in successive 'crowns'. Thus, at very least, they are part of four separate contexts, or in Koestler's terms 'matrices of meaning', each with their own chain of associations and rules of combination. Again this surplus of meanings

S. Ivo della Sapienza. The Chigi mountain and star (or globe and sunburst) is a decorative element that is transformed into a unifying formal motif. On the inside the round mountains, in a pyramidal massing are surrounded by flaming crowns while on the outside, the globes and crosses become, on the spiral, twisted crowns plus globes – thus reversing the theme. The spiral ends in the flaming crown holding another type of globe – a negative formed by the iron cusps. The Chigi theme and its variations unifies one level after another thus making the whole 'dome' into an argument for a particular papal family. But the heraldic signs are also so tranformed into cosmic and abstract ones, and so the meaning can be reversed from propaganda to philosophy.

causes consternation and excitement, as our mind tries to decode a single answer and finds instead clues to many possible solutions.

The next level, that of the 'lantern', is also a little temple, or *tempietto* as it was called, a pun on Bramante's building of that name. In its sweeping concave shapes and columns it also recalls the ancient Roman temple at Baalbek, so again a present Christianity is being united with a previous paganism. The formal unifications also become apparent at this level as the six-sided shape of the drum, and its centre window, are played in a different key: the pilasters have come together as paired columns, convex has become concave and the general bay rhythm of A, B, A is repeated. Thus the *tempietto* is being equated with the drum semantically, an equality which is confirmed on the interior, where the lantern is a little dome. This redundancy of forms heightens their visual potency since it doubles the interpretations of each one. Furthermore, the *tempietto* intensifies the vertical thrust by gathering these visual forces in a tighter space.

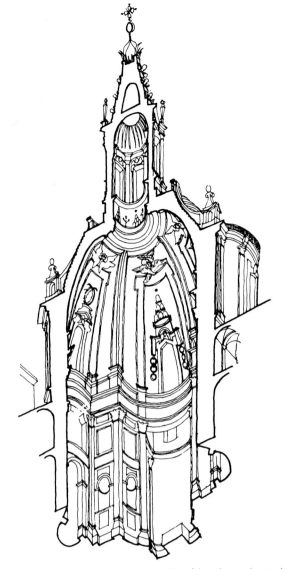

S. Ivo della Sapienza, cut-away axonometric of interior and exterior. (Paolo Portoghesi).

We are not prepared, however, for the next transformation which is, or was at the time, truly extraordinary; the turning of these vertical forces into an ascending spiral. We might expect instead either a repetition of the 'steps' or a continuation of the pilaster and buttress lines of thrust. But we get a shape that is both and neither; the spiral 'ramp' echoes the steps, while on its surface in low relief are 'frames' which echo the pilasters, and hold the vertical lines. These variations on a theme have the effect of pulling together all the previous visual forces for their final burst of energy – the explosive crown, the thin almost invisible iron cusps which hold the globe and topmost cross.

The spiral is also semantically ingenious, recalling a variety of cultural and natural allusions. Perhaps it personifies Wisdom, appropriate to the name and function of this university church (della Sapienza). Since the spiral surrounding a pillar was also a symbol of the Church we have a rather obvious bisociation of Divine Wisdom – The

Church. The spiral also naturally signifies time and growth, meanings inherent in the collection of spiral, conch shells that Borromini built up and kept at home. Architectural meanings alluded to were the spiral columns that Imperial Romans built to celebrate their victories; Babylonian temples and ziggurats, as well as the great mosque at Samarra. The most obvious allusion, the Tower of Babel, might be intended as well, with the ironic twist that now this pagan form has been crowned, or subjugated, or redeemed by the superincumbent Christian cross. An alternative bisociation is that the spiral form represents Divine Wisdom, and that we see here the moment of Pentecost when the Holy Spirit descends and the original confusion of tongues is cleared away by the Gift of Tongues. This interpretation is supported by the fact that the conventional meaning of the Tower of Babel form, the spiral, had reversed itself (in certain quarters) and that by 1650 it meant the Gift of Tongues, understanding and the Pentecost. Thus there is a dual, contradictory meaning to the form: both Tower of Babel and anti-Babel. Whatever its precise emblematic meaning, it has these various references, and they once again bring together opposite cultures under the dominance of Rome.

The references, and distinct layers, are often quite explicit and allowed to keep a certain autonomy. It is true the layers are also merged by intermediate forms – the vertical scrolls and flaming torches – but they still keep an identity. This gives the whole 'dome' its curious eclectic feeling, as if it were a piling up of distinct cultural symbols into a *summa* of wisdom and theology. Yet because most of these layers and symbols are cross-referenced, the result is not an encyclopedia. Rather it is a coherent whole and, I believe, an argument for a pluralistic world view and syncretism.

The last supposition is, however, not crucial to my exposition which concerns multivalence. Borromini's S. Ivo has to an excessive degree the three aspects of multivalence which I've mentioned: a series of inventive combinations that unite previously separate meanings (e.g. 'dome', steps, *tempietto*, Tower of Babel); a great amount of meanings, both syntactic and semantic, which can be related; and a great deal of linkage between these meanings (between the visual layers, and the themes such as Christianity/paganism). It is this kind of integrity we value in works of art and architecture, an integrity based on a sure working out of imaginative links. And whether this linkage is present in impoverished systems, such as Eisenman's, or eclectic ones such as Borromini's, its importance is to set up a rich density of interrelated meanings which keeps the eye and mind at work. This 'organicity' of architecture ultimately keeps it alive to each generation, or to put it another way, stimulates the sensual and intellectual appetite of succeeding generations. All great art stimulates growth of the mind as well, no doubt a highly moral function for it. Clearly there is more to morality in architecture than this – it matters what the meanings are – but surely not less.

NOTES

1.1 Introduction

1 *The Language of Post-Modern Architecture*, Rizzoli, New York; Academy, London, 1977, revised 1980, p. 9.

1.2 Late-Modernism and Post-Modernism

1 A general point about historical periodization. The length of a creative movement is often not more than twenty years. The High Renaissance or High Baroque only lasted about this length, so by comparison High Modernism, if we want to call it that, was longer lived – roughly from 1920 to 1960. The second general point concerning historical periodization concerns its discontinuity and the excellence of individual architects. By and large the best architects work when a movement is young, or has just started, but there are exceptions to this rule. Thus good High Renaissance buildings were produced in provincial centres right up until 1620. Indeed English architects such as Inigo Jones practised it *after* the country had gone through a 'kind of' Mannerism. High Baroque flourished in parts of Spain, Northern Italy and Bohemia long after it had died in Rome. Today of course movements travel around the globe with the speed of an issue of *A & U*, so time disjunctions tend to disappear; but they are replaced by the plurality of styles and approaches. The previous historical discontinuity and the present pluralism should warn us that good architecture, formally creative, can be found even after a period has 'died'. This leads us to the conclusion that some form of Modernism, or rather the International Style minus its utopian and social ideology, will be practised into the twenty-first century. It needs to be called Late-Modernism to distinguish it from the previous mode and ideology of the Pioneers.

The last general point concerns the classification of schools, movements and entire periods. How do historians ever come to agree that any period as diverse as the Renaissance should be fixed by one, or at least a very few labels? First of all the classifying process is a long and cumulative one created by a few individual historians – Vasari, Wölfflin come to mind – and then spelled out and modified by much subsequent research, which shows, for instance, the exceptions to straight-line development. The general categories or periods may remain, but are modified in shape. Thus the Mannerist period is shown to have mini-Classicist revivals, the Baroque is seen to be distorted by the influence of Gothic and exotic sources. The general rule is, I believe, that in any one cohesive movement there are many lesser trends as well as conflicts within the reigning approach. We can never find complete agreement or unity and thus we classify on the basis of a constellation of related motifs and ideas rather than a completely integrated system. Out of ten or so aspects of the Renaissance, only seven or eight are shared by diverse architects such as Alberti, Palladio and Inigo Jones. Classification into groups is thus a matter of statistical degree, of loose overlap, rather than exact correspondence between architects.

2 Portoghesi explained these meanings in a lecture at the Architectural Association, October 1978. Further interpretation, especially concerned with his notion of 'place', can be found in Christian Norberg-Schultz, *On the Search for Lost Architecture*, the works of Paolo Portoghesi, Vittorio Gigliotti, 1959–1975, Officina Edizioni, Rome 1976, pp. 55–64.

3 In Italy his battles with Bruno Zevi and Marxist critics are well known. Outside of Italy his work is not very well known.

4 The Crooks House, 1977, is the first key building where Classicist historicism becomes apparent. How much this is due to other Post-Modernists, including myself, is hard to say, but Michael and I had many discussions on implicit versus explicit metaphor in London and Los Angeles over a period of two years. No doubt since his two year stay in Rome years ago he has always been aware of this bank of historical reference. The influence of Robert Stern and the exhibition on the Beaux-Arts should not be discounted.

5 Conversation April 1978, looking at his drawings. My analysis here is partly based on the references he mentioned and those which are implicitly coded.

6 For the idea of suggested metaphor and the 'penumbra effect' see *The Language of Post-Modern Architecture*, Academy, London, 1978, p. 48, p. 117.

7 In *The Language of Post-Modern Architecture* I gave several historical examples including the classical temple pediment which mixed representational and abstract codes. Dual-coding and a desire to communicate, rather than stylistic qualities, distinguish Post-Modernists as a school.

8 See the *New York Times*, March 31, 1978, p. B.4. This project was also featured on the front page of the *New York Times* that day; in its *Sunday Color Magazine*, May 14, 1978, and on the front page of *The Times*, London, May 13, 1978. Its 'news' value as the first historicist skyscraper was obvious.

9 From their descriptive brochure, *Pavillon Soixante-Dix*, 1978.

10 Yasufumi Kijima 'Making an Image Sketch After the Building is Finished' from *The Japan Architect*, Oct/Nov 1977, p. 48. The issue is, incidentally, on 'Post-Metabolism'.

11 Letter to author, March 12, 1978, after our discussion on the Long House.

2.3 The Supersensualists I and II

1 *Pasolini on Pasolini, Interviews with Oswald Stack*, Thames and Hudson, London, 1969, p. 142.

2 See John Weightman's very sympathetic but ultimately incomprehending review of Pasolini's *Theorem* in *Encounter*, June 1969, pp. 41–2.

3 See *AD* 4/70.

4 See *AD* 7/70.

5 Unpublished manuscript, 1970.

6 Superstudio's twelve ideal cities are even more the *end* of a process – 'the supreme achievement of twenty thousand years of civilisation, blood, sweat and tears; the final haven of Man in possession of Truth, free from contradictions, doubts, equivocations and indecision; totally and forever replete with his own PERFECTION'. *AD* 12/71, pp. 737–742.

2.4 The Pluralism of Japanese Architecture

1 See Robert Venturi, *Complexity and Contradiction in Architecture*, Museum of Modern Art, New York, 1966.

2 Robin Boyd, *New Directions in Japanese Architecture*, Studio Vista, London, 1968, p. 34, p. 102.

3 See pages 88–98.

4 Michael F. Roess has written two excellent articles on this subject. See 'Architechnics' in *Architecture Plus*, May/June 1974, pp. 88–97; also 'Modern Technology changes the Built Environment: Japanese Values and Architechnology', in *The Japan Interpreter*, 1973, pp. 334–351.

5 See Arata Isozaki, 'About my method', *The Japan Architect*, August 1972, pp. 22–28.

6 Arata Isozaki, *op cit*, note 7, p. 38.

7 I have treated this theme in my essay 'Architecture and Morality', as well as 'Irrational Rationalism – The Rats Since 1960'.

8 Of course these theorists recognized a cultural role for architecture, but they still overemphasized natural determinisms and confused custom with natural law, form with function, signifier with signified. To say that the relation between these two sets of oppositions is 'arbitrary' is not to say it is irrational, 'free' or unpredictable, but rather that it is not set by nature. It is open to premeditated change.

9 For a statement on this view from an anthropological perspective see Amos Rapaport, *House Form and Culture*, New Jersey, 1969, pp. 58–60, p. 135.

10 Mayumi Miyawaki, 'Are the Young Architects Changing Course?', *The Japan Architect*, Nov/Dec 1974, pp. 19–26. An excellent article on the forces that shape the urban house and Miyawaki's response with 'Primary Architecture'.

11 Takefumi Aida, 'Twelve Memoranda on the House like a Die', *The Japan Architect*, April 1974, p. 83.

12 Takefumi Aida, 'Speculation in the Dark', *The Japan Architect*, November 1972, p. 101.

13 Mayumi Miyawaki, 'Why Primary Forms?', *The Japan Architect*, January 1972, p. 31.

14 Takefumi Aida, 'When Architecture Disappears', *The Japan Architect*, April 1974, p. 42.

15 The Face House and anthropomorphism are further discussed in *The Language of Post–Modern Architecture*, section under 'Metaphor' and *Bizarre Architecture*, Academy and Rizzoli, London and New York, 1979.

16 Letter 'My Way of Architecture', April 1975. Miyawaki has also been critical of the Metabolists, or at least the 'high–rise slums that resemble long chicken coops' which have been copied from Metabolist building. See note 10 for the reference for this attack – part of the healthy dialectic which is underway.

17 Mayumi Miyawaki, 'Why Primary Forms?', *The Japan Architect*, January 1972, pp. 29–31.

18 Mayumi Miyawaki, 'White Triangle', *The Japan Architect*, February 1975, p. 86.

19 Mayumi Miyawaki, 'Declaration in Favour of Primary Architecture', *The Japan Architect*, October 1970, pp. 34–5.

20 Minoru Takeyama, 'Emotional Notations', *The Japan Architect*, April 1974, p. 28.

21 Juan Pablo Bonta, *An Anatomy of Architectural Interpretation*, a semiotic view of the criticism of Mies Van der Rohe's Barcelona Pavilion, Barcelona 1975.

2.5 Irrational Rationalism – The Rats Since 1960

1 See Karl Popper, *Conjectures and Refutations, The Growth of Scientific Knowledge*, London, 1963, partly the entries under 'Intellectualism' which correspond to Rationalism. Popper's *Critical* Rationalism should not be confused with this intellectualism, because it is rooted in refutation, in criticism.

2 See Giulia Veronesi, *Difficoltà Politiche dell'Architettura in Italia, 1920–1940*, Milan, 1953. Leonardo Benevolo, *History of Modern Architecture*, Volume 2, London, 1971, pp. 561–576.

3 See *Architettura Razionale*, 'XV Triennale di Milano', by Aldo Rossi, Franco Raggi, Massimo Scolari, Rosaldo Boncalzi, Gianni Braghieri and Daniele Vitale, Franco Angeli Editore, Milan, 1973.

4 Colin Rowe, 'Collage City', *The Architectural Review*, August 1975 and following letters. The book is published by the MIT Press, 1979.

5 The main criticisms in English are: Alan Colquhoun, 'Rational Architecture', *AD*, June 1975, pp. 365–6; Manfredo Tafuri, 'L'Architecture dans le Boudoir', *Oppositions 3*, May 1974, pp. 42–8; Vittorio Savi, 'Aldo Rossi', *Lotus 11*, 1976, pp. 42–52; Vittorio Savi, David Stewart in *A+U* No. 5, 1976, issue devoted to Rossi with bibliography.

6 Aldo Rossi, *A+U, op cit*, p. 74.

7 Manfredo Tafuri, *Oppositions 3, op cit*, p. 45. See also his *Architecture and Utopia, Design and Capitalist Development*, MIT Press, 1976, pp. 170–182.

8 Massimo Scolari, 'Avanguardia Nuoval Architettura' in *Architettura Razionale*, quoted from Alan Colquhoun's translation, *op cit*, p. 366.

9 Takefumi Aida, *The Japan Architect*, November 1972, p. 101.

10 Leon Krier, 'Projects in the City', in *Lotus, op cit*, p. 73.

11 Richard Meier, 'My Statement' is an issue devoted to his work of *A+U*, No. 4, 1976, p. 76.

12 Susan Whittig pointed out the 'foregrounding' of certain themes in Eisenman, Graves and Venturi in her paper 'Architecture about Architecture' delivered at the Semiotics Conference in Milan, June 1974.

13 Colin Rowe and Robert Slutzky, 'Transparency: Literal and Phenomenal', *Perspecta*, No. 8, New Haven, 1963, pp. 45–46.

14 I have written on the 'Los Angeles Silvers', *Progressive Architecture*, December 1976; *A+U*, October 1976.

15 My own guess is that the movement will split evenly in two directions.

16 These quotes from John Hejduk actually refer to a discussion of Mondrian, Van Doesburg, Le Corbusier's Carpenter Centre and the paintings of Juan Gris, but they apply equally to his Diamond series. See his 'Out of Time and Into Space' in an issue of *A+U* devoted to his work, 1975, No. 5, pp. 3–24.

17 Ken Frampton, 'Frontality vs Rotation', *Five Architects*, New York 1972, 1975, pp. 9–13. See also his 'John Hejduk and the Cult of Humanism' in the *A+U* cited, note 16. Frampton isn't altogether supportive of the Five and Hejduk, but he confines his analysis to formal concerns and then jumps a mile to pure iconological interpretation.

18 The Hejduk quote from *A+U*, p. 4; the Frampton one from *Five Architects, op cit*, p. 10.

19 This chronology Hejduk outlined in a lecture at UCLA in April 1976.

20 Robert Frost, in 'Mending Wall': 'Something there is that doesn't love a wall. That wants it down'. Of course, as Hejduk shows, walls unite neighbours on a line and are therefore basically ambiguous, half bringing together, half dividing.

21 Rem Koolhaas formed OMA, The Office for Metropolitan Architecture, on January 1, 1975. This office includes his wife Madelon Vriesendorp, and Elia and Zoe Zenghelis and sometimes O. M. Ungers: two Dutch, two Greeks and an occasional German. Their work has been published in *Lotus 11, op cit*, and Koolhaas has published *Delirious New York*, New York and London, 1978.

22 Rem Koolhaas, *Lotus 11, op cit*, p. 36.

23 *Ibid*, p. 34.

24 Elia Zenghelis, *Lotus 11*, p. 36.

3.2 Bruce Goff – The Michelangelo of Kitsch

1 See *The Architecture of Bruce Goff* by Jeffrey Cook, Granada Publishing Ltd., St. Albans, 1978, p. 96.

2 *Ibid*, p. 30.

3 See Robert Kostka, 'Bruce Goff and the New Tradition', *The Prairie School Review*, Second Quarter 1970, p. 11. A student at the AA and Miami University, Paul S. Brown, who worked for Goff for the

summer of 1976, supplied me with some of this information, including that on Goff's method of design.

4 See *Adhocism* by myself and Nathan Silver, pp. 84–87, where several examples are given with descriptions by Goff which show his enthusiasm for out-adhocing the next guy and being cheaper than thou (*Adhocism*, Academy, London, republished 1977). Reyner Banham refers to the 'Army and Navy Surplus Aesthetic' in his *Guide to Modern Architecture*, 1962, re-edited as *Age of the Masters, a personal view of Modern Architecture*, Architectural Press, London, 1975, p. 79.

5 See Cook, *op cit*, p. 121.

6 *Ibid*, p. 63.

7 Admittedly Goff used these parts as scaffolding on the Bavinger House whereas Gaudí used them as decorative grill-work on his Güell Chapel. But they both revel in refusing industrial or commercial waste, whereas Wright steered clear of this adhocism. For the sewing machine see Cook, *op cit*, p. 46.

8 For a discussion of this natural, empathetic co-ordinate system see Kent C. Bloomer and Charles W. Moore, *Body, Memory and Architecture*, Yale University Press, London and New Haven, 1978. Renaissance architecture, after Vitruvius, codified the body metaphor.

9 See Herbert J. Gans, *Popular Culture amd High Culture*, an analysis and evaluation of taste, Basic Books, New York, 1974, pp. 84–8.

10 Kostka, *op cit*, p. 11.

4.2 Architecture and Morality

1 For examples see the section 'Straight Revivalism' in my *The Language of Post-Modern Architecture*, Academy and Rizzoli, London and New York, 1978, pp. 90–96.

2 *Op cit*.

3 See *Architettura Razionale*, Franco Angeli Editore, Milan, 1973; 'Formalisme-Réalisme', *L'Architecture d'Aujourd'hui*, Paris, April 1977; *Lotus 11*, Milan, 1971; *Rational Architecture*, Archives d'Architecture Moderne, Brussels, 1978, and my 'Irrational Rationalism – The Rats Since 1960' in this volume.

4 *The Language of Post-Modern Architecture, op cit*, pp. 118–122.

5 Not surprisingly either, since Eisenman was greatly influenced by Colin Rowe, whose work and essay 'Mannerism and Modern Architecture' has influenced so many others interested in Post-Modern space. See his *The Mathematics of the Ideal Villa and Other Essays*, MIT Press, Cambridge, 1976, pp. 29–58.

6 See Rudolf Wittkower, 'Carlo Rainaldi and the Architecture of the High Baroque in Rome' in *Studies in the Italian Baroque*, London, 1975, pp. 9–53; N. Pevsner, 'The Architecture of Mannerism', *The Mint*, London, 1946; as John Shearman has pointed out, however, Mannerism was just as involved with contrary principles of 'elegance', 'skill' and 'artistic virtuosity'. See his *Mannerism*, Harmondsworth, 1967, pp. 19–35.

7 See Shearman, *op cit*, p. 212, pp. 52–3.

8 For Late-Modernism see pages 31–80. We haven't looked at the minimum differences in glazing which convey interior use, nor analyzed the colouring as a representation of interior conditions, but these would show further ambiguities.

9 House 10 Peter Eisenman told me in 1978 was 'decentered' and without a 'heart'; glass was put in the floor etc. An 'absurd' axonometric model of it was made. Eisenman's talks in 1977–8 in Chicago and New Haven stressed disturbing and anti-humanist aspects of the twentieth century such as concentration camps, the principle of uncertainty etc., but perhaps he would term his work more Quietist than Nihilist.

10 Nikolaus Pevsner, *An Outline of European Architecture*, Harmondsworth, 1970, pp. 426–431.

11 Many histories of recent architecture show this; I've shown five traditions in *Modern Movements in Architecture*, Harmondsworth, 1973, as well as six different ones in *The Language of Post-Modern Architecture, op cit*.

12 See both texts cited in the previous note.

13 See Siegfried Giedion's chapter 'Mies Van der Rohe and the Integrity of Form' in *Space, Time and Architecture*, Cambridge and Oxford, 5th Edition, 1967, pp. 587–617; the investment of form with moral attributes such as integrity is also typical of Pevsner's many writings on Mies.

14 Before an art object can be valued it must be put into a system, that is into relation with other objects. Thus art history and the art market grow together, as Joseph Alsop has recently argued in his Mellon Lectures, delivered in Washington D. C., Spring 1978, partly published in the *TLS* and *New York Review of Books*, 1978.

15 To avoid monotony and also to point out its connection to other concepts, other critical terms will be used such as depth, density, texture, unity in variety, tension and the most inclusive terms such as irony and tragedy.

NOTES

16 For a critical comparison of many interpretations see Morris Weitz, *Hamlet and the Philosophy of Literary Criticism*, Faber and Faber, London, 1965.

17 See Paul Frankl, *The Gothic Literary Sources and Interpretations through Eight Centuries*, Princeton, New Jersey, 1960.

18 See Erwin Panofsky, *Meaning in the Visual Arts*, Anchor Books, Garden City, New York, 1955, pp. 26–54.

19 His main work on the subject was published in Stuttgart, 1888, see George Kubler, *The Shape of Time*, Yale University Press, New Haven, 1962, pp. 80–1.

20 For short historical discussions see I. A. Richards, *Coleridge on Imagination*, Routledge and Kegan Paul, London, 1934, and Cleanth Brooks and W. K. Wimsatt, *Literary Criticism: A Short History*, New York, 1957. The idea in architecture has been reiterated in all classical revivals as well as in the movements of functionalism, organic architecture and Art Nouveau.

21 For the 'Role of the "Concetto"' in Baroque see Rudolf Wittkower, *Art and Architecture in Italy 1600–1750*, Harmondsworth, third revised edition, pp. 169–170.

22 E. H. Gombrich has shown the psychological coherence behind such mixed critical terms in his essay 'Visual Metaphors of Value in Art', *Meditations on a Hobby Horse*, Phaidon Press, London, 1963, pp. 12–29.

23 Quotes are from *Biographia Literaria*, XIV and XIII.

24 I. A. Richards, *op cit*.

25 See Christopher Alexander, 'A City is not a Tree', *Design*, February 1966.

26 See Arthur Koestler, *The Act of Creation*, London, 1964.

27 Much of the factual and interpretive material for this analysis comes from Rudolf Wittkower, *Art and Architecture in Italy 1600–1750*, Harmondsworth, first paperback edition, 1973, pp. 206–212; Paolo Portoghesi, *Borromini*, New York, 1968, p. 149 ff, and Leo Steinberg, *Borromini's San Carlo Alle Quattro Fontane*, A Study in Multiple Form and Architectural Symbolism, Garland Publishing Inc., New York and London, 1977, pp. 374–396. The further important symbolic studies of Dr H. Ost and P. de la Ruffinière du Prey are discussed by these authors.

28 Paolo Portoghesi pointed this out to me in conversation, 1978.

BIBLIOGRAPHY

BIBLIOGRAPHY OF CHARLES JENCKS. . . . . . . .1963 – January 1979

1963 November. The magazine *Connection*, The Visual Arts at Harvard, is founded by myself and Gordon Milde. The idea was to 'connect' the different areas of specialization concerned with the visual arts at Harvard. Among our contributors were Edouard Sekler, Stanford Anderson, Walter Gropius, James Ackerman, Jerzy Soltan, Daniel Moynihan and James O'Gorman.

November 26. – 'Specialization and Dyspepsia', an editorial attack.

– 'The Architect in an Overpopulated World', review of Chermeyeff and Alexander's *Community and Privacy*, pp.21-5.

December 18. - 'G.S.D. Juries Judged', another editorial attack, pp.1-2.

– 'The Architect in an Overpopulated World II', review of C. Doxiadis, *Architecture in Transition*, pp.13-16.

1964 January 28. – 'Esprit Nouveau est mort à New Haven', an intemperate attack on Paul Rudolph's Arts and Architecture building.

February 28. – 'Vacuum at the Top', an editorial attack on the lack of leadership in American architecture.

– 'The Architect in an Overpopulated World III', review of Konrad Wachsmann's *The Turning Point of Building*, pp.14–18.

March 27. – 'Exhortation to the Unreasonable Planner', an editorial of quotes from Shaw, Nietzsche etc.

– 'Mr. Mumford and Mr. Eliot', a review of two books, pp.27–30.

May 4. – 'Variety and Architecture', concerned with Van Eyck, Bakema, Le Corbusier, etc., pp.22–30.

May 25. – 'Polar Attitudes in Architecture', pp.5–12.

December – 'Harvard Architecture', pp.39–43.

1965 April – 'No Revolutions, Please', pp.20–26.

June – 'Procrustes on the Wilbur Cross', p.62.

After coming to England and the Architectural Association, I started writing for *Arena*, the AA magazine, a series of articles on the major Modern architects which were later collected and revised as parts of *Modern Movements in Architecture* (1973).

1965/7 Articles which were never published because they led to ideas in my PhD thesis: 'The Function of Criticism and Architecture' based on theories of M. Weitz and T. S. Eliot; – 'Multivalent Architecture'; – 'A Picture of the Tradition'; – 'The Modern Sensibility'.
– 'Safety First, Then Crisis', a review of John Jacobus' *Twentieth Century Architecture, The Middle Years 1940–65*.
– 'Dr Pevsner's Interludes', a review of his 'Architecture in Our Time – The Anti-Pioneers'.

1966 May – 'The Problem of Mies', *Arena*, pp.301–4

June/July – 'Gropius, Wright and the Intentional Fallacy', *Arena*, pp.14–20.

1967 May – 'Charles Jeanneret – Le Corbusier', *Arena*, pp.299–306.

June – 'Meaning in Architecture', issue with George Baird.
– 'Complexity and Contradiction in Architecture', review of the book of Robert Venturi, in *Arena*, pp.4–5. This review supported Venturi's ideas, but criticized the lack of a psychological argument which could justify complexity.

November – 'Alvar Aalto and Some Concepts of Value', *Arena/Interbuild*, pp.29–45.

1968 Winter – 'Pop-Non Pop', *AAQ*, Vol.1, No.1, pp.48–64; Part II, April 1969, Vol.2, No.2, pp.56–74.

January – 'Wading Through the Oleaginous Lagoon of Gooey Platitudes', a review of *The Architecture of America*, by J. E. Burchard and A. Bush Brown, *Arena/Interbuild*, p.47.

July – 'Adhocism on the South Bank', review of the Hayward Gallery and initial conception of adhocism, *The Architectural Review*, pp.27–30.

1969 Spring – 'The Silent Zone', review of Barbara Miller Lane, *Architecture and Politics in Germany, 1918–1945*, *AAQ*, pp.80–1. Discusses the political compromise of Bauhaus members, Mies, Gropius etc., with the Nazis, a compromise that had been passed over in silence.

June (?) – 'Architecturology the Ultraquistic Subterfuge', review of I. M. Goodovitch, *Architecturology*, in *The Architectural Review*.

October – 'The Religious Con-Version of Herman Kahn', a review of Kahn's address to British businessmen, written in the Neo-Hysterical Style, *AAQ*, Vol.1, No.4, pp.62–9.

November – 'Pigeonholing made difficult', on the use of numerical taxonomy as a more delicate way of classifying architects. *Architectural Design*, p.582.

December – 'Points of View', on Venturi and Scott-Brown's visit to the AA, in *Architectural Design*.

December (or Jan?) – 'After Functionalism, What?', review of Frei Otto, *Tensile Structures* (Vol.2), *The Architectural Review*.

– *Meaning in Architecture*, a collection of essays edited by George Baird and myself, Barrie & Rockliffe, London; George Braziller, New York. Includes 'Semiology and Architecture', pp.9–25 and 'History as Myth', an analysis of recent historians, pp.245–65.

1970 – 'Modern Architecture - The Tradition since 1945' a thesis under Reyner Banham submitted to the University of London which was revised as *Modern Movements in Architecture*, minus the chapter 'A Theory of Value'. This chapter was the interpretive position behind the book and it was based on the ideas of imagination and multivalence developed by S. T. Coleridge and I. A. Richards; printed in part here as a section of the last chapter.

April – 'Does American Architecture Really Exist?', a review of Vincent Scully's *American Architecture and Urbanism* which raises the difficulty of defining a plural American architecture, and discusses Scully's interesting use of metaphorical description. *AAQ*, Vol.2, No.2, pp.62–4.

– 'Architecture Becomes Political', in *The Year's Art, 1969–70* edited by Michael Dempsey, Hutchinson, pp.87–97. Review of the plural trends, the six traditions, later incorporated into *Modern Movements*.

– 'Le Diable est dans les détails', review of the heavy, later works of Marcel Breuer, *New Buildings and Projects, 1960–70*, *The Architectural Review*.

September – 'The Modern Fragmentation', review of several books and a discussion of the break up of the Modern Movement. *Encounter*, pp.73–8.

– 'Student Dorms on a Scottish Coast', a discussion of James Stirling's buildings at St. Andrews, a semiotic analysis where the role of metaphor is seen as a primary agent in communication, *Architectural Forum*, pp.50–7.

October – 'The Evolutionary Tree', first approximation at classifying the six traditions of Modernism, *Architectural Design*, p.527.

1971 April – 'Revolution in the Art in Revolution', a review, (in French, of the show on Constructivism at the Hayward) discussing the irony of reactions and attitudes, for *L'Oeil*, pp.20–5.

Spring – 'The Missing Link', review of *Programmes and Manifestos of 20th Century Architecture*, edited by Ulrich Conrads. Discusses two aspects of the Modern Movement which have been overlooked: creativity and politics. *AAQ*, Vol.3, No.2, pp.54–8.

– *Architecture 2000, Predictions and Methods*, Studio Vista, London; Praeger, New York.

April – 'Towards the Year 2000', a satirical profile of coming events based on my book, *Landscape Architecture*, pp.207–15, also *AAQ*, Winter, Vol.3, No.1, pp.56–60.

May 5. – 'E Pur si Muove', review of *Kinetic Architecture*, by William Zuk and Roger H. Clark, for the *Architects' Journal*.

June – 'The Supersensualists, Part I', a discussion of Superstudio, the Italian *Domus* scene and Pasolini, *Architectural Design*, pp.345–7.

September – 'Libertarian and Authoritarian Views of Revolution', a discussion of Constructivism and the two opposed left-wing traditions, *RIBA Journal*, pp.389–91.

– 'Heutige Architektur und Zeitgeist', the perpetual treason of the clerks, part of *Architecture 2000* with additions on political fatalism, in *Archithèse 2*, pp.25–40.

1972 Winter – 'Giedion's Last Bible', review of Siegfried Giedion's *Architecture and the Phenomenon of Transition, AAQ*, Vol.4, No.1, p.67.

January – 'The Supersensualists, Part II', a discussion of Archizoom and death, Hollein, Sottsass, *Architectural Design*, pp.18–21.

– 'GRRRRRR', review of Peter Collins, *Architectural Judgement, The Architectural Review*.

– 'Life and Architecture', a review of Phillipe Boudon's *Lived-in Architecture, Times Educational Supplement*.

April 13. – 'Kitsch Hikers', review of Justus Dahinden, *Urban Structures for the Future, New Society*, p.76.

Summer – 'Rhetoric and Architecture', first general statement on semiotics and architecture, address in Barcelona at Semiotics Conference, *AAQ*, Vol.4, No.3, pp.4–17.

– *Adhocism, the Case for Improvisation*, with Nathan Silver, Secker and Warburg, London; Doubleday, New York.

October – 'The Case for Improvisation', with Nathan Silver, but 90% my own serious joke about adhocism, *Architectural Design*, pp.604–7.

Autumn – Spring 1973 – Letters between Stirling and Jencks on metaphor and Art Nouveau, *AAQ*, Vol.5, No.1, p.64.

1973 January – 'Mainstream Modernism', review of Dennis Sharp, *A Visual History of 20th Century Architecture, Times Educational Supplement*.

Summer – 'The Triumph of the Muddle Class', review of Robert Maxwell, *New British Architecture* and Philip Drew, *The Third Generation, The Changing Meaning of Architecture*, discusses spelling mistakes and boring Modernism, *AAQ*, pp.59–62.

August – 'Mutations in the Avant-Garde', review of *Archigram*, edited by Peter Cook, and Barbara Plumb, *Young Designs in Colour, The Architectural Review*, p.129.

– 'The Urge to Destroy', review of *Vandalism* edited by Colin Ward, and *Defensible Space*, by Oscar Newman, *Times Educational Supplement*, p.14.

September – 'Ersatz in LA', the first statement of four kinds of phoney but funny Los Angeles types, *Architectural Design*, pp.596–601.

Winter – 'The Candid King Midas of New York Camp', a Neo-Hysterical account of the life and work of Philip Johnson, *AAQ*, Vol.5, No.4, pp.27–42.

– *Le Corbusier and the Tragic View of Architecture*, Allen Lane, Penguin Books, Harmondsworth; Harvard University Press, Cambridge.

– *Modern Movements in Architecture*, Penguin Books, Harmondsworth; Doubleday, New York, (finished in 1971 as revised PhD thesis.)

1974 March/April – 'James Stirling's Corporate Culture Machine', *Architecture Plus*, pp.96–103.

– 'A Semantic Analysis of Stirling's Olivetti Centre Wing', an analysis of metaphorical reactions, *AAQ*, Vol.6, No.2, pp.13–5. Also to be reprinted in *Signs, Symbols and Architecture*, edited by Geoffrey Broadbent, Richard Bunt and myself, John Wiley and Sons, London and New York, 1979.

May – 'Adhocism Misunderstood', reply to Ken Frampton's review, *Oppositions* 3, pp.106–7.
– 'Meaning in Architecture Misunderstood', reply to Mario Gandelsonas and Diana Agrest, *Oppositions* 3, pp.110–1.

June – 'A Detonation in Glass and Brick', review of James Stirling drawing-show analysing the 'controversy', *Times Educational Supplement*, p.21.

September 8. – 'Cracking the Codes', review of the First International Congress of Semiotics held in Milan, *Times Educational Supplement*.

September 27. – 'Modern Architecture Collapses', review of Malcolm MacEwen, *Crisis in Architecture, Building Design*, pp.26–7. Also published in *AAQ*.

October – 'Architecture that Speaks', an early version of *The Language of Post-Modern Architecture*, given as the Melbourne Oration, Melbourne.

October 12–19. – 'A Trip to the Antipodes', diary, unpublished of the trip to Australia.

1975 February – 'An Interview', concerned with Oration and current views, in *Architecture in Australia*, pp.50–7.

May 16. – 'In Undisguised Taste', interview with Reyner Banham about his *The Age of the Masters*, showing his bias and bringing up taste as the great undiscussable, *Building Design*, pp.12–3.

June (?) – 'The Language of Architecture', *Sunday Times*, pp.24–5.

June 6. – 'Sex and Communication', a Neo-Hysterical take-off of sexologists and their baneful influence, *Ghost-Dance Times*, pp.1 and 4 (written Feb. 1970).

July – 'The Rise of Post-Modern Architecture', an initial formulation of the new tradition, *Architecture Inner-Town Government*, Eindhoven, pp.78–103, reprinted in *AAQ*, issue partially devoted to the subject, Vol.7, No.4.

– 'James Stirling versus the Komfy Style', commissioned for the *Sunday Times*, not published; ditto 'Norman Foster'.

September – 'Trompe L'Oeil Counterfeit', *Studio International*, pp.109–13 (Part of *Ersatz*).

– 'Reflections on Mirrors', concerning Norman Foster's work and the qualities of mirrors, *A&U*, pp.58–60.

– '125 Years of Quasi Democracy', a discussion of AA politics in *A Continuing Experiment, Learning and Teaching at the AA*, edited by James Gowan, The Architectural Press, London, pp.149–59.

1976 February – 'The Pleasure House of the Rising Sun', on the Japanese Love Hotels, *Sunday Times*.

March – 'The Enigma of Kurokawa', *The Architectural Review*, pp.142–53, also in *Kisho Kurokawa* as introduction, published by Studio Vista.

– 'Isozaki's Paradoxical Cube', *The Japan Architect*, pp.46–50.

June – 'ArchiteXt and the Problem of Symbolism', *The Japan Architect,* pp.21–8.

July 5. – 'Bricolage', an answer to Reyner Banham on Adhocism, *New Society.*

- 'The Revisionists of Modern Architecture', on the English Post-Modernists, RIBA conference, July 14–16, published in *Architecture: Opportunities, Achievements,* RIBA publications edited by Barbara Goldstein, pp.55–63.

– 'Fetishism and Architecture', a discussion of the erogenous zones, parts reprinted in *Daydream Houses of Los Angeles, Architectural Design* 8, pp.492–5.

October – 'Review' of Juan Pablo Bonta's *An Anatomy of Architectural Interpretation. A Semiotic Review of the Criticism of Mies van der Rohe's Barcelona Pavilion, JSAH,* pp.226–7.

November – 'The Los Angeles Silvers', Pelli, Lumsden, Kupper etc., *A&U,* pp.13–4.

December – 'Fear, Asceticism and Suicide of the Avant-Garde', paper to Art Net.

– 'The Pluralism of Japanese Architecture', in French and Japanese versions of *Modern Movements.*

1977 January – 'Isozaki and Radical Eclecticism', *Architectural Design,* pp.42–8.

March – 'MBM and the Barcelona School', *The Architectural Review,* pp.159–65.

May – 'Genealogy of Post-Modernism', an early evolutionary tree, *Architectural Design,* pp.269–71.

May 27 (?) – 'More Modern than Modern', on Post-Modern architecture and exhibit at Art Net, *Sunday Times,* pp.30–1.

– *The Language of Post-Modern Architecture,* Academy Editions, London; Rizzoli, New York.

– 'History as Myth II', address to Delft Symposium.

– 'Irrational Rationalism - The Rats since 1960', *A&U,* 77, 4&5, reprinted in Dennis Sharp, *The Rationalists,* London, 1979.

– 'Venturi et al are almost all right', *Architectural Design,* 7/8, pp.468–9.

– 'Le Corbusier on the Tight-Rope of Functionalism', a speculative soliloquy on Le Corbusier's defense of architecture, in *The Open Hand, Essays on Le Corbusier,* edited by Russell Waldon, MIT Press, pp.187–214.

1978 January – 'Typology, Context and Post-Modernism', an answer to S. Cantucazino, *The Architectural Review.*

January – 'The Language of Post-Modern Architecture', *Architectural Design,* incorporated as new last chapter to the revised edition.

February – 'The Tory Interpretation of History', on D. Watkin's *Morality and Architecture, The Architectural Review.*

March – 'On Fame as the Engine of Architects and Architecture', unpublished paper delivered to seminar at Yale University.

April – 'What is Post-Modern Architecture?', an answer to S. Stephens' review, *Progressive Architecture.*

April, May, June – 'The Architectural Sign', general considerations on semiotics and architecture, *A&U,* republished in *Signs, Symbols and Architecture,* op. cit., 1979.

June – 'Architecture as a Peculiar Language', unpublished lecture at Darmstadt.

July – *The Language of Post-Modern Architecture,* revised and enlarged edition, with new introduction and last chapter, Academy and Rizzoli.

– 'The Return of the Missing Body', a review of Kent Bloomer, Charles Moore and Robert Yudell, *Body Memory and Architecture, The Architectural Review,* and also another review of this same book and *Dimensions* by Charles Moore and Gerald Allen, for *JSAH,* March 1979.

October – *Daydream Houses of Los Angeles,* the erotic, largely self-built houses of various districts in Los Angeles, Academy Editions, London; Rizzoli, New York.

October – 'Bruce Goff - The Michelangelo of Kitsch', *Architectural Design,* pp.10–4, and a reworked version for the *Sunday Times Colour Magazine.*

December – 'Late-Modern and Post-Modern Architecture', a set of distinctions, *Architectural Design,* pp.592–609.

– Contributions and conclusion to *The Chinese Garden* by Maggie Keswick, Academy Editions London, Rizzoli, New York.

PHOTOGRAPHIC ACKNOWLEDGEMENTS

All photographs are by the author or from Academy Editions archives except as listed below:

Gil Amiaga 20 top left; Archizoom 91 top right, 92, 94 left; Atelier Braun – Ruth Kaiser ABCV 96 top and bottom left; Atelier Hollein *frontispiece*, 20 bottom left, 20 top and bottom right (photos Jerzy Surwillo), 33 bottom left, 96 right, 97; Ricardo Bofill 136; Brazilian Embassy 77 centre left; Brecht-Einzig Ltd. *front flap, back cover*, 34, 53, 58, 60 top right, 80 bottom, 81 bottom, 82 top, 83, 86 top, 172 top and bottom left (photos Richard Einzig); Peter Carl 139 top and centre right; Louis Checkman 64 top; John Donat 7 bottom, 38 bottom right, 60 centre left, 61 top right, 140 bottom; Peter Eisenman 56 top, 137, 177, 178 centre, 179; Craig Ellwood 48 bottom; Ralph Erskine 180; Foster Associates 7 top, 9, 43 bottom, 60 bottom, 61 top left; French Government Tourist Office 52 top (photo G. Karquel); Reinhard Friedrich 77 centre right; Hiromi Fujii 117; Giuliano Gameliel 60 top left, 94 left, 95, 132 bottom right; Alexander Georges 156; German Embassy 48 top right (photo NOWEA); Bruce Goff 160, 161, 162, 163, 164, 165, 166, 169; Jordi Gomez 52 bottom; The Soloman R. Guggenheim Museum 77 bottom (photo Robert E. Mates); Hardy Holzman Pfeiffer Associates 40 bottom and top right; Yasutaka Hayashi 119 top; Herman Hertzberger 10, 45 top; Lucien Hervé 44 top left; Arata Isozaki 112, 113, 114, 115 left, 140 top; Italian State Tourist Office 48 top left; *The Japan Architect* 56 bottom right, 69 top, 119 bottom (photos Masao Arai), 120 (photo Taisuke Ogawa); Japan Information Centre 99 top left (photo E. Benn); Philip Johnson *front cover*, 54, 62, 70, 151 centre, 152 left and centre; Louis Kahn 132 left; Phokion Karas 44 bottom; Yasufumi Kijima 24; Kiyonari Kikutake 100 right, 102 top left; Rem Koolhaas 144, 145; Leon Krier 135; Kisho N. Kurokawa Architect & Associates 103 right (photo Hideki Hongo), 56 bottom left, 103 left, 104 left, 106 (photos Tomio Ohashi), 55 top, 102 right; Denys Lasdun 75 top; Nathaniel Lieberman 14b; Anthony Lumsden 66 bottom, 72 bottom; Norman McGrath 139 bottom right; Ryuji Miyamoto 121; Kaneaki Monma 109 left; Monta Mozuna 116; Ugo Mulas 88; Osamu Murai 49 top right, 102 bottom left, 116 top left, 124, 125; C.F. Murphy Associates 47 top right and bottom, 59 top left; Tatsuhiko Nakajima and Gaus 105 top; Taisuke Ogawa 37 left; Tomio Ohashi 37 top and centre right, 49 top left, 100 left, 104 right; Richard W. Payne 64 bottom left; Cesar Pelli & Gruen Associates 67 bottom; Photo Lang 14c, 14d, 73 inset; Plura Edizioni 72 top left; John Portman 14e; Paolo Portoghesi 15; Marvin Rand 65 top right; Jo Reid 61 bottom; Retoria 99 bottom right, 101 top (photos Y. Futagawa); James Volnay Righter 21, 22 bottom, 23 top left; Kevin Roche 14a; Ruth Rogers 59 bottom; Alberto Rosselli 45 centre left and bottom right; National Monuments Record 130 bottom (Mrs. J. Cox), 130 top (J. Saunders); Paul Rudolph 45 bottom left; Kuniharu Sakumoto 69 bottom, 116 bottom left; SAUP slide library, UCLA 51 top; Oscar Savio 16; Gordon H. Schenck 73; Nikken Sekkei 110 right, 111; Shinkenchiku-Sha Co. Ltd 49 bottom (photo Masao Arai); Shokokusha Publishing Co. Inc. 101 bottom (photo Fumio Murasawa), 99 bottom left (photo Shigeo Okamoto); Thomas Gordon Smith 27; James Stirling 84, 85 top, 86 bottom left, 87 top, 172 bottom right; Ezra Stoller Associates 31, 76 bottom, 138 left, 147, 148, 153 top and bottom left, 154 left, 158, 159; Tim Street Porter 66 top; Studio di Porta Pinciana 17 top; Roy Summers 146; Superstudio/Architettura e Design 91 left and bottom right; Minoru Takeyama 128 bottom, 129; Kenzo Tange 40 top left; Usis 41, 65 top left, 151 top, 153 right; Bernard Vincent 12, 36 bottom; Deidi von Schaewen 30; Yoji Watanabe 109 right; Albert Weber 96 centre left; Colin Westwood 64 bottom right; Kazumasa Yamashita 122; YRM with SOM Chicago 59 top right.

INDEX